THE SEVEN SPIRITS

Greg J. Stenger

THE SEVEN SPIRITS

A Zodiac Revolution Within The Bible

GREG J. STENGER

The Seven Spirits: A Zodiac Revolution Within the Bible by Gregory Joseph Stenger
Copyright © 2024 by Gregory Joseph Stenger
All Rights Reserved.
ISBN: 978-1-59755-810-5

Published by: ADVANTAGE BOOKS™ – Orlando, Florida USA
www.advbookstore.com

All Rights Reserved. This book and parts thereof may not be reproduced in any form, stored in a retrieval system or transmitted in any form by any means (electronic, mechanical, photocopy, recording or any other mechanical or electrical methods without prior written permission of the author for commercial gain or profit, except in the case of brief quotations or occasional page copying for personal or group study, except as provided by United States of America copyright law.

Neither the author nor the publisher can be held responsible for the use of the information provided within this book.

Unless otherwise indicated, all Scripture quotations are from "ESV," the "Global Study Bible," and the ESV logo are registered trademarks of Crossway, registered in the United States of America. Use of any of these trademarks requires the prior permission of Crossway.

Library of Congress Catalog Number: 2024950660

Name: Stenger, Gregory Jospeh

Title: ***The Seven Spirits: A Zodiac Revolution Within the Bible***
Gregory Joseph Stenger, Author
Advantage Books, 2024

Identifiers: ISBN Paperback: 9781597558105
ISBN eBook: 9781597558266
Hardcover: 9781597558358

Subjects:

Author Contact information: gregjstenger@gmail.com

First Printing: December 2024
24 25 26 27 28 29   10 9 8 7 6 5 4 3 2 1

The Seven Spirits: A Zodiac Revolution Within the Bible

Table of Contents

INTRODUCTION 7

1: EARLY LIFE 9

2: QUESTIONING 15

3: THE NIGHT 19

4: PROCESSING 21

5: WANDERING 25

6: THE CALLING 29

7: THE HUNT 33

8: ZODIAC 39

9: HYPOTHESIS 43

10: INVESTIGATING 49

11: BIBLICAL CONSIDERATIONS 53

12: SEARCHING FOR TWELVE 65

13: ANYTHING ELSE? 73

14: MODALITIES 81

15: THE HEART OF THE ZODIAC 85

16: GRAVITY 93

17: DARKNESS 99

18: NOW WHAT? 103

19: LIFE GOES ON 107

20: 2019 113

21: WAITING 119

22: PROPHECY CONFERENCE 123

23" ONWARD 133

APPENDIX 137

THE TWELVE ZODIAC SIGNS 150

Greg J. Stenger

Introduction

    Have you ever read the Bible and wondered why you see some of the symbols and numbers that you do in the Bible used repeatedly? Most of us wonder that at some point. We see God do things a certain, borderline obsessive-compulsive way. He'll do things in periods of 7, or has things set up in sets of 12. Never in my life did I think I would understand why, but here I am, writing this book, at God's direction, with what I am confident is THE answer to the question. It's hiding in plain sight, but takes a decent amount of searching if you're willing to undertake the journey as I was years ago. The result of the answer could quite possibly help to lead to the next biggest move of God and preaching of the gospel since the times that Jesus walked the earth. The result is that there is potentially scientific evidence not only that God exists AND created us, but at the same time also proves that Jesus is the Messiah.

    The main idea being presented, is that the numbers twelve and seven in scripture point to the twelve Zodiac signs, namely what would commonly be called "sun sign" psychological traits in modern astrology. The evidence of these being real can be seen by every person alive, and thus you get tangible, real evidence that God exists. You can argue that point from a secular perspective, but it's through the symbology in the scriptures that you get evidence that there is a divine mind behind the Bible, as well as confirming many Messianic accounts in the texts.

    The effect that this should have on people who are skeptical or searching for God is similar to what Amanda Walsh shared on her podcast "Astrology Hub" (Renstrom, Christian Astrology? w/ Christopher Renstrom, 2023):

"I'm sure you've heard me tell this story ad nauseam, but my first astrology reading after twelve years of catholic school, studying every world religion in college, getting my master's in psychology, just really trying to answer this question like "who are we and why are we here?". My first astrology reading was my first tangible evidence of God, for me. Like I sat there with tears just going, there has to be a divine intelligence if that can be deduced from this piece of information, like it just made complete sense to me."

    While I did not come to know God through such means, rather through personal experience of the supernatural, I had a similar experience later on while looking for evidence of the supernatural and stumbling upon Zodiac signs. Many supernatural events however are highly debatable as to their authenticity to onlookers. That, and the lure of evolution, newer naturalistic thinking, the problem of evil, doubt about the authenticity of scriptures (both inside and outside of Christianity) are leading many to become agnostic, atheist, have some vague sense of spiritualism, or other odd belief. The Zodiac signs are static, ever-present, smoking gun evidence of not just a god, but the God of the Bible. I believe due to the nature of this evidence and the argument, we can potentially once and for all *definitively* answer the big question, "Is there a god, and if so, who are they?"

    Now that I've set the bar very high, what you will actually find in this book is mostly my personal testimony and walk with God over the years, with much of the central theme being what I discovered in the Zodiac. I believe strongly in sharing personal testimonies, as it is written in Revelation 12:11:

"And they overcame him by the blood of the Lamb and by the word of their testimony, and they did not love their lives to the death."

    I hope it will be much more entertaining and interesting to read it this way. I know I enjoy reading testimonies and life stories more than a list of arguments. The central argument in this book is what has seemed like my life's calling ever since I discovered it. I have never written a book before, and wasn't necessarily eager to do so. There's a lot of work involved in writing including publishing, advertising, and uncertainty about how well it will be received. However, one day I felt like God was telling me to write a book about it. Then less than a week later he confirmed it to me through other people who had no idea I had heard that from God, as I had not shared that with anyone at the time.

    All of that said, I do want to be respectful of your time if you don't think you have time to read all of my testimony. So, here is a generic cheat sheet for this book: Chapters 1-7 highlight my life leading up to the point of discovery of the Zodiac. The subject matter transitions over to the Zodiac in chapter 8, and the argument for this continues through chapter 17. Chapters 18 through the end is what happened afterward and spans roughly thirteen years, leading up to God confirming all of this to me as well as the publishing of this book.

1

Early life

I was born and raised in southeast Indiana, in what would be considered part of the greater Cincinnati area. My father was a carpenter by trade, and my mother did a few different odd jobs to help make some extra money, as well as taking a few jobs for insurance purposes. Most of her life she was a bank teller, but she took time off to be a stay-at-home mom for a few years, and also spent time as a teacher's aide for elementary school. I have 2 sisters, one older, and one younger.

My father grew up farming and learned to enjoy it, so we did that on the side to make a little extra money. We primarily raised cattle, but my dad also grew field corn to be used to feed the cattle, and had also grown soybeans as well which he would sell. Summers were spent baling hay. I learned how to drive the tractor at a young age in order to help with raking, tethering, and eventually mowing/baling hay, etc. We were always busy with something involved with the farm. School nights often involved chores such as helping to feed the cows, or herd the cows, or check on the cows, count the cows. It was all about the cows, to the point where I started to loathe all of it. Equipment broke down, we had to help fix it. On weekends we would do more involved things, such as clean the barn, or catch the cows to give them shots, or castrate the calves. There was always something to do, to the point where I started to wonder if my dad was just making things up to stay busy, and in the process trying to keep us busy as well.

All I had wanted to do was just sleep in on Saturday morning to watch the Saturday morning cartoons. We had cable television a few different times, but mostly just local stations via antenna, so cartoons were typically only during certain times. There were cartoons on at different times throughout the week, but all the best ones were on Saturday morning. When I would watch the other cartoons throughout the weekdays, they would advertise all of the Saturday morning ones, and hype them up. I was very rarely able to watch the Saturday morning cartoons, because of…. the cows. Always something to do.

As much as I hated it then, it's something I'm glad I went through. It built character, so to speak, and I learned a lot of good practical skills. It instilled a good work ethic, which carried over to school and several other things. When I did start to hang out with friends more in high school and college, it felt out of place how much leisure time they had to do things; I was not used to it. It felt weird hanging out and playing video games for hours, I rarely had the opportunity to do such a thing growing up. While moving into my first apartment with some friends in college, one of my roommates remarked,

"Your dad gets stuff done."

"Yea, I know," I replied. I had begun to realize my childhood experience was not necessarily the norm.

****

God makes everyone unique, and as a kid if you were to ask me, or probably any of my peers what was special about me, they probably would have answered, "He's smart." I remember as a young kid about to go into kindergarten or first grade, my parents gave me all kinds of advice like any typical parent would. They told me to study hard and do well in school so I could grow up and get a good job. So as far as school was concerned, that was my assignment. I wanted to make them happy, or probably more accurately, I didn't want to get in trouble. I wanted to be a "good boy."

So I tried my best in school, and did well enough. Reading and English were not my best subjects, but I seemed to be doing decent in math, it came somewhat easily to me. I had just kind of wanted to fit in. Above all else, I did not want to be last in class. I wasn't too concerned where I would end up as far as the intellectual pecking order was concerned, as long as I was not last. That would be failure and devastating to me, after my parents had told me to do well in school.

I remember distinctly in first grade the first, and probably only time I cried during elementary school. We were doing some sort of craft, and students were being taken out a few at a time to do some sort of vision or hearing test, then would come back in and resume where they had left off at with the craft. My turn came and I was taken out for the test. I had often made it a habit to look around to see where everyone else was at with their progress on things, and this time noticed that most were ahead of me on the craft, not many were behind me. By the time I had come back I resumed the craft and looked around again, and noticed that everyone was further on it than I was. I was dead last. I tried to keep going but was panicking. I had failed. I started to cry, which bothered me even more because now I just looked weak and pathetic sitting there crying. I had been bested by the first grade crafting project, all the other kids beat me in the craft.

Third grade came along, and Mrs. Scane, a random teacher, would come in and administer this "Continental Math League" test a handful of times a year (Continental Mathematics League, 2023). I wasn't sure what the point of it was, but it was just another part of school I guess so I had to try to do my best like everything else. She handed out a sheet of paper with six-word problems, and we were supposed to answer them within a certain time limit, and then turn it in. I did my best and moved on. We never heard much about the results though.

Then at the award ceremony later that year. Mrs. Scane was back and started talking about how one of the students at the school had won first place in the Continental Math League. At the time our school district was broken up into 3 different elementary schools, all K through 5, and then they all came together in sixth grade. I didn't know much about the other 2 schools, but I knew that ours was the smallest. Mrs. Scane may have even mentioned that while building it up. I thought to myself while she was talking, "sounds like this kid is pretty smart." Then she finally announced the person, and I was quite surprised to hear my name called. I reactively got up with a big grin on my face and started walking down to the stage. My teacher lit up and smiled and congratulated me on my way down. I ended up graduating in a class of about 330 students.

The event set me apart in both my own mind as well as the other students who were there. I had just wanted to fit in, and didn't want to be "the dumb kid". I preferred that I was on the smarter end of course, but it wasn't the end of the world. Well as it turned out, I wasn't just towards the top, I more or less was the top at least when it came to math at our school. I went on to win 1st place more times than not up until we stopped doing it altogether in 7th or 8th grade. I didn't completely dominate everything as some of the other super smart kids did in grades above and below me, but I placed number one quite a bit when it came to anything involving math.

About middle school and up, I hung out mostly with other smart kids. Since we were all in the same AP classes, they just naturally became my circle of friends. I still tried to be "a good kid." It wasn't all nerds, many of them were very athletic. I did well enough in sports at a very young age. Being able to sprint helped. Looking back, I think most of it was just because I was smart and could see openings and plays better than others; I had a better read on things. Once everyone got older my insights became commonplace, and my tactics didn't work as well as they used to. Then the natural athleticism others had took over and I faded into mediocrity

The main reason I share this story is not to brag, but so that you understand a big part of my identity growing up. I would argue most people who excel quite a bit at something have a similar experience. It becomes a part of who you are. I was "the smart kid", the one others would come to for the right answer for hard math questions. Others might be "the star football player", or "the best juggler", etc. It becomes a point of pride and sinks into your identity. I don't think a whole lot of it much anymore, I didn't do anything special to be born the way I was, it was all a gift from God. I could have been born a much different way. Ultimately, life goes on and becomes what you make of it.

****

As for religious upbringing, I would put that in the realm of conservative Christian. When my parents got married, they were both Catholic, and thus I was raised Catholic. That meant attending mass once a week on Saturday or Sunday, and then Sunday school at our local parish. Not going to church was considered a sin, so we attended church every week without fail. When I became of age I completed the typical expected sacraments of Communion and eventually Confirmation, as did everyone else whose parents were part of the Catholic faith. Even though I am no longer Catholic, these are some of the things I do appreciate about the church – the weekly partaking of communion and dedication to church attendance. Ultimately though, church, like life, is what you make of it.

I read my Bible periodically, that was what my mother wanted me to do and told me to do. I wanted to be a "good kid" so I did what I was told. In doing so I acquired a decent knowledge of scripture for my age. I remember my mom telling me different things about God and Jesus quite often. I once had a bad dream to where I couldn't go back to sleep, so I snuck into my parents' room onto the opposite side of the bed where she was at and asked her to tell me about the story of Jesus again. I don't know why but it just felt comforting to hear about God at such a time when I was pretty terrified; just hearing about this larger-than-life person/thing that was on my side. She sat there awake and kept going on and on about His life after I had stopped paying attention and slowly drifted off in the middle of the night.

She told me how God does things in seven, and twelve, and forty, with the most important one being seven. I wondered why God would put importance on certain numbers. It didn't make sense, but then again no one else seemed to have a good answer to the question past what I would consider generic, unsatisfactory answers. There seemed to be a lot of unsatisfactory answers in religion. We just kind of believed things. I wasn't sure why, but that's what everyone wanted me to do, so I kind of did. I certainly wanted God to be real, so I kind of just played along.

I was playing outside one day, and my mom came out and pulled me aside. I can't remember what she said, but I know she explained to me how to get saved and told me the guts of the gospel. Then she told me to repeat after her, and we recited the sinner's prayer. She was very serious and getting emotional, started crying, so I did too, feeding off of it. I felt different afterwards. "So this was what it was like to be saved." Still, I didn't really choose any of it, I just was kind of doing what I was told, and I knew that. I felt changed for a moment, but sooner or later the moment was gone.

Still one thing kind of puzzled me about all of the "god stuff". After my parents got married, my mother's side of the family left the Catholic church, though it was either before I was born or too young to remember, likely the former. My grandma had started watching Jimmy Swaggart on television, and in the process saw some truth in what he was preaching. They became non-denominational protestants, and eventually started attending an Assemblies of God church. They were different though. At family gatherings, they would talk about God in casual conversation, which I had never seen anyone else do. They would talk about God as if it was all just without question true – from healings to speaking in tongues, etc. They talked about it like it was a fact. I didn't get how they could be so sure about God's existence; it just didn't make sense.

While we were still catholic after this, my mom would watch different televangelists on TV to learn more about God outside of Catholicism. Her favorite was Benny Hinn, so I saw a few of his miracle services as well, with people speaking in tongues and being "slain in the Spirit." It seemed very odd to me. Part of it seemed like a show, while at the same time it didn't make sense that all those people were actors. How could they be sure all that stuff was God, and not just the power of suggestion or hypnotism or something? The healings seemed more legit, but a lot of the healings also seemed to be able to be explained by other, natural means, or maybe the power of psychology. I wasn't sure what to make of all of it. My mom would for the longest time be considered my spiritual rock. To this day I would say she still is truly one of the nicest people I know. I was hard pressed to find anything malicious in her.

****

All of this considered, I was still "the smart kid." I wasn't sure exactly what smart people did when they got older, but I knew it involved science. That was all the talk in the

1: Early Life

day; science was the authority. With me being good at math, it seemed like that was my life's path; to join the realms of science, whatever that meant.

However, I knew the scientific community's general take on "god." He wasn't needed, and therefore didn't exist. Almost none of them believed in God. They were smart like me, and therefore must have thought it through very well. Belief in God seemed to be at odds with science, or at least none of the other adult smart people seemed to think God was real.

The people in my life that believed in God seemed to be gullible or naïve to me in some way, which was especially true of my overly trustful mom and a lot of her family. I wanted to believe in God, but at the same time I had no good reason to, other than my upbringing and environment. There were people across the globe with different upbringings too though, and they typically believed what they were raised to believe. Many of them believing full-heartedly in the beliefs they were born into. Most of the religions conflicted in some way as well. There seemed to be no logical conclusion to draw from all of it.

2

Questioning

Junior year of high school came along. My friends and I were all sitting in classroom, and I couldn't help but overhear two of my friends having a conversation. I thought I heard the word, "god." My ears perked up. It wasn't something I had often heard in class, especially coming from my friends, particularly these two friends. I couldn't hear all of the conversation, but I distinctly remember one friend talking about if there was a god, and that he wanted to get that settled in his life so he could move on without the uncertainty. I knew he was raised catholic, and I think the other one might have been as well, but I wasn't certain.

The conversation struck a chord in me. For the first time it prompted me to take a look at my beliefs. I knew I hoped there was a god, but that was about it. I had no logical standing or reason to believe in a god. I played the part around my family and other religious people. I even prayed often, hoping that God was there, that maybe he would hear my prayers, that after I died, I would exist in hopefully a peaceful state. I had positive emotional encounters with God through that. But deep down I wasn't sure. I was told to pray, so I did. All of what I was told about God seemed too good to be true, like I was being sold a car or something and the salesman was overhyping it up. At heart, I believe I was an agnostic.

Getting a lot of closure on the subject was just so appealing. Then I could stop wondering and live my life according to what I had found to be true. It could maybe cause ties to break in my family; to let my parents down potentially if what I found wasn't what they believed. I didn't want to disappoint my mother, but at the same time living a lie seemed to be just as bad. In any case, I knew I needed to do this.

So my journey started. I began with the natural place, the necessity of explaining our existence – the origins of life. The argument for intelligent design was simple enough, and it made sense. No one in the scientific community was promoting that though, which at the time was a bad sign. Later on I began to understand why, which I would argue is mostly a mix of political reasons, and a heavy bias towards naturalism and applying it in a field of study where it didn't necessarily make sense.

I was no expert on evolution, but I understood the basics. I was getting a better understanding of what science was. I understood the evidence for evolution – supposedly millions of years, all biology being very heavily related through DNA, fossils, etc. At the end of the day though, evolution had to actually *happen*, and that is where I could not make sense of it. There had to exist some kind of path between a single celled organism such as bacteria, to something as complex as a turtle, with each intermediate stage being more or less fully functional. Just finding any theoretical solution to that seemed impossible.

I had played with Lego Mindstorms quite a bit as a kid. I built and programmed my own robots using plans that only existed in my head, and getting things to work the way I envisioned them in my mind was often difficult. Many projects I had to give up on or re-envision completely because the motors didn't have enough power, or the motors would break the robot apart due to stress, or the programming logic wouldn't work due to lack of sensors or sophistication of sensors. Here, the "molecules to man" theory of evolution being pushed was relying on a lot of random chance to build the most sophisticated technology known (if you would for a second consider biology to be technology, then by any objective measure it most certainly is still the most sophisticated technology on the planet). It was just practically impossible. I couldn't believe it; it was intellectually dishonest for me to do so. If I had believed in the theory of evolution being pushed, it probably would have been the nail in the coffin on God, but none of it made any practical sense. It is still my sincere, scientific opinion that "macroevolution" is for all practical purposes, science fiction. It's taking something that is factual (microevolution) and pushing it to an extreme, unrealistic end, much like what you read in comic book backstories or sci-fi novels.

So intelligent design of some sort seemed to make the most sense. I didn't have all the details figured out with that but it was definitely the most promising, and there was still a lot more to consider. Next up on the list, was more theological questions. Who, or what is God? How would we know which god(s) are responsible, and what is their nature? Is God more of a clockmaker who just sets the universe into motion and lets things unfold as they would? That didn't make a whole lot of sense from a standpoint of purpose - why would you create something and then make a strict vow to not touch it? At the same time though, I had a hard time seeing God interacting with the world, at least in my life.

There were several different belief systems and religions, both now and in the past. I was born into Christianity, but I could have easily been born into Hinduism or something. Which of these systems was correct, if any of them? Was Zeus god? I highly doubted it, but for all practical purposes he could have been. Anyways, the easy place to start was with what I knew, Christianity.

I considered the problem of evil. I was able to get around that; the existence of freewill was sufficient to get around that barrier. Natural disasters were harder, but I could see the "fallen world" and other things I had heard make some sense within the Christian framework. There did seem to be some good that came out of natural disasters; it made people re-evaluate things. I'm sure I considered other things as well, though I can't recall all of them. Overall, I was able to logically work my way around all of them, except for one.

Hell made no sense. First and foremost, hell was terrifying and cruel. Secondly, I could see hell making sense in only one scenario: it was temporal. If it was temporary, it could serve as a means of redemption and breed an eagerness to live right and do good. Everything I was taught about hell was that it was eternal, unending. I could not see how any kind of God could do such a thing. I would rather not exist at that point and go back to nothingness.

I had much to consider in other religions, but that would require a lot of research. I couldn't logically get on board with Christianity completely because of that reason. I was at a temporary impasse, but it was late at night, and I needed to rest so I went to bed discouraged.

****

My two friends' journey would eventually lead them to atheism as far as I could tell. Years later in a different friend's basement, that same friend said something that struck another chord in me. He said, "How can anyone know that there's a God? Like how could they possibly know that". When he said it, he put into words better than I could something that I had believed growing up. Even at the current stage I was in at that point, I still didn't know how someone could possibly have it all figured out. After all, they all more or less had the same information I did. Little did I know that I was soon about to get the answer I had been searching for, in less than a few weeks' time, in a way I never imagined.

3

The Night

It was a school night and starting to get late. I was in bed, trying to get sleep. My older sister and I lived in our basement at the time. My mom was in the basement 'living room' outside of our bedrooms pouring her heart out to God. I could hear it. This time was different though, she had started speaking the gibberish "tongues" that I had heard so much of.

This was an interesting development in my quest for truth. I knew that there was much to think about here, either this was real, or my mom had lost it. The latter was not out of the question. It didn't seem reasonable that she had gone insane, but she came off very gullible and naïve in many ways to me. For right now though, I was tired. I'd think about it tomorrow. My older sister Sheryl unfortunately had a different idea. She came into my room.

"Greg! Mom's speaking in tongues!"

"Yea, I can hear her."

"Come on! Come out here."

"That's ok. I'm tired. I'll think about it in the morning."

That answer wasn't good enough. She grabbed my arm and yanked me out of bed. Now I'm awake and seeing this firsthand. Mom just kept going in tongues. After a short time, my older sister Sheryl's countenance changed completely. She started laughing joyfully, I would describe it as an almost angelic, altered state. I had never seen anything like it, possibly even to this day. She started speaking in tongues as well.

My mom I wasn't so sure about, but my sister seemed to have a pretty level head. I don't think she would have lost her mind. I had seen similar stuff on TV happening to strangers I knew nothing of, but this was starting to get personal, these were 2 of the people I knew better than most others. Like I said there were 2 choices: either they had lost it, or this was real. In the moment, I had decided that this was real.

I started praying, but this time was different. For the first time in my life, I prayed as if God was in the room standing in front of me. Most of my life I had prayed hoping He was there. This time there was no question if He was real.

I even told God, "You can't hide from me, I know you're there! I don't believe that you're a passive, clockmaker God. That doesn't make any sense. Why would you create something then deliberately ignore it? Even if you were, there's nothing preventing You from interacting if You wanted to. God you did something with my mom and sister, you could give me some kind of supernatural sign to prove you're there. I believe in you now in this moment, but if all I leave here with is an emotional experience, then days, months, or years later I will doubt it. I need You to do something. I'm not going to speak in tongues because those people look foolish, but just do something else. I'm not leaving here until you do something!"

I paused. I wasn't sure where to go from here. I waited a little bit. Nothing happened. I had laid my demands and argument before God, but I had offered nothing in return. I got the idea, that maybe I need to come to Him now. I knew enough about Christianity to know how to come to Him. I can't remember all that was running through my head, but I know at one point, I told God that I trust Him with my life, that I just wanted what He thought was best for me. After all, He is God and knows much more than I do.

Once I had surrendered to Him, a short while later, something very odd started happening. My hands and possibly legs started to feel on fire. It's very hard to describe to someone who has never felt it before, as up until that point in my life I had never felt it either. It's a physical feeling, almost like a soothing electric current is running through your limbs, or possibly if your arm was vibrating and had gone numb but you retained complete feeling. At the same time it was nothing like those at all. Then, it was almost as if an invisible force was lifting and controlling my arms. I still had control of them, but they were just kind of being gently guided or lifted up, like one would do in worship at a church service. Again, it's very hard to describe.

Shortly after this, the deep love of God just started to pour over me. I had heard televangelists and others talk about how deep and endless the love of God was. Every time I had heard about it, it just sounded like a typical salesman would talk, trying to overhype something so that the consumer would buy into it. It all sounded like a fairytale, and as we all know, fairytales are just that, tales, and for the most part not real.

But now that I was experiencing it firsthand, what I had heard started to make sense. Every time I would try to comprehend it and go deeper into it, it just got more and more intense, to the point where it started to become unbearable or incomprehensible. Words couldn't do it justice. Not only was the 'fairytale' I had heard so much about true, it was better than what I could imagine or comprehend! Everything I had heard about it fell way short.

God had spoken back and answered me. I knew He was real, but none of this necessarily proved who He was. So I asked Him, "Who are you? Zeus?", more as a rhetorical question. The answer I seemed to get back was that he was Jesus/God the Father/Holy Spirit. It made the most sense since that was who my mom and sister had prayed to, but I wanted to be sure. Was I so lucky to have been born into the "correct" religion? The odds were not in mine or anyone's favor, but at the same time it was hard to deny what was happening right in front of me.

Later on, I would get the gift of tongues through faith in God. That was much easier to get, as I had already experienced something supernatural in my life. God had moved my hands and limbs; it wasn't too much of a stretch to have Him move my lips and tongue.

4

Processing

I woke up the next morning and went to school as usual. There was much to think about, but for the moment life went on. I had just experienced something supernatural as far as I could tell. Was this really God? I had turned to God, asked Him for a sign, then received said sign. The sign I received was unlike anything I had ever experienced. The only naturalistic explanation I could come up with was that I had some undiagnosed medical condition, and the symptoms came up for it the first time that night. Perhaps being in a euphoric state had caused it to come on?

There were a few problems with that argument. One was coincidence. That whole explanation just made the religious aspect of it seem as a coincidence. It was possible, but it just seemed very unreal. Secondly, I'm not sure what medical condition would fall under what I had experienced. I've heard of ghost limbs that have a mind of their own, but this was not like the typical symptoms of that. I had full control if I wanted, and the movements were not random. That didn't explain the tingling though either.

Every way I could argue against it I had to do some kind of mental gymnastics to invalidate it. I didn't want to believe a lie, but the non-supernatural argument was more error-laden than the simple explanation of "God did it." And most importantly, I had poured my heart out to God. It was more intellectually dishonest and stupid to deny what was happening in front of me and explain it away, than to just accept it. I didn't want to be stupid, especially in my own eyes. There have been days that I've doubted if what had happened is real, but it always came back to just the common-sense argument. What else was I going to believe, sudden onset ghost-arm tingling syndrome?

I didn't think others would believe me. After all, I had heard testimonies about odd things like that for a large part of my life, and I didn't fully buy into a lot of them, even from close family members. I would have doubted my story if I was them. For me personally though, there was no other rational option. I couldn't play dumb.

Little did I know that God was going to teach me an important lesson just hours after the whole experience. It was either the very next day, or potentially the day after that at the lunch table with my friends. I got my lunch and went to sit down, and I couldn't help but hear the word, "God" come from a few lips in conversation. I didn't hear a whole lot, but I knew they were having a heated discussion on the existence of God. I sat down, and without much time to comprehend what was going on, someone looked at me intently and popped the question.

"Greg, what do you think about God?

I've rarely been good at thinking on the spot with personally involved issues. I was totally not prepared and blindsided by it. What did I think about God? I had never been more sure of the answer to that question in my life. If you had asked me several days before, I'm not sure what I would have said. Probably something agnostic, or how I didn't think evolution was a good theory. That day I knew there was a God, and who He was. The only way I could defend what I believed though, was to share my experience, and come out as a crazy person. My place in the group wasn't cemented in my opinion, so doing so could be social suicide. I didn't want to be labeled crazy at the moment either. Still, I was one of the "smart kids." My opinion probably had some weight for that reason alone. I was one of the people that they went to for the answers to the hard questions.

One scripture came instantly to mind as well. It was drilled into me a few times and was one of the verses that was talked about a lot at, mostly to help people that were faced with a martyrdom choice. Matthew 10:33:

"But whoever denies me before men, I also will deny before my Father who is in heaven."

I knew I couldn't say I didn't believe in God and deny Him, but I was so unprepared for that question that I really wanted to dodge it. So, I told a different lie.

"I'm not sure where I stand with that." I said quickly in a very dodgy way.

They looked away and moved on with the conversation. I felt so terrible, I begged forgiveness from God, felt as if I had failed Him. It wasn't technically denying Him, but close enough. In my mind, I knew better. Looking back, it would have been an almost perfect witnessing opportunity, but I blew it. There were 2 positive things I learned from this though: 1. When you move towards God, He moves as well. 2. I learned the meaning of 1 Peter 3:15:

"But in your hearts honor Christ the Lord as holy, always being prepared to make a defense to anyone who asks you for a reason for the hope that is in you; yet do it with gentleness and respect"

****

Following my experience, I naturally developed a deep hunger for God. Those who have had relatable experiences will understand. You get a taste, and you want more. A lot more. You want to live in it. If I couldn't feel the fire/tingling, I worried if God was still there. Obviously, scripture is sufficient to put this fear to rest, as it says in Deuteronomy 31:6,

"Be strong and courageous. Do not fear or be in dread of them, for it is the Lord your God who goes with you. He will not leave you or forsake you."

but I couldn't help but feel like that. After all, He could give me the experience constantly, so why not? Why couldn't I live here? Therefore, if I wasn't feeling it, was He really there? More or less what happened was, when I felt it start to go away, I would pursue Him more until I felt it again.

Eventually, it got to the point where I just stopped doubting. Whenever I sought God, it would come back instantly. I started to just have faith that God would be with me, and from then on it just stuck and came whenever I thought of Him. From then on, I've felt it pretty much every day of my life. It would be a very bad day if I didn't feel it, and even on my worst days I still would feel the fire in my hands, though often in a different tone. There are often different "tones" of it, which I believe God uses to guide me. For instance, when a thought I have or something I'm doing is wrong, I'll often get a mildly painful tingling sensation, or if I'm doing something right or in worship it will feel like a very good and uplifting, or soothing tone. God became a consuming fire in my life, and I often couldn't get Him off of my mind, I just wanted more.

At different times through prayer, it was even able to be transferred to other people. I prayed often with my mother, or more accurately, she prayed with me. She was not only able to speak in tongues, but was able to interpret, and I was blessed to have such a person to pray with me regularly. I often doubted her gifting, and didn't always trust the interpretations, more just because of my skeptical nature. Over time though I saw things come true and I started to pay more attention. Through prayer she did get the tingling as well, as did a few other family members or close friends, and possibly others that I'm unaware of.

****

There is one story concerning the "fire feeling" that is prominent. I was praying in our hot tub late at night, as I had often done. I would get in, listen to my iPod and just think of God and/or pray. I often questioned my salvation, as I wasn't living right, though I still spent a lot of time with God for the most part. In part of that wondering and thinking things through concerning that, I just started pondering things. I realized how big God was, and powerful, and all-knowing, and then it just came to me that God really does know everything that's going to happen. He holds it all in His hands. Most importantly, He knew it before the world or anything was set into motion. The most minute details He knew before the world began. Then the logical conclusion of that, was that He knew before the world began, that at this exact moment in time, I would be sitting here in this hot tub thinking about this exact thing.

I found it very funny (ironic) and peaceful at the same, just knowing that God holds it all in His hands, everything is thought out, and nothing takes Him by surprise. But it was more than just "head knowledge" to me, it became imparted into my reality, I fully believed and understood it. In this experience, God's presence fell very heavy on me, and the "fire" intensified to consume my whole body. Usually when the fire would fall, (and it fell pretty much every day to some extent, several times a day,) I'd always have final control over my limbs if I so chose. This time, I tried to move my limbs, and my fingers, but I could not. I'm wide awake and more or less paralyzed in God's presence. It was exhilarating and a bit scary at the same time if I was honest.

I decided to take the opportunity to ask a question, since in this state I knew I didn't have any influence in the outcome. First, I should clarify that I usually heard from God by asking Him to move my limbs in a certain way. For example, I would ask a question and would ask God to move my left hand to the right for "yes", or to the left for "no", and things like that. I still had control of my limbs though through it all, so I often wasn't sure I was hearing correctly in case my bias had influenced the outcome. Only if I was in a strong presence of God would I likely not doubt it. This time was different though, as I had lost the ability to move my limbs of my own free will, so I knew I couldn't influence the outcome.

The only thing that came to mind to ask was "who are you?", and I asked them to spell it out as I went through the alphabet using my index finger to mean "no" and middle finger to mean "yes", and what I received was T-A-H-A-Z. Well, it passed the first test in that it has syllables and is not gibberish. Some time later after praying about it more, I believe it was the name of my guardian angel. The whole experience was a little out of my comfort zone, though I thank God for it.

5

Wandering

    I would like to say that after I found God, that I did my best to live for Him and obey what He said in scriptures. My heart, who I was, was always with Him, but my actions and my lifestyle were not necessarily a good reflection of that, at least in the traditional way that people would think of when they thought of "Christian values." I thoroughly enjoyed trying new things, be it new foods, new experiences, and challenging myself. I learn the most when I just dive into things and become immersed in the various aspects of them, and this carried over into a generally negative lifestyle commonly described as "the norm" for young people.

    It was probably just a month or two after I had had my lifechanging encounter with God. A friend of mine had invited me over to a party he was having at his house "to play video games" and spend the night. Obviously the video games were not the main appeal of the party. I knew that; it wasn't hidden, but that's what I told my parents. Drinking was going on, and I had kind of wanted to try it. It would be the first time for a few other friends of mine, as well as myself, so we were kind of in the same boat. I didn't have much of a social life outside of school, and I kind of wanted one. I wanted to get out and be part of the "fun crowd" in some sense, or at least see what it was all about and then go from there. I knew where I stood with God, and I didn't think just trying it could change that. If I didn't try it, I knew I would just want to do so at some point, wonder what it was like, and who knows what else.

    I went out to eat with my friends at a restaurant for the first time, which was nice. Penn Station is always good. They told me to just take it slow, just drink beer the first time, etc. They seemed sincere in just trying to help out, like most people are. I got to the party before they did, and by the time they had got there I was several shots in. I've always been a "go with the flow" kind of person as the default, for better or worse, so when I was offered something I didn't turn it down. It didn't take long before I was hooked after just a fraction of the night had passed.

    Afterwards while talking with a friend, we discussed how it was fun but we didn't want to do it all the time, just like maybe every other month or something. That seemed reasonable enough. Of course, every other month turned into every month, then every couple of weeks, then almost every week if there was a party somewhere or a hangout location. After high school and into my college years, every week turned into multiple times per week.

    Probably a year or so later after I had started drinking, I was coerced into trying marijuana while drunk. How bad could it be? I didn't feel much the first time, and I didn't have plans then to do it anymore after that, just more of a one-time thing to try it out as fit to my curious disposition. I got coerced again though a few days later, so I tried it again, and this time I felt it, and I liked it, probably more than alcohol. So began another dive into drug use, though that is where it stopped for the most part. In a way I kind of became the poster child for marijuana use among my friends who also smoked pot. I became somewhat of a regular pothead, but at the same time I still excelled in school for the most part, which was often counter-culture to what people typically thought of when they think of potheads – hence the "posterchild."

****

All of the "fun" came to an end in the fall of my senior year of college. My friend and I were leaving someone's apartment as the party was dying down. I could have walked to my apartment, but it was starting to get cold out, so I drove there instead. I pulled out onto the road, and forgot which streets were one-way streets. I didn't have a whole lot of time to figure it out before the one-way street turned into a 2-lane, one way bridge, by which time it was too late to turn back. I saw red and blue lights behind me, but at the moment I was more concerned about dodging the 2-3 cars that had come across the bridge, using my turn signals as best I could. As soon as I got to the other side I pulled over right away into the first parking area I could find.

I quickly cracked the window, shut the car off, and asked my friend to look for the registration and insurance. By that time 2-3 cop cars had pulled up, and I was a little surprised to notice a gun pointed at my head in my peripherals. I froze up, and did everything the officer had told me, as they escorted me to what I assume was the police department for processing. By that time the officers had become friendly, I was just remorseful and in shock. I was very close to causing an accident. The officer said he probably wouldn't have pulled me over if I hadn't went across the bridge, even though he saw me pulling out going the wrong way and could probably assume I'd been drinking. It was a college town, I'm sure drunk driving was a common occurrence. The last thing he asked me before taking me to jail to sober up was, "Why didn't you pull over when I turned my lights on?"

I was quick to reply, "I didn't want to block traffic."

Now the whole gun thing started to make sense to my drunk mind. They had to assume the worst since I was kind of running away from their perspective, and had put people in danger. Hence, the gun.

My friend that was with me was free to go, and had my sister's number. He had told her what happened, and she told my parents. I still remember my dad's response: "good." I had often driven drunk. To be honest, I enjoyed it; something I probably wouldn't openly admit at the time. Every time I got in the car, I made it a habit to remind myself of the fear of it, and the seriousness of what could happen in order to help prevent such a thing from happening and get my act together. My luck had run out, and my method failed me.

I plead guilty to the DUI on my birthday. One receptionist noticed and wished me a happy birthday. Since I had already gotten one charge for underage drinking, classes were mandatory, as well as community service. I also had to have alcohol monitoring for 6 months, so I chose to have the breathalyzer installed on my car. The alternative was to have a take-home one where you had to blow into it at random times during the day. I had no desire to spend the last part of my senior year of college without alcohol, so the car was the obvious choice. Even having done the "better" choice, the car version was absolutely humiliating. Besides just it being present in my car, it sounded like a kazoo when you had to blow into it. Having to do it in public was embarrassing, it was fairly obvious to anyone who was halfway paying attention. It was a constant reminder of my sin.

The class started soon enough. They started off by asking why we were all here, to which the answer was almost unanimously, even from the teacher, that we got caught. That being said, I had to be there. So, I figured I might as well pay attention and see if I could take anything positive away from the class.

The main thing that stuck with me, was this scenario that we all had to ponder. There were several things listed on our pieces of paper: money, family, religion, self-respect, career, health, friends, and probably a few others. The idea was that drinking/drugs could take away some or all of these things. We had to go step by step and cross out things that we were willing to lose, crossing out more things as we went on, until we were down to just one thing that we could hold onto, which we then shared with the class. Most people had family at the end, with religion 2nd or 3rd. One person had self-respect. Only a MMA fighter and myself had religion last. I know that no one can take that away except me, but that's besides the point. What stuck with me was that it helped to prioritize things in my life. I wanted God to be first, and if the typical college lifestyle was going to get in the way of that, maybe it wasn't for me.

Once, I had seen an older gentleman, probably 50-60 years old or more at a bar, drinking by himself. I didn't know much about him, but he was by himself and looked like he might be single, and like this was the highlight of his week. I realized that if I kept on that path, that this could be me someday, and I didn't like that thought at all. I don't mean to offend anyone who might be living in such a way, but I didn't want that to be me in thirty years. It was a sobering moment.

I did continue the lifestyle until a little while after I graduated college. I had my fun, but I was ready to move on. God had taken the desire to drink and do drugs away from me, so quitting alcohol and marijuana was very easy – I just did it cold turkey with no difficulty. I had somewhat regularly started chewing tobacco every couple of days in my latter college years, which took a little weaning off just because of the nicotine fits/headaches, but it was not that hard either because God was in it.

I was kind of living a double life through it all, up until I graduated. On the outside, there were still probably many friends who questioned if I believed in God – I almost never brought it up. I lived the typical party life. On the other hand, I thought about God constantly and prayed often, though I didn't go to church at the time. The hardest part of all of it was I stopped seeing many of my friends after I quit that lifestyle. Hanging out almost always involved drinking or pot, and without me partaking in that we just didn't have much else in common at the time. I don't think they saw it coming, it was hard.

Like many people will tell you if they've gone through something similar, God does not leave you during the sinful years. He didn't leave me either. In fact, much of God moving in my life happened during this time. Jesus says in Matthew 15:11:

"it is not what goes into the mouth that defiles a person, but what comes out of the mouth; this defiles a person."

I still believe that to be true. The problem with drugs and alcohol though is that it makes you more likely to do bad things or say bad things. It may also become an idol, where you waste your life and your time or opportunities chasing the high. This is alluded to in 1 Peter 5:8:

"Be alert and of sober mind. Your enemy the devil prowls around like a roaring lion looking for someone to devour."

Drugs and alcohol numb your senses and makes you susceptible to sin. There's been times where I've been drinking or high and I've not sinned, or even come closer to God in some way, though more often my former statement is what typically held true. That, and I do believe God wants us to take care of our bodies. Paul states in 1 Corinthians 6:19-20:

"Do you not know that your bodies are temples of the Holy Spirit, who is in you, whom you have received from God? You are not your own; you were bought at a price. Therefore honor God with your bodies."

This is more in response to sexual immorality from the previous verses, but I would say the general principle still applies to poisoning that could result from drugs/alcohol.

6

The Calling

During spring of my freshman year of college at Purdue University, for whatever reason, I was under a lot of demonic attack. I was very busy in school at the time with finals coming up and projects coming due. I didn't have much free time, and besides being very scary, the demonic attacks were eating up a lot of my sleep time. I kept praying every night for God to give me rest and keep the demons away. I knew I wasn't living right, but didn't want to change at the moment. I would pray and feel somewhat good about it all before I went to bed, then something would happen and I'd sense just an evil presence or something. Rinse and repeat each day or attack.

The attacks seemed to keep getting progressively worse as time went on, and I just didn't get it. Why was God allowing this? I had been attacked by demons before this time, but prayer and faith in God had always worked. That didn't seem to be the case anymore, at least at the time. I had at times questioned my salvation, especially because I wasn't living right. Was I not saved? I was just at a loss of what to do, and why this was happening.

Everything kind of came to a tipping point one night. I prayed and went to bed as usual. At some point, I woke up and there flashed the image of some demon face inches from my face. It terrified me. I prayed even longer. I felt pretty good about things after I prayed, and only went back to bed because I felt good. There was still a little fear, but I felt like God was with me, so I could go back to bed.

After a little time, I was asleep again, or at least I thought I was. It seemed like I was maybe in some start of a dream state. My eyes were closed, but in my dream state I was exactly where I was while sleeping, in my bed staring at the ceiling. The dream suddenly turned into a bit of a nightmare for me. The scenery didn't change much, and I didn't see anything scary, but it was as if I had suddenly been pulled from my body. It wasn't like a dream – in a dream you could control things. Here I felt powerless to do anything, and it seemed very real. It felt like my whole being was being dragged somewhere by my feet. I was quickly pulled through our (closed) dorm room door, and took a hard left down the hallway.

My mother had often told me that if in trouble, to call on the name of Jesus. Romans 10:13

"For everyone who calls on the name of the Lord will be saved."

I knew what to do. But, how does this whole being out of body thing work? If I speak the name of Jesus here, will it be said in my body as well, in which case my roommate might hear it. If he does, he'll probably think I'm nuts. I thought about it for a half second, but what was in front of me was much more important. Where was I being taken to? Was I going to hell? I knew I didn't want to find out; it couldn't be good. I didn't know that it would work as praying hadn't seemed to work either, but it was the only thing I could do. I quickly said, "Jes-"

As soon as it had started, it was over. I was instantaneously back in my body. I didn't even have the chance to finish saying His name, and I was back. I tucked that bit of knowledge of the power of His name in the back of my mind, but I was still much more concerned about what just happened. Even more so, I was concerned about what else might happen if I was to fall back asleep again.

This was the last straw. Praying wasn't working. It's been said by a few that insanity is doing the same thing over and over and expecting different results, and I was tired of doing that. I was done with praying like I had been. I knew God could stop it, but he wasn't. Why? So, I asked God,

"What do you want?"

At this point the only thing I could do was sacrifice, or something. The only thing that came to me was to give my life.

"Do you want my life?" I said.

I interpreted this as my will for how I wanted my life to go. My career was not mine to choose. My life was not mine to choose. I figured it meant a life of ministry, as that's what God wants people to do, to spread the gospel. The answer I seemed to be getting back was, "yes." I didn't want to do this at the moment, but I was running out of options.

I had a lot of reservations, but I wanted to ask God a few questions about my concerns. I asked God,

"Will it be harder?"

"Yes."

I didn't like harder, who does? I was used to it though, at least in my mind.

"Will I enjoy it more?"

"Yes."

I figured as much, but I wanted to ask. I trusted God had good things in store. I had one more question. Something I wanted more than anything. Everything else I could probably go without if I had to.

"Will I have a wife and kids?"

"No."

The answer hurt in a very real way. I didn't want to give that up at all. God did say I'd enjoy it more. I didn't understand how I would enjoy it more without my own family, but I trusted God. I thought about it for a minute. What other option did I have though?

"Alright God, I'll give you my life," as I jumped in to it.

After I had committed, I felt God's presence come over me in a powerful way. Fire came all over my body. I became happy and at peace. Soon after that, Abraham and Isaac came to mind, and how God had tested Abraham and told him to sacrifice his son to see if he would do it for Him. Maybe God had done that to me, to see if I would follow him unconditionally. So I had to ask God again,

"Will I have a wife and kids?"

"Yes."

I was so relieved. I thanked God. I did ask God one more question that was eating at me.

"When will this happen (as in what age)? When will I be in ministry?"

I was hesitant to settle on a specific answer, as I didn't want to be let down if I heard or interpreted it wrong. What I thought God said was 33 or 34. It was definitely a thirty, and I thought three was next, but the double three seemed too repetitive. I know it couldn't have been anything after thirty-five by the way it sounded. The takeaway I had here was that it would be between 30-35 years old.

As an important side note, I should explain how I usually hear from God. Since God could move my hands, I would ask Him often to move one of my limbs to the left or right to mean yes or no when I asked a question, which I explained earlier. Later on though when I started speaking in tongues, I just let God guide my mouth in a similar way, but when I got answers it would come out in English. Here I knew the second number was not anything after 35 by the way my mouth moved.

I sat there and just basked in God's presence awhile before going to bed, and sleeping like a baby. I had no fear or concern that the demonic attacks would come back. They didn't. I haven't had any since that time, except for the occasional nightmarish dream, and even those were very rare. When they did happen, I knew how to fight back with praise and worship and it wasn't a big deal. Eventually you realize it's mostly just lies and putting on a show to inspire fear. It only works if you let it. Standing on God's truth and your identity in Him works.

****

I woke up a changed person. I was now supposed to obey God and follow Him, so I did. I lived with God 24/7, sought Him at all times. In class, while hanging out with friends, and still partaking in things I probably shouldn't have been. Praying in all of my free time. It was exhilarating and exhausting at the same time. School was still very busy too. The demonic attacks were over, but I was still exhausted because now I was staying up late praying. I didn't want to go to sleep unless God said I was finished.

About a week after all of this had happened, I made a fatal mistake. I told God that I still wanted to follow him, but I asked if I could just have a little bit of a break to kind of collect myself and get some sleep. I envisioned just having like 2-3 days off to just recollect myself, but what happened was the presence of the Holy Spirit seemed to have left me. For the first time in several years, I didn't feel the fire or "tingling." I doubt He ever really did leave me, but it sure felt like it. I didn't like it, but at the moment I just kind of wanted to rest physically, mentally, and emotionally.

Praying or thinking about God didn't bring it back like it used to. This went on for several months. I began to sink into despair. Having felt God's presence constantly for several years, and then losing it was devastating. The biggest high of my life had just turned into the biggest low. In time I did cry out to God again, and the Holy Spirit did come back. The fire returned, and things were well again.

7

The Hunt

The Holy Spirit was back, but I didn't want to lose Him again. I started thinking about how this calling to ministry would work out. I knew that meant preaching the gospel, and leading people to Jesus, but how to do that was just a big question. If this meant I had to persuade people that God was real, I didn't want to do it from a point of weakness. When I say weakness, I typically mean that you shouldn't have to do it from a point of blind faith. Once you've reached that point in persuading you're probably going to lose your audience. I've seen a lot of people try to explain why you should believe in God, or specifically in Jesus, and while they weren't necessarily wrong, they often came off as very naïve, or just lacking reason. I had no interest in "blind faith" as a reason to believe. You should have a reason for whatever you believe, and they should be good ones. That's where I was when I was searching those few years ago. I had my reasons, mostly personal experience as the primary one, but a lot of the other arguments I heard made sense as well. Unexamined faith to me was not worth it at all, and if it was to be my job to try to convince others that God was real, I wanted to have the upper hand in those arguments.

Because I was an intellectual, witnessing to me was in many ways an intellectual thing rather than a heart one. After I got saved, I tried to come up with arguments for God and intelligent design. Atheists did put up a lot of valid arguments, and I knew that if God was real, there was a reason that things were the way that they are. I did know that God was real, therefore the reasons exist, and I could maybe start to find them if I thought things out more. So I did. I thought things out, and I came up with what I thought were some good arguments and answers to many of the valid points that atheists made. I hadn't heard of others put things the way I did either, so maybe they would be effective.

At the same time though, the goal was to get people to believe in Jesus. These arguments would really only potentially get people to accept the possibility of God existing. That is a huge step, to just open the door to God, and over time maybe they would come to Him. However, they could just as easily turn the other way too and go to atheism / agnosticism. They were probably just equally as likely to go the other way. I wasn't satisfied with it. It wasn't good enough. The whole evolution vs. intelligent design debate was still just a bunch of people trying to make educated guesses at what happened over the last thousands to billions of years. There's a good chance you're just going to believe whatever you want to.

I was determined to find answers. I thought about my own conversion. At the end of the day for me, it was a supernatural encounter with God that won me over. I think that would honestly probably be the best way for anyone to come to God. I'd argue that over the years it has been the best at producing well-grounded believers more than anything, at least in knowing that God was real. Once you experience something like that, it's hard to deny what's happening in front of you. I couldn't think of a more powerful way to bring someone to Jesus.

A few years after I had my first supernatural encounter with God, I was reading the book of Hebrews in the Bible, when a verse jumped out at me. This verse to this day is probably my favorite verse in the Bible, as it describes almost perfectly How I came to know God. Hebrews 11:6

"And without faith it is impossible to please God, because anyone who comes to him must believe that he exists and that he rewards those who earnestly seek him."

In the moment that I got saved, I both fully believed that He exists, and I believed that He would reward me if I sought after Him. This formula to me, backed with scripture, seemed to be the key to experiencing God in a supernatural way firsthand. If people could believe that God existed, then it was a short leap of faith to believe that He would reward them if they sought Him. At that point I could use my own testimony, as well as that of others, to convince them to diligently seek after God themselves, and encounter Him in a tangible way like I had.

The big question though, was how do you get them to believe that God exists, and not doubt? In my own experience, I had seen my mom and sister experiencing supernatural things which caused me to believe. The intellectual arguments for design and all that were good, but at the end of the day it wasn't enough for me, and I could see many people like me not buying into those and going the other way. It wasn't until I saw something supernatural that I believed in God. Because of all of this, what I settled on, was the mantra that "seeing is believing," and went from there.

People had to see that the supernatural was real, that there was something else out there that was real and didn't fit into the atheistic worldview. It was clear. What I needed to do now, was dig into all things supernatural. It didn't matter what it was. If it was supernatural, it could almost certainly be used as an argument for God. Anything out of the ordinary was evidence of something bigger out there, it was an open door that could lead to God. Before I started this search, I told myself that I'd dig into anything – good, bad, or ugly. I knew I needed to possibly explore anything supernatural; it didn't matter where it came from. I had a firm foundation of my faith, and didn't think that could be shaken. I understood that "opening doors" could be a bad thing spiritually, but at the same time, why should I fear knowledge? That didn't make any sense. I didn't believe in fear mongering Christianity. Truth is truth, you just need to make sure you understand why it's true or why it works, and go from there. I was confident that I would know when to stop too, before I opened any doors that might lead to negative outcomes.

****

So, I started digging into supernatural phenomena. The first and most obvious was miracles. After all, that's how I first believed. Miracles are very effective in bringing people to God, probably one of the best, if not the best way that people come to God. There's nothing quite like the laws of physics and logic breaking in front of your eyes to make you question your worldview and open your mind to a world unseen. This is especially when they happen in a religious context. You typically put two and two together and then you can get a glimpse of who God is. The main issue I ran into here though, is that this was already being heavily preached. It's nothing new. Miracles should continue to be preached, and with God's power and presence they will continue to happen and be effective. For me personally though, I wanted to look for other ways, as I didn't have much I could add to this.

Also, there was obviously a limit to the effect that miracles were having. People weren't believing in droves. Miracles are typically one-off events. They're hard to reproduce, at least in a scientific way. While it's fairly obvious to me why they aren't reproducible in the scientific sense, I get the skeptic's point to some extent. Many of the miracles that happened could be explained by natural means. For example, people prayed for someone, and they recovered naturally. God still very well could have been in it, and it could have literally been a miracle (act of God), but it also could have been due to natural means. Other miracles could be argued as people being gullible, naïve, easily persuaded, or even downright lying. All of those and everything in between have happened in the past.

There was also the issue that other religions had supposed miracles as well. Miracles weren't exclusive to Christianity. This fact is present in the Bible as well, in both the New and Old Testaments. In Exodus, Pharaoh's magicians were able to replicate many of the miracles God did through Moses. In the New Testament, we hear of people performing miracles through witchcraft. I'm sure other religions probably have supernatural things happening as well. I would argue Christianity has the largest share of them, and in matters of supernatural authority Jesus always comes out on top, which I'd say should be a compelling argument. At the same time I see the bystander skeptic's point. Miracles supposedly happen in all religions, yet religions seem to be in conflict with one another over this or that point. How do you begin to pull apart the weeds if you don't know any better either way? The best way is to just pray to the one true God to reveal Himself to you, whoever He is. Most people for whatever reason just don't get to that point though, or they don't want to take the next step and seek Him with all of their heart as they suspect that there's personal cost involved (which isn't untrue).

I myself had somewhat questioned the miracles I had seen reported on television and by others, and I had grown up in the church. I imagine it'd be even more difficult for someone who didn't, or had grown up in a different religion. Because I experienced miracles firsthand, I typically didn't doubt when others reported some of their own, but my old self probably would have, so I get where they're coming from. All this being said, I didn't have much to offer here other than my own testimony and that of others. It's something myself and every believer definitely needs to keep in mind, but I wanted to look at other things as well, as you don't know what else could cause someone to believe. I had to move on.

****

The next most obvious thing to me was the opposite of Christian miracles, the demonic. I knew I needed to tread carefully here. I was just interested in arguments and evidence of it. Demonic things, from what I knew of them, tended to be more in-your-face kinds of things; which for argument's sake did appeal to me. I much prefer to be in your face when it comes to arguments, and "go for the jugular" if I see that it's unprotected. Demonic possessions from what I'd heard could potentially involve things flying across the room without reason, perhaps very odd bodily things, etc. Christian miracles tended to be more subtle, though just as powerful of an argument, while demonic tended to be more overt.

Evidence of the demonic was also to me ultimately evidence of God once you run the logic out it's full course. A very malevolent deity that also created us doesn't make a whole lot of sense, therefore, there must be some other deity that has more benevolent interest in us that created us, and that deity would be much more likely to have more power on the other side. Otherwise, the evil deity could just overpower the benevolent one and destroy everything on a whim, in which case we wouldn't be here.

This has also been tried before, but it wasn't looked into as much as I thought it could be for apologetic's sake, so I decided to take a dive. Before going on, I cannot stress enough for the average person, to not do this. To take on the demonic successfully, you need to know where you stand with God. Your identity must be firmly established without doubt in the blood of Jesus, knowing that God is with you. Opening yourself up to such things can just inspire fear, and give Satan an entry point into your life. I used to love the thrill that horror movies gave me, but now I hate watching them. I'm not saying that I was perfect when I went searching, but I knew to tread very carefully. I had my encounters with demons, and they could be terrifying.

Anyways, I started looking online for evidence of demonic activity. The holy grail here was video evidence, as that would be harder to disqualify. This was before video editing and AI became what it is, and it was harder to manipulate videos in a convincing way. Nowadays it probably would mean little if I found such a thing. I eventually found a video where the person had a somewhat believable story and evidence. I watched it a few times. What it consisted of was a still-camera pointed in their kitchen. Then all of a sudden a drawer or 2 flew open, silverware coming out. Perhaps a plate flew across the room out of a cabinet. Some of the comments claimed fake, some supported it.

The evidence to me, even if it was real, quite honestly looked like a joke. I sarcastically thought to myself, "This is supposed to make me believe in God?". It looked like it could easily be staged, even if it wasn't. There were enough things off-camera to easily discredit it. I imagined myself trying to use this to convince my friends, and I imagined the looks I'd get, and that was enough to call it quits here. I had spent a decent amount of time trying to find that, and that was the best I could get. Besides, demonic activity suffered from all the other pitfalls of miracles. They're typically one-off events. Often people involved seem very gullible, naïve, easily influenced. The lack of trustworthiness is definitely there in most cases.

****

I decided to move on. There was a little bit of a problem though. I was stuck. The two most obvious things to me were out. I would have to get a little creative in thought here. Had I known more at the time, I probably would have pursued near death experiences (NDE), where people had supposedly died, seen the other side, and come back to life to tell about it. Most people who I had heard about who had that experience typically had something happen to them that fell in line with their current belief system, and therefore their testimony has a lot of the potential pitfalls that go along with miracles that I mentioned earlier. On the other hand, many came back with knowledge of things that they couldn't possibly have known otherwise, which in any case helps to validate their experience was real, and therefore evidence of the supernatural.

In today's world, you can find tons of stories and videos online about near death experiences. Many people who were atheist or somewhere on that spectrum have had such experiences as well, and woke up as changed people. A few stories I would highly recommend for the skeptic are those of Howard Storm, an atheist art professor, as well as Dr. Eben Alexander, neurosurgeon. "Imagine Heaven" by John Burke is also a good read which is more of a compilation of NDE's.

Like I said though, that's not what happened. I did have a mild curiosity that ate at me for a while though. To this day I couldn't say for sure if it was God or myself leading me to it. It all stemmed from a memory I had from back in second grade.

Greg J. Stenger

8

Zodiac

The memory stood out to me, because at the time it seemed like I was in the twilight zone. The year was roughly 1997, and the internet was starting to become a regular household service. The school had given each family with a student of a certain age a desktop computer. In addition to that, computer class was becoming normalized. It started as any other computer class, we walked into the computer lab and logged in. Then as an activity for "fun", we were all instructed to go to this specific website and look up our Zodiac signs, and read the descriptions to see how much it matched us.

Since I was raised in a fairly conservative Christian home, alarms started going off. I didn't know much about Zodiac signs but for all practical purposes they might as well be demonic. I had probably heard of horoscopes by that time, which was divination, which was clearly against what God said in scripture. At best, it was not Christian from what I knew. My teachers were both very nice, I didn't have a problem with either my regular teacher, or the computer lab teacher. I remember sort of liking them. Ultimately though, I wasn't comfortable at all proceeding with the assignment. However, I was a good, obedient kid, so I just kind of did what I was told.

The Zodiac signs, if you're unfamiliar with them, are broken up into twelve signs/groups, one for each month. Depending on your date of birth, you were placed into one of these twelve signs, and that meant that you tended to have certain characteristics associated with that sign. Then based on some other things that I didn't understand, it also affects certain things in your life, such as how your day would go and what would happen in the future, through horoscopes. If you went into the larger field of astrology under which all of these are contained, things got even more complex. The very premise of it seemed like a joke. Like palm readings or tarot cards. Why would that ever work? Class went on though, and so did I. So, my birthday was November 22, 1989. I looked it up and the website showed it was Sagittarius, but barely. It was the start date of Sagittarius. The teachers had special instructions for such cases, but I couldn't remember, so I called one of them over to clarify.

"It's whichever one seems to be right," she said.

Well that didn't make any sense. If I get to choose which one I am, then how could this system be reliable at all? Things went from bad to worse. I was supposed to read both of them now, and then choose one. Keep in mind that this was second grade, and reading was work. Time was starting to run out. I had skimmed both of them. Scorpio mentioned things about being emotional. It was an immediate turn off. I was a man, and men weren't supposed to be emotional. Clock still ticking, and I was behind because my birthday was difficult in this system. I decided to just pick Sagittarius and go with it, after all that's what the website said I was. My teachers probably just didn't know as much as the people who put the website together. They weren't the experts, the website was.

I read the description, and none of it was close, at all. A lot of it I would even say was the opposite of me. Well that went about how I expected it to. A superstitious, irreligious system didn't work. Surprise, surprise. At the end of class, and even after class, the teacher asked everyone if they felt like the description fit them at all. I was expecting a large majority of "no." What I heard surprised me quite a bit. I would say a large majority of the class said yes, theirs did fit them. Probably only a handful, including myself, said it didn't fit them.

This puzzled me quite a bit, but I didn't think much of it at the time. I had heard adults, including my parents, say that kids just don't understand things. Kids were often stupid. Maybe everyone in class was just easily swayed by things, or superstitious. I wasn't sure, but I knew it didn't work for me. If it didn't work in my case, how could it possibly be real? It bothered me for a short time, but I let it go and didn't think about it much after that.

****

Here I was though, years later, searching for evidence of the supernatural and out of ideas. It was the next thing that I had some experience with, so I decided to look into Zodiac signs again. I was always a little curious too as to how it had such a large following, when from just a basic glance it seemed to be so clearly false or illogical. Being older and more experienced, I went through the whole drill again, but this time with a better grasp on things. On some websites, I did see that Scorpio was listed as being on November 22, though most still had my birthday as being in Sagittarius. So I first decided to look at Sagittarius again.

I looked into some Sagittarius traits – they seemed to bounce around a lot from one thing to the next. Did I do that? No, not really. I tended to be more hyper-focused. They tend to not have a filter when they speak. I tended to overthink things to the point where I would end up not saying anything at all, or by the time I thought of something to say the moment had passed. Optimism was big, I tended to be pessimistic. Some of the negative traits were a lack of commitment or consistency. Again not really me. I was committed to things that I was invested in. I tended to be more committed than not anyways. Then of course there were the generic buzzwords – honest, philosophical, lively, passionate, adventurous, direct/blunt, intellectual. Half of those fit in some way, but were too generic. I was honest for the most part, philosophical, intellectual, probably passionate, but those were all too generic. They fit me because I was academically smarter. I'm sure no Zodiac sign had a monopoly on intellect, so I had to ignore those things. I read 3-4 descriptions, and just being perfectly honest, I had to say it didn't fit me at all. Some things did, but they were too generic to say with any accuracy that Sagittarius fit me. So just like when I had looked into it all those years ago in computer class, I had to say it was false. I guess I should move on.

I had a thought though. I still remembered what my teachers had said all those years ago. "It's whichever one fits you better." Years ago that didn't make any sense to me, but now that I was older, a student of science, and understanding how science is actually done on a practical level, that logic made a lot of sense. Suppose that the Zodiac signs were accurate – the way that we would study them would be some pseudo-scientific way. Like many things in science, if it was true, there's a good chance that we just don't quite understand exactly how it works. It would then make sense for people on the cutoff date to judge which sign is more accurate, because if you don't fully understand it, you couldn't say for sure what exactly defines the cutoff between signs. It made sense, so I decided if I was going to cross this off my list with good conscious, I needed to look at Scorpio to see if it was at all accurate. So I started again, but with Scorpio.

So I looked up some Scorpio traits. Determination – yea I was determined. It was my perseverance and determination that had gotten me through many things. When most people probably would have given up, I kept on. It was a big key to my success in everything from school, projects, sports, etc. I wouldn't say this was generic, at least not for my personality. I knew I had more determination than many others.

- Loyal – yes I was very loyal to people. That could be generic though.

- Honesty – somewhat generic, but yea fit for the most part.

- Ambition or single-mindedness – yes, this goes along with determination. I often got tunnel vision on things. I'd get so focused that I could tune other things out. "Where there's a will, there's a way." That was a big theme in my life. I had the will and determination if I really wanted something, so I was usually pretty good at finding a way to achieve my goals.

- Secretive – yes I was very secretive. I never thought of that as a defining trait in my life, but I had to admit it fit very well and I knew it to be true. I thought this was just being smart. I learned at a young age, that once you know what someone is attached to, you know what motivates them. You'd know what they are likely to do based on that. All of that meant that those things could be used against them. I didn't want to get hurt, so I kept everything that I held dear close, and didn't share it. It was the best defense mechanism I had. Yes everyone keeps their secrets to some extent, but I was much better at it, and I knew it. In school, even at a very young age, I didn't want to tell others simple, stupid things like what toys or TV shows I liked, or my favorite color, etc. I watched people share things I never would have said, both my peers and adults. This was a fundamental way that I operated throughout my whole life. It was a big reason why I didn't share my faith with anyone, it would open me up to the potential for a lot of hurt. This was a big, unexpected hit here.

- Brave/fearlessness – yes I was brave and fearless in some aspects. The way some articles put it is that they rush into danger without a second thought. Yes this was me, and it came out a lot in sports or video games. I would be the person that drove or dove in to try to make the play happen, or go for the hard play – an all or nothing approach in many cases. In video games, it meant that I died quite a bit trying to secure the kill or the objective – I would take on suicide missions. I saw what needed to be done, and figured if no one else was going to do it, I'd have to.

- Psychic – a weird thing, but yea it did fit. My way of interpreting people around me often rested on trying to figure out their emotional state, what they were thinking, their mood, etc. Similar to the secretive thing, I tried to figure out others' secrets. Not to share, more to just know so that I knew how to better deal and interact with them. It helped me to get a better read on them. People's emotional state was usually the first thing I picked up on.

Moving on to negative traits – jealousy, resentful, unforgiving, moody. I supposed I could get jealous, that seemed natural though. I could get resentful, I knew it was wrong though so I tried to get through it. My mom had told me to try to look for the best in people, so I used that to help get through those times. It was better to stay positive. Unforgiving – yes I struggled with that. As a Christian it's fundamental, not optional and tied to your salvation, but I struggled with it. From my perspective, I could easily see the potential outcomes of people's words and actions. They should be able to see that too I thought, so why did they do it in the first place? They should have known that would happen. Because I saw the hurt coming, I had a hard time with forgiveness, because the person who caused harm should have known better. Related to all of this, I would hold grudges occasionally, and no one could bring me out of them. I had to bring myself out.

I went on to look at other things, such as relationships, sex, etc. I had not been in a relationship, but everything that was written about those things was how I had imagined it; it was my ideal relationship in my mind. I went on down the list. To be honest, I got chills down my spine as I was reading things. Point after point was not just kind of me, or generic, but it was all just like hammer on nail accurate. Every little thing was me, or if it wasn't me, I could see myself behaving like that in certain situations, or thinking that way. It wasn't just the generic buzzwords that were accurate, the reasoning for "in what way is Scorpio this way or that way" hit home pretty hard.

I was surprised at what I found. I did not expect to actually find anything here, at least not to the degree that I did. If I did find anything, I expected it to be like maybe 60-70% accurate, with a lot of generic things added in. It was more like 90%+ accurate, with very little generic descriptions, and many things were dead on. If I was to be unbiased and honest, I'd have to say that it worked for me. The Scorpio personality fit me to a "T." I don't think I ever thought of these things to be defining characteristics of me, but at the same time it's hard to know how to truly define yourself when "who you are" in a philosophical sense is a bit of an enigma.

It was definitely true for me, but there was still a lot of room for error in just one person, when there were billions of people on the planet. If this was a real thing, and had the potential to be evidence of the supernatural, it had to be true for everyone. I had found a hit on my quest for supernatural things. I had to look into it more.

9

Hypothesis

At this point in time, you need to understand a few things. There were so many thoughts going through my head all at once. Many trails I needed to think about and research. So, at this point I'm going to try to compartmentalize each trail in order to make it easier to understand, but at the time these were all happening more or less simultaneously in many regards.

My immediate thought went to scripture. I couldn't help it. I knew it was the "wrong" way to study scripture. Many have made the fallacy of trying to make scripture mean what they want it to. The most common way of doing this was to come to scripture with preconceived notions. You would then try to justify your thoughts by searching for scripture that supports it. The danger in this is that you can easily take things out of context and make it mean whatever you want it to mean. The correct way was to understand the setting of scripture, and then let it speak for itself in context. That's the correct way to study any kind of writing.

The number twelve was very significant in the Bible though. The only more significant number is seven. There were 12 signs of the Zodiac. At the time I understood that the number seven was a sign of completion. For the number 12, I knew there were 12 tribes of Israel, and 12 disciples of Jesus. So far in our understanding of God and prophecy, if you buy into that, God often does things a specific way in order to illustrate a greater spiritual truth. Sometimes in prophecy, God will just come right out and say things that will happen, and that is rather straightforward. "This event X is going to happen", and those are easy to recognize as prophecy.

Other times, God uses symbology to demonstrate spiritual truths. These symbols oftentimes can go unrecognized as prophecies or having deeper meaning, as they often serve a needed purpose in the context that they're written, which makes sense. However, there is often a deeper, or greater spiritual meaning/purpose that God has for doing things a specific way. I'll give a few common examples. Numbers 21:8:

> *"And the Lord said to Moses, "Make a fiery serpent and set it on a pole, and everyone who is bitten, when he sees it, shall live."*

There was an issue here: the people grumbled against God, were afflicted by serpents as a result, and this was God's solution to heal them. Now, God could have done this any way. They could have taken the manna/bread he gave them and rubbed it on their wounds. They could have eaten bugs. There were limitless possibilities. God chose this way though, because later on when we see Jesus dying on the cross and us being saved, healed, and forgiven by looking upon what He did for us, we see the parallel with the snake on a stick mentioned in Numbers. The real-life significance becomes evidence that Jesus is the Messiah by fulfilling scripture. Similarly, we see this in Numbers 20:11

"And Moses lifted up his hand and struck the rock with his staff twice, and water came out abundantly, and the congregation drank, and their livestock."

Here we have Moses striking a rock, and water comes out. In scripture, the Messiah is often pictured as a rock. When Jesus was stabbed on the cross, we get the report that water mixed with blood came out. We see the parallel symbology, and when we see the fulfillment, the purpose is more evidence that Jesus fulfilled the scriptures.

I'll do one more – the feast of Passover. In Exodus 12, the nation of Israel is instructed to take a lamb and keep it in their household, and then kill it, and eat it. They were to take some of its blood and spread it on the doors of their dwellings. Then when the Spirit of the Lord passed through that night, He would kill all the firstborn except for those who had the blood on their doors. Similarly, when we see the Gospel message of Jesus, we see that God will judge everyone, and that we are passed over in judgement by applying His sacrifice to our lives and to cover our sin. John the Baptist even said of Jesus in John 1:29

"Behold, the Lamb of God, who takes away the sin of the world!"

God could have done all of this in many different ways, but He did it in specific ways in order to show greater spiritual truth. When you see the fulfillment of the symbolic prophecy, the result is we see evidence of a higher being orchestrating things, and it causes faith in God and the events . The takeaway here, is that God not only does prophetic things through direct prophetic words, such as those recorded in Isaiah chapter 53, but He weaves prophetic signs and symbols into what might otherwise be considered random, or "odd" ways of doing things. At first glance some of these things may seem random, but they're oftentimes not. They point to something specific, and once you see the connection, the result is further proof of what God has said, and it gives more reason for faith in God.

Similarly, I would argue the numbers twelve and seven follow the same format. They're not generic methods of communicating certain things, they're symbols. That's just how God does things. Yes they could have double meanings. God often does that, but there ultimately is a primary meaning. Passover had a very real meaning to the Jews at the time (and still does today), but the greater meaning of it was to point to the Messiah's sacrifice. If the number 12 in the Bible was meant to represent the 12 signs of the Zodiac, it would fit with the way that God operates in prophecy. How?

1. It's specific, not generic. If the number twelve is just some generic number that God made up or has an affinity for, then there is no real-life significance to anyone. It is meant to signify something. The number twelve in the Zodiac is also specific to the Zodiac itself and how we interpret it. If Jesus died by stoning, then the snake on the stick wouldn't fit very well. Jesus died suspended from a wooden structure though, high up for all to see, fitting the symbology.

2. It has a real-life connection and is not some abstract concept. If it's an abstract concept, then it doesn't mean anything to someone outside of Judaism or Christianity. God

does use some symbols like this to represent metaphysical things such as the Trinity (will get to that later), but most of the major, significant symbols are not this way. Most importantly though,

3. What this ultimately means, is that there's more evidence of God. If it was in scripture, it could go one step further and be considered evidence that the God of the Bible is the true God. If the Zodiac was a real thing along with it matching prophecy in the Bible, it could potentially confirm that it all was orchestrated by God and point people to Jesus.

That was the primary purpose of all scripture from a Christian perspective: to point people to the Messiah. The Zodiac could fulfill that purpose. That hypothesis rested on two major contingencies. The Zodiac had to be real; it must be true for everyone. It also had to fit in scripture. After that, the rest of the logic fell into place easily, because of Revelation 4:11

"Worthy are you, our Lord and God, to receive glory and honor and power, for you created all things, and by your will they existed and were created."

All things exist because God created them. If the Zodiac was true, there was only one logical explanation in my mind, because God created all things, including the Zodiac. That logic works for me and hopefully most Christians, because I know that I know who God is. I do understand that doesn't work for everyone; I'll get to that later.

****

The other big question of the Zodiac and its almost synonymous field of astrology is the question of why it works or how it can exist. I would argue that the Zodiac signs, and even astrology if you buy into all of it, can only exist in a reality where we were created. All of it exists supernaturally, there is no logical way around that.

In modern astrology, everything is typically based around a birth chart. That is, where the heavenly bodies – sun, moon, planets, etc. all line up at the time of birth. Because of this, one of the hypotheses is that the heavenly bodies somehow have an influence on the human psyche. I understand where this is coming from, it is an attempt to tie it to the natural. Perhaps there's some unknown force or connection to it all. While this is not necessarily false, it's insufficient.

Here's why: at the end of the day, all forms of astrology are interpreted through the twelve signs of the Zodiac, or 12 houses, etc. How do you begin to tie that to something natural? I don't think it's possible at all. Why not have 9 signs, 21, 3, or 15? Also, if it was due to some natural force, you would expect there to be a smooth transition between them. That's arguably not true as the change seems to be more abrupt. I'm right on the cutoff and was not Sagittarius at all, though I was raised by them more than any other sign. The only logical way the Zodiac or astrology could exist was if it was supernatural. I don't think there's any logical way around it because it's all interpreted through 12 signs, which defies any kind of natural explanation.

****

There are also many different theories and subfields of astrology. I was highly skeptical of it all. The worst-case scenario was that I'd believe a lie. I looked at all of it this way and tried to pick it apart as best I could.

There were horoscopes. Those were in part a result of the line of thinking that the planets had influence on people, and apparently not just at birth but throughout their whole life. This is kind of taking it to the next step that I don't quite think is there, notably the logic. My sun sign described how I tended to think. I would call it my default method for interpreting and interacting with the world around me. How you are is different from what will happen to you on a fundamental level. There's no connection necessarily. If it's not a necessity, then logically speaking it's probably not there at all. Furthermore, scripture is clear on divination in several places, probably most notably in Deuteronomy 18:10

"There shall not be found among you anyone who burns his son or his daughter as an offering, anyone who practices divination or tells fortunes or interprets omens, or a sorcerer"

If God forbids us from doing such things, why would He create a method of divination? Horoscopes were definitely out for me, from both a logical and Christian perspective.

There was Numerology as well, which generally attempted to tie the number of the day you were born on to your personality. The system itself was full of self-contradiction, as the result you would get depends on which calendar you use and which numbering system (we use base ten numbering system, but you could have the base set as anything you want – base 5, base 8, etc). It was very easy to pass on.

There were also all of the planets and moon that affected one's personality in their birth chart. For me starting off, this made things infinitely more complex. This took it from twelve archetypes to twelve to the tenth power number of possibilities, well over one trillion possibilities. With so many possibilities, you could almost get whatever you want out of such a system. Again, while not necessarily false, this was way out of scope of my hunt for evidence of the supernatural. I do also believe that there's more to one's personality than just their sign or birth chart. I highly doubted that was everything.

There was the possibility that all of that was just taking it too far. Like I said before, it existed supernaturally. Using the planets and other heavenly bodies was an attempt to tie it all to something natural, as a natural force causing it would beg the question "why wouldn't other bodies have influence using this natural force?" Because it exists supernaturally, there was a real possibility that the sun didn't have anything to do with it at all, and that whatever was responsible for its existence just set it up to take place over a year. Or the sun could have been set apart as "special" in this system, and the other planets were not made special or made to have any significance at all. From my perspective, the logic didn't necessarily flow to include anything other than the sun because of the supernatural contingency. What caught my eye was the 12 "sun signs," as that's all that I could reasonably validate for myself. I was mostly interested in just that. In any case, I didn't have the time or resources to investigate that far into it and reasonably be able to validate the results.

****

9: Hypothesis

Now all of this culminates into the question of why the Zodiac is true. Since it exists supernaturally, the cause of it is likely supernatural as well. As it's supernatural, its cause is also most likely from an intelligent source, rather than from an unknown supernatural "natural" phenomenon. Any cause related to the latter is pure speculation, and one can hardly even do an educated guess. Here, I proceeded with the former assumption of it coming from an intelligent source. Another thing to note here, is that this system is more or less incompatible with a worldview that espouses biological evolution as the primary cause of life on earth. Life being the result of random chance, then also being characterized and influenced by the Zodiac makes very little sense. So here, assuming the Zodiac is true, we are dealing with a realm where life on earth was either created, or perhaps transplanted from somewhere else. Either way, life on earth was the result of the actions of more intelligent being(s) in a reality where the Zodiac was true. From here, the most logical path is that whatever started life on earth is almost certainly also responsible for the Zodiac. This brings us to the primary question, "What could be the possible purpose of such a thing to a creator?" To understand this, you need to think about the purpose of such a system.

When you look at it this way, again horoscopes drop out quickly, there's no point. That doesn't serve a creator any purpose, that serves us a purpose – magic and divination. It could be that the creator put that in place for us to use to help us live our lives, or to help things play out a certain way, but there's still no good purpose for it other than a means of having people experience this or that through forcing circumstances around them, etc. I would still put horoscopes in a category of "no good reason."

In asking this question of purpose, we need to consider the facts within the system. What I first found to be true was that Scorpio fit me, as in it fit how I processed and interacted with the world around me. It described how I thought. As we look throughout biology and life on earth, we see that we don't eat food and it magically turns into excrement. Offspring don't magically appear from the stork. It's all governed by biological, physics-based processes set in place by the creator, if you'll accept that statement. Likewise, I don't for a second think that our minds or our spirit is "magic." I'm sure there is a method to the madness, whether it all exists in the brain or outside of it. We're not promised to know the answer, but knowing is not out of the question.

Since the Zodiac described how I processed and interacted with the world around me, the main benefit of this to a creator, as well as the theme of it all, appears to be tied to how we think. Therefore, it's likely tied to how we were created, or how our minds or spirit/soul is wired to work. That is the most obvious and only real necessity of such a system to a creator. By having 12 different signs, you're creating 12 different archetypes of people. It would allow for intentional diversity of personality, thought, etc. By separating it from DNA and tying it to time, you're ensuring that diversity of thought will be scattered finely among all people, where if it was tied to DNA, you could get populations that are very much set in their ways, only able to see things or process things this way or that. This would also allow for the possibility of "intellectual extinction" if one race or so was to be wiped out, then so would that way of thinking be. Certain populations could overpower others in numbers as well, creating a lopsided distribution. Tying all of this to time instead of something like DNA or geography therefore ensures a fairly even spread of diversity and ensures that each "type" would continue to prevail.

I'm sure there's more than one way to achieve something like that, but that is the most basic, logical conclusion I could draw from all of this. This was the prevailing hypothesis as I moved forward in my research: that the Zodiac was tied to how we were created to think or behave.

10

Investigating

So began my search to see if the Zodiac was true for other people as well. If this was a real thing, it would have to be true for nearly everyone. Being true for some people and not others would not work well given the hypothesis I had come up with. Do some people breathe and others not? Of course not. If it was tied to our creation or design, it needed to be applicable to all humans, not just some, or 70% of them.

One of the biggest hurdles was just trying to understand what each sign meant, and what to look for. I did a lot of reading on each sign, got a decent feel for many of them based on articles I found online. I knew the big things to look for. I was sort of able to get a grasp on a little bit about what the signs were about.

- Aires tended to have the 'go-getter' attitude as a big thing that stuck out.
- Taurus I read a lot about stubbornness, being practical, and reliable. I struggled with how that definition was special.
- Gemini were big communicators, and juggled a lot of different things, explored different avenues.
- Cancer was nurturing, sensitive.
- Leo's liked to be the center of attention.
- Virgo traits were logical, practical, analytical, hardworking. Those seemed generic to me as well.
- Libra's were extroverted, and maintained balanced. Could be diplomatic.
- Scorpios were easy since it fit me. Secretive was big (or not revealing too much or anything of value). Kept to themselves. Sneaky maybe. Emotional, though that's harder to tell.
- Sagittarius were travelers, tended to be all over the place, lively, blunt.
- Capricorns were determined, dedicated, loyal. I struggled with how this one stood out as well
- Aquarius was humanitarian, intellectual, creative, independent.
- Pisces was very sensitive, compassionate, sympathetic. Dreamers.

Now it came down to looking out into the world and trying to see if it fit the description of others. Very early on I decided that I was only going to look at people that I knew fairly well. I had no interest in second-guessing if the things that I had noticed about a person were true. I wanted to at least be somewhat sure about the accuracy of the data I collected, and that would not necessarily be possible if I didn't know the person very well.

Because of this, the easy place to start was with close friends and family. I had enough experience with much of my family, so I could use memories for that. My current environment was also college, so I studied many of my friends there. It was what I had to work with. I would go to parties and just study people. Obviously, alcohol was involved. It was actually kind of helpful. People tended to be a little unfiltered under the influence. Their natural or "raw" self came out, which is exactly what I was looking for. Their guard was typically down, and you could often have more meaningful conversations with them. You could see their reactions, and the way they were thinking a little easier. A lot of the negative traits of the signs also tended to come out when under the influence. I'm probably a natural pessimist, though I prefer to call it realism, so this helped me personally quite a bit in my studying. I could see what a lot of their default methods of dealing with negative situations or emotions were.

Facebook was a great way to birthday stalk so that I would know what their sign was, and then see how well they matched up to it. It was invaluable in helping to greatly expand the number of people I could study. Otherwise, I would have been severely limited in my studying, and would have had to resort to weird ways of asking about someone's birthday. Knowing myself, I probably wouldn't have done this, and instead would have just tried to pay close attention to anything they might have said that would hint at their birthday.

In addition to this, probably one of the more effective methods was comparing people of the same sign to each other and looking for similarities. I would try to see what stood out and matched up with their signs. My data pool was restricted a bit when doing this, but it was the best way to confirm things. I could see that people of the same sign often had similar tendencies. I read what the articles said about such people, but you kind of need to see it for yourself to get a better judge of the thing.

One of the bigger questions that naturally came up, is "what does it mean to be a Scorpio?" Of course it's the same question for all of the other signs as well. This is where the articles were a little limited for me, it's something I had to see for myself to really be able to understand. It's not that the articles were inaccurate, but it's like trying to learn a foreign language without speaking it regularly. You can learn a lot from textbooks, but at the same time you have to live it a little to really get a grasp on it. This is why comparing people of the same sign was most effective, it potentially offered real-world experience to know what things were.

There were signs that I had a little bit easier time seeing people match up with, as well as signs that I had a harder time matching people up with. Libras, Geminis, Scorpios, Cancer, and Pisces were probably some of the easier ones. Libras and Geminis tended to talk quite a bit which helped. Scorpios tended to not share too many personal details. Cancer and Pisces were emotional in different ways which I could pick up on – more so Cancer. I didn't know too many Aquarians. Aires and Leo weren't too hard. Sagittarius, despite knowing many of them, was a little bit of an enigma. Some fit the description quite a bit and I could see some similarities, though not always. Taurus, Capricorn, and Virgo I struggled with.

10: Investigating

****

There was another big pool of people that I could tap into and study as well. People that openly displayed their lives and their birthdays for all to see – celebrities. Film actors and musicians were the most common type of celebrity. Now, one could write several books on this subject alone, but I'll mention a few.

For instance, look at the romantic genre in film. When I was growing up, Titanic was the big romance hit. Leonardo DiCaprio became a household name, and did well in romances. He's a Scorpio. Looking at other big names in romance – Ryan Gosling, Emma Stone, Julia Roberts, Rachel McAdams, Matthew McConaughey, Owen Wilson. They were Scorpios, and highly regarded as doing very well in romances. Scorpio tends to be emotional, so romances would tend to be a natural fit for excellence. One other thing I always thought was interesting was how Leonardo DiCaprio tended to keep to himself outside of acting, more so than other actors who would go on television shows and whatnot. Many of those actors also did that as well – a very Scorpio trait.

A lot of the bigger names in rap tended to be Libras or Geminis as well. Kanye West, Eminem, The Notorious B.I.G., Lil Wayne, Snoop Dogg, Andre 3000, Kendrick Lamar, Will Smith, and Ice Cube were all top rappers that were Libra or Gemini. Both signs tended to be a little chatty, which is a good trait for rapping.

If you're looking for someone to take on an odd role in films, Gemini were also a good bet. Think of Johnny Depp and all the strange roles he's played – Edward Scissorhands, Captain Jack Sparrow, Alice in Wonderland. Helena Bonham Carter did a great job playing the unhinged Bellatrix Lestrange in Harry Potter, as well as Dark Shadows with Johnny Depp, and the Red Queen in Alice in Wonderland.

A lot of the larger "pop queens" tended to be Sagittarius. Miley Cyrus, Taylor Swift, Britney Spears, Christina Aguilera, Nicki Minaj. I think the free-spirited nature here might help to command a presence on stage as well as with song flow or lyrics, but I'm not quite sure on that one. The abundance of talent that tends to dominate certain genres does help to build a case for something statistically significant here though.

****

What I was ultimately doing was trying to guess how people were processing and interacting with things based on their behavior. A big part of the hypothesis that I had was that the Zodiac was tied to how people's minds operated at a fundamental level – that it was part of our mental wiring or creation. Some people in astrology say that the sun sign only affects certain aspects of your life, or sets your generic goals or the moon is more affecting this or that, or perhaps this planet affects this aspect of your life, etc. Many of these presumptions went against my hypothesis in some way, though not necessarily. If it was true, it's ultimately how you're wired to think, which means you live it every moment. For example, as I'm writing this, a certain aspect of Scorpio is coming out in my writing style in some way since it all stems from my mind. That's one of the implications of my hypothesis. Looking at the macro, big picture, or tendencies helped. What I was looking for though was to see if it worked in just everyday conversation and the way that they carried themselves. The micro scale would be the big win.

All of this considered, my results were that I could see probably a little better than half of the people I studied matching up somewhat well with their sign. I didn't keep written tally's or anything, just more in my head. This was way better than what it should have been if the Zodiac was all garbage. It's hard to calculate what the percentage should be in a control group assuming the Zodiac isn't real, but you would think it'd be fairly low. The fact that I was at about 50% or better was definitely statistically significant and gave a promising lead. However, it wasn't good enough - not good enough for what I was trying to find. I was looking for almost everyone to fit.

11

Biblical Considerations

As a disclaimer, most of what I wrote in this chapter I found out after writing most of this book, so this chapter may seem a little out of place. It's important though to consider what is written in the Bible about astrology and the Zodiac signs. In modern Christianity, astrology and all forms of it are often shunned, with opinions ranging from nonsense to demonic to everything in-between and beyond. I'm not necessarily interested in peoples' opinions though, I'm interested in God's opinion.

The first thing that many biblically versed people will think from reading the next couple chapters is that I'm taking things out of context in scripture. While this was originally what I was doing in some regards because I didn't have a good basis for tying astrology to the bible, I no longer think that is the case. I will explain further.

First of all to demonstrate this, I want you to stop reading and check what time it is. Seriously, go do it. As I'm writing this it's 4:59pm on December 21st, 2023. How do I know that? I checked my phone. How does my phone know that? It probably measures vibrations in quartz, and has to be calibrated against a more sophisticated time source from the internet. How does the internet time source get the correct time? It probably uses some sophisticated mechanical measurement, but ultimately, especially in regard to the calendar day, people have to look up to the sky and see where we're at in our revolution around the sun.

In ancient times, they didn't have the ability to use quartz vibrations. They didn't even have more rudimentary pendulums to keep time. They had to look up to the sky. The sky was their clock, and they could discern hours of the day using it - even months and years. Think about how often we check to see what time it is today. They asked the same question back then, and every time they did that the answer was in the sky. For this reason, the practice of astronomy was widespread in all ancient civilizations, Hebrews included.

How do you tell time with the ancient clock? You have to track movements and positionings of stars and planets. Since most of the stars are relatively fixed in location relative to each other, they are used as a backdrop. Wouldn't it be easier though to find certain locations in the sky if you were to group them by star patterns though? This is exactly what we get with the constellations. Ancient cultures, including Jews, knew about the constellations, if nothing else but for keeping track of time. I say this to demonstrate the point that ancient Jews and Christians surely had a working knowledge of astronomy. Therefore, it is not completely out of line if some biblical references point to the Zodiac – the original audience likely would have picked up on it. I'll expand on this some more with scripture.

****

The first major reference and basis for astrology in the bible arguably comes from Genesis 1:14

"And God said, "Let there be lights in the expanse of the heavens to separate the day from the night. And let them be for signs and for seasons, and for days and years"

Here we have the stars being dedicated for signs and for season, days and years. Here God ordains the heavenly clock that we just spoke about – the Zodiac. Perhaps it wasn't quite in the same way as the Zodiac, but just as a means to tell time. After all seasons, days, and years all are perfectly well contained within the realm of "just time," or just a clock. The word "signs" here is one point of debate, and the Hebrew meaning of the word here is very important. It can mean "sign, pledge, token", or even a prophetic sign, omen, miracles, a pledge of covenant (such as Noah's rainbow), tokens of changes of weather and time. The interpretation here doesn't necessarily have to do with dabbling in astrology. At the same time it's also very much there, and probably the most fitting interpretation given the word choice.

Likewise, the word "season" here is not exactly accurate. The word used here for "season" is the same word used for "feast" as in "Feast of Passover", or any other of the Jewish feasts. Many translations therefore refer as this to mean "appointed times," as that's more fitting with the other uses that we see of the word. This actual meaning as well is also more in line with a possible astrological interpretation as an "appointed time" would suggest a symbol in the sky having a deeper meaning.

Next let's examine another commonly referenced support for the Zodiac, Job 38:31-33 and arguably after that.

"Can you bind the chains of the Pleiades or loose the cords of Orion? Can you lead forth the Mazzaroth in their season, or can you guide the Bear with its children? Do you know the ordinances of the heavens? Can you establish their rule on the earth?"

A few things to keep in mind here. First of all, this is God talking, not a man or prophet. This is the part where God answers Job out of a whirlwind. In the previous verses, God points to parts of creation and life surrounding Job, and quizzes him on what he knows about it, and what he's able to do concerning them. Verses 16-18 speak of the depths of the sea and expanse of the earth, and 22-30 speak of the weather. Now in these verses he shifts to the sky.

The Pleiades and Orion references almost surely point to constellations. If this wasn't enough, the word Mazzaroth literally means "constellations". The bear and cubs is likely a reference to the Ursa major and Ursa minor constellation, possibly more. This is likely the correct interpretation here, as it fits with "Mazzaroth", and also fits with the next verse which talks about the heavens. Verse 33 goes a little more into it, giving birth to the idea that the heavens have ordinances, and that they have a rule on earth. If this is to be interpreted as having a tie to the Mazzaroth verse before it, then this is suggesting that the heavenly bodies (stars/constellations) have a rule on earth, and it's coming from God himself. It certainly sounds a lot like astrology.

There is probably very much a non-astrological interpretation here: if heavens is meant to be the "invisible" dimension where God lives, the place of life after death, etc., then that means just God's rule coming to earth, more akin to what Jesus prays in the Lord's prayer. "Thy kingdom come, thy will be done, on earth as it is in heaven." The problem with that interpretation though, is that from a literary perspective it doesn't make as much sense. The subject matter here from verses 31 and 32 is clearly the constellations, so it makes more sense that verse 33 is following along with that pattern, rather than shifting to the "invisible heaven" where God resides. The Hebrew word here for heaven means "heaven, sky." Also, consider this: If what you were reading here in Job was not considered scripture, but instead a typical "pagan" historical writing of the time, would you think that it was talking more about astrology or "thy kingdom come"?

In the most extreme case, both the passages in Genesis and Job give biblical justification for the basic idea of astrology: that there's more to the sky/time than just balls of matter in orbit that are visible from earth. If you do buy into this interpretation, a major question is "to what extent", which is a much more involved question. In the least extreme case, it confirms what I pointed to originally: that the Hebrews were very much familiar with the constellations and Zodiac signs.

****

If we look at some other ancient writings by Jews outside of scripture, we start to see that according to Jewish sources, astrology may have gotten its start from god-fearing people, or that many followers of God fully believed in astrology. This idea is consistent with the passage we just looked at in Job, but it seems to be confirmed by other sources.

The first bit of evidence comes from Jewish historian Flavius Josephus's "Antiquity of the Jews" (Josephus, 93). For those unfamiliar with his work, this is a pretty highly regarded source in Christian and Jewish circles. When talking about Seth (Adam's son) and Seth's offspring he mentions the following:

"They also were the inventors of that peculiar sort of wisdom which is concerned with the heavenly bodies, and their order. And that their inventions might not be lost before they were sufficiently known, upon Adam's prediction that the world was to be destroyed at one time by the force of fire, and at another time by the violence and quantity of water, they made two pillars, the one of brick, the other of stone: they inscribed their discoveries on them both"

The point of contention here is the "peculiar sort of wisdom concerned with the heavenly bodies". Whether this is astronomy or astrology is unclear, but since it was described as peculiar, the more likely explanation of it would be astrology. Astronomy I don't think would strike most people as peculiar, even back then (whether Josephus means peculiar to his time or peculiar to Seth's time is subject to debate) – it's just using geometry to navigate time and space. Astrology is a little more peculiar. They thought it was important enough to engrave in a monument so that the knowledge wouldn't be destroyed, per the prophecy that Adam had of destruction coming.

It should also be noted here that Seth was always spoken of as being an upright person, virtuous, and passing his character onto his descendants. They are mentioned in a positive manner by Josephus. These were likely followers of God.

If you look at another source that dates to around 100-200 BC, Pseudo-Eupolemus (probably a Samaritan, Jewish ancestry) (Pseudo-Eupolemus, Hyatt, & Kirby, 2013), we get an account of Abraham that describes him as an astrologer. He learned it from the Chaldeans (Babylon), where he was originally from, and then taught it to the Phoenicians and Egyptians. This script also states that Enoch was among the first to learn astrology. Enoch was a descendant of Seth, so this does agree with Josephus's account.

Looking again at Josephus (Josephus, 93), but now later on into what he says about Abraham, we can see more pieces of the picture. First off, we have the confirming account that Abraham came from the land of Chaldea (Babylon) originally, which is often regarded by secular modern sources as the birthplace of astrology. Back then, cultures worshipped the stars and planets as deities, and Josephus states that Abraham argued against this idea using apologetics by saying that the stars and planets all follow a predetermined course, so they couldn't be free agents, and that there must be a higher god than them because of it. Josephus states that because of this idea, along with God's command, he left the country and went to Canaan. So we know right away he was an astronomer (a pretty good one for his time too), as he was able to ascertain that the heavenly bodies followed a preset path.

Josephus quotes another historian before him as well right after this passage:

> "Berosus mentions our father Abram without naming him, when he says thus: — "In the tenth generation after the Flood, there was among the Chaldeans a man righteous and great, and skillful in the celestial science." "

Again this is more confirmation of that. In modern times we can separate astronomy and astrology easily. In times past, while they would know the difference between the two, the two were very commonly married together. We know the Chaldeans practiced astrology. Secular history tells us that the Chaldeans practiced astrology. The passage Josephus mentions about Abraham arguing against one of the commonly held fundamental beliefs of astrology, that the stars and planets are deities, tells us that Abraham was part of a culture that practiced astrology since he was arguing against part of it. Doesn't that then sound like Abraham was arguing against astrology in a way? If you look at the text in Josephus you don't necessarily draw that conclusion, actually quite the opposite. He seems to be confirming astrology while arguing against the idea that the planets are gods. Consider the quote that Josephus seems to accredit to Abraham:

> "If [said he] these bodies had power of their own, they would certainly take care of their own regular motions; but since they do not preserve such regularity, they make it plain, that in so far as they co-operate to our advantage, they do it not of their own abilities, but as they are subservient to Him that commands them, to whom alone we ought justly to offer our honor and thanksgiving."

He states that they co-operate to our advantage, which appears to allude to astrology, though it could mean astronomy as well. In the passage just before this, Josephus states this though:

"for he was the first that ventured to publish this notion, That there was but one God, the Creator of the universe; and that, as to other [gods], if they contributed any thing to the happiness of men, that each of them afforded it only according to his appointment, and not by their own power."

Here the subject matter is clearly astrology, as it talks about the happiness of men in relation to celestial bodies, so it makes sense to assume that the next passage that I quoted earlier is also referring to astrology. Thus, it's likely that Abraham was not just an astronomer, but also an astrologer on some level. It does not stop here though, astronomy comes back up in Josephus concerning Abraham later on during his trip to Egypt:

"He communicated to them arithmetic, and delivered to them the science of astronomy; for before Abram came into Egypt they were unacquainted with those parts of learning; for that science came from the Chaldeans into Egypt, and from thence to the Greeks also."

It's fairly accepted in modern times that the Egyptians learned astrology from the Chaldeans (Whitfield, 2001). The account in Josephus offers a plausible explanation for this. Since we know that both the Egyptians and Chaldeans practiced it, and according to Josephus Abraham was the transmitter of astronomy, it likely follows that Abraham was also the transmitter of astrology as he was certainly familiar with it, and therefore in some way a practitioner of it.

If we were to take a look at one of the banned books of scripture, but also one that early Christians seemed to esteem, the book of Enoch, we see another picture. I don't want to argue for the legitimacy of the book of Enoch, though there is a good case for it (and there's a good case against it too). I just merely want to state that it came from somewhere (meaning that it's probably not all completely made up), and that for a time it was held in esteem by Jews and early Christians, which I don't think you can argue against too much. Anyways, in verse 8:2 the book mentions that the fallen angels that created the giants also taught men a bunch of things, including astrology, constellations, signs of the sun, course of the moon, metalworking, enchantments, and more. Whether or not you think astrology is true or beneficial, based on this passage it seems to have its roots from angelic beings, though these are probably fallen angels here, or angels who sinned. Note however that during the time all of these things were regarded as having validity to the Jews, even enchantments, though they were forbidden from practicing enchantments. Not all of the things listed here are necessarily bad either such as metalworking, though at the time what the angels did in teaching mankind this was considered a sin. It's said in a conversation between the good angels just a little bit later in 9:6-7:

"Thou seest what Azazel hath done, who hath taught all unrighteousness on earth and revealed the eternal secrets which were (preserved) in heaven, which men were striving to learn"

So much of what was revealed to mankind through these demons was likely just hidden knowledge that they weren't supposed to learn about, or perhaps not learn about *at the time,* but were meant to figure it out on their own or in due time.

If you look further into the Book of Enoch, the whole section 3 from chapter 72 to 82 talks about Enoch being taught astronomy by the angel Uriel. This would seem to confirm the account of Pseudo-Eupolemus who states that Enoch discovered astrology along with others, though one of these sources could be feeding off of the other. Enoch is a descendant of Seth though, which also confirms Josephus's account of a *"peculiar sort of wisdom which is concerned with the heavenly bodies, and their order"* being invented by the descendants of Seth.

Also, if you're going to take a look at the non-Hebrew possible origins of astrology, consider the following: Mesopotamian tradition speaks of divine teachers who dwelled on earth in the past and taught men many different kinds of knowledge and wisdom, including astrology (Whitfield, 2001). At least, that's the claim.

If you were to put all of this together, then it's likely that from an ancient Jewish perspective, astrology originated with Seth's descendants, likely Enoch. It was likely taught by either angels or demons depending on which version of the story you believe. We know Enoch was highly regarded as a prophet, so if he's the source it would come from God or angels. Then when you take that bit of knowledge you can see how many of the passages we see in scripture that supposedly come straight from God (Genesis, Job), or Jesus talking (mentioned soon) start to make more sense if at least parts of astrology are true and originate with God.

Furthermore, if we look at some historical evidence after the time Jesus walked the earth, we see that Jews and early Christians actually seemed to practice astrology! Consider the text from a letter of Roman Emperor Hadrian to Servianus (Gregorovius, 1898):

"There is no chief of the Jewish synagogue, no Samaritan, no Christian presbyter, who is not an astrologer, a soothsayer, or an anointer."

It should be noted that Hadrian does not think very highly of these groups obviously, and does say that all of it is worship of Serapis (a supreme Greek-Egyptian god). This is also in the context of those who lived in Egypt. It's possible they confused Jesus with Serapis or God the Father with Serapis, we aren't sure. The point though is that both Jews and Christians practiced astrology.

Consider the texts of Rabbi Samuel in Berachot 58b (3rd century AD), where he talks about if a comet were to pass through the constellation of Orion the world would be destroyed. He makes other allusions to things we would consider to be astrological in nature.

Some of the best evidence that Jews had a bigger connection to the Zodiac in times past actually comes from archeology. At least seven synagogues in Israel have been uncovered that have Zodiac mosaics contained within them, or some wheel pattern similar to the Zodiac (Gilad & Schuster, 2020). These were all built in the 3rd-5th century AD. This suggests it played a much bigger role than you might think, and that it very much was part of ancient Judaism in some manner. To try to separate it entirely from the Bible, Judaism, or

Christianity for this reason simply put just does not make sense, you're losing context instead of gaining it.

There is an argument that many of the early Christians and Jews of the time were following an impure, or corrupted form of Judaism/Christianity that is referred to as Hellenistic Judaism, which is estimated to have started between 305 to 30 B.C. This form of Judaism incorporated astrology into it. Some evidence for this would be Emperor Hadrian's letter where he said Christians and Jews were worshipping Serapis in Egypt. The letters of Pseudo-Eupolemus of the time might hint at that as well, as he is thought to be a Samaritan, who we know didn't follow the same Judaism as the typical Jews in Jerusalem based on the context of the Bible. However, we still have the writings of Josephus who was born in Jerusalem. His father was of priestly ancestry, and his mother claimed royal ancestry. He very much fit into one of the "purer" forms of Judaism at the time. While he doesn't outright embrace astrology from a Jewish perspective, much of what he's written alludes to such a conclusion based on what we know of the time that astrology was being widely practiced in conjunction with astronomy. Furthermore, and I could be wrong on this, but I don't think we can demonstrate a Judaism that existed at the time that we know for sure did not incorporate astrology. That conclusion in today's world is heavily influenced by the general condemnation of astrology in the forms of religion that came about much later. This condemnation was mostly influenced by the Renaissance where astronomy became science, and astrology got left in the dust for the most part (Whitfield, 2001). We also still have the passages from Genesis and Job in scripture that seem to confirm the basic thesis of astrology.

****

"Okay, they knew about astrology, and were fairly familiar with it, possibly practiced it, but it's still not from God, or is a part of an offshoot of Judeo-Christian religion that was false." Well, let's look a little deeper.

Many people forget that the prophet Daniel was most likely an astrologer, or that he was at least trained in it. He was grouped in with the "wise men", the magicians, enchanters, sorcerers, and Chaldeans that king Nebuchadnezzar tried to kill when they could not interpret his dream. He was even made chief prefect over the wise men, who were certainly practicing astrology. Astrology was the respected science of the time, and would remain so for thousands of years up until the last few centuries. We will talk more about Daniel in a little bit.

Furthermore, Jesus hints at astrological signs that would mark as a sign of the times in Luke 21:25:

"And there will be signs in the sun and moon and stars, and on the earth distress of nations in perplexity because of the roaring of the sea and the waves."

Perhaps this is just talking about what God spoke of at the beginning of Genesis, that the stars were for "appointed times" (commonly translated as "seasons"). That certainly seems to be in line with what Jesus said, though at the same time we would traditionally call this a form of astrology, not astronomy.

The biggest piece of evidence in my opinion though, comes from the nativity scene in the early gospels. The three wise men followed a star to find Jesus. The three wise men were almost certainly astrologers. They knew which star it was, and knew how to follow it, so they were well versed in astronomy and navigation. They also knew that the star would lead to the Jewish King.

How they knew the latter is subject to debate, but one possible reason is that they were partly following the prophecy laid out in Daniel 9:20-27, which talks about periods of "weeks" (Durham, 2021). I say "weeks" here, because the actual word is "heptads", or "a seven". Most translations have it listed as "week", as that is the most common interpretation, but it's not necessarily a week. You then have to be careful about which translation you use, as which translation you use and how the wording is laid out will make or break what comes next – I was looking at the Lexham English Bible for this. It speaks of the time between the going out of the word to restore Jerusalem until an anointed one would be seven weeks and sixty-two weeks. The decree was issued by king Cyrus to restore it in 444BC, and it was completed in 395 BC, 49 years later, or seven heptads, if a heptad is taken to mean seven years. Then 7x62 = 434 years later (62 heptads), an anointed one would be cut off (Messiah killed), then the temple would be destroyed again. Guessing at the age of the Messiah to be roughly 30 years old, as that age was considered a mature adult, you can guesstimate the time of birth.

How did they know the book of prophecy of Daniel though? It's likely that they came from the Babylonian or Persian culture, which was "from the East." Remember Daniel was the chief over them years ago; it's likely that they had copies of his writings. They may even have been part Jewish, as not all the Jews returned from exile. They likely knew some of the prophecies.

They still were following a star though, how did they know about that? The only biblical reference that scholars found was from Numbers 24:17, though honestly I'm not sure it's technically applicable and able to be used for the wise men's purpose. The only good explanation for this seems to be either divine revelation, or that they were using parts of astrology to know that this certain sign in the sky meant this or that (basically astrology). If they did come from Babylon and were using the prophecy left behind by Daniel, they were again almost certainly astrologers as it was widespread in that area. In the end, the simplest and most likely explanation is still some form of astrology.

Note also that Herod and all of Jerusalem was troubled. Why were they troubled? Well the most logical explanation is that they bought into what the wise men were saying, that there was a star that foretold the arrival of the Messiah (astrology!). Herod inquired of the chief priests as to where the Christ was to be born. After hearing about Bethlehem, Herod directed the wise men to go there. Moreover, the early gospel writers thought it was important to include this story. If they did believe in astrology to some extent, to them this would have been seen as objective proof that Jesus was the Messiah, and would expect that it would have such an effect on their audience. If they didn't believe in astrology at all, then this would just be something miraculous that God had done, but would lose much of the effect on the audience since the audience wouldn't necessarily buy into the premise of it all outside of the Daniel prophecy or the testimony of the wise men.

11: Biblical Considerations

The fact that they were following a star gives merit to certain parts of astrology, namely that God does use the sky to point to certain things, though this part of astrology has nothing to do with my thesis. This story plainly shows some aspect of astrology in action in scripture in a way that glorifies God. This in itself from a Christian perspective is solid ground that God does use the sky in some prophetic way.

****

Doesn't the Bible forbid astrology though? That's typically what you'll hear in mainstream Christianity. There are a few verses that would suggest so, and need to be addressed. Well let's look at the first commonly quoted one, Deuteronomy 18:10-11

There shall not be found among you anyone who burns his son or his daughter as an offering, anyone who practices divination or tells fortunes or interprets omens, or a sorcerer or a charmer or a medium or a necromancer or one who inquires of the dead"

This verse in my opinion is pretty weak as an argument against astrology. It mentions divination, fortune telling, and omen interpretation. Much of these things are commonly affiliated with astrology, and for good reason as astrology has been used for all of these things. Please make note that astrology is not directly mentioned here though. This point can't be stressed enough. Divination is the thing that is banished, not astrology. There were other methods of fortune telling, interpreting omens, and divination at the time, that very likely involved consulting demons or other things such as reading entrails. A black bird flies a certain way, and that's an omen of something. Astrology was more than likely one of the means of divination at the time, though it is not explicitly stated here. God specifically mentions three things that are related to telling the future (arguably more as a medium or inquirer of the dead could do such as well) and astrology is not on the list. Since He was being so exhaustive in listing all these things individually, which we could wrap up with just one broad word "divination", don't you think that if it was meant to be banned, that He would have just listed it explicitly here? Again, don't forget that Abraham likely practiced astrology as well.

You also must understand that Christians, Jews, and most religions believe in divination – we just call it a different thing: prophecy. Prophecy could come from any being that has knowledge of future events. We typically only approve of prophecy where God is the source, which we call "true prophecy", and kind of label everything else as divination or false prophecy. That's really the only difference between the two: the source. Then the results and nature help to prove the source. In modern Christianity, it's somewhat commonly accepted that God speaks to us through our circumstances and even other people. Well isn't that kind of like interpreting omens? What about Joseph interpreting Pharaoh's dream, or Daniel interpreting Nebuchadnezzar's dream? Wouldn't that be considered divination if it was done by some pagan? There is a line here somewhere which takes discernment to find in each case, but ultimately whether or not it's divination or prophecy depends on the source.

Also, keep in mind though that here the main message God was sending was to not participate in these practices as the nations around them were doing. God was trying to separate the Israelites from them and not have the cultures blend together, lest the Israelites get taken off course.

Yes, I do get the point being made here. The problem though is that we have to weigh that against the biblical evidence that we just went over in Genesis, Job, the Gospels, as well as the historical evidence that Jews were practicing it. Jesus said there would be signs in the sun moon and stars. God made the stars for signs and for seasons. The most literary coherent interpretation of the verses in Job point that the heavens/constellations have a rule on earth. Then we have an aspect of astrology pointing to Jesus in His infancy with the star in Bethlehem and three wise men. We have evidence of the Zodiac being a part of Jewish synagogues and Jewish life, even reaching back to two of the most revered men in scripture: Abraham and Enoch. There is a good case here that God has ordained at least some parts of astrology. We must reconsider the question then and ask if astrology (at least in certain aspects) came from God, and is therefore closer to prophecy and not divination. Because of all of this, I don't think it's biblically sound to group astrology or Zodiac signs in with the divination that is being mentioned here. It's very shaky grounds to use to condemn all of astrology, though you could possibly pick apart certain aspects of it using these verses. In any case, the part of astrology that I'm going to discuss in this book I would not consider to be flirting with divination – I'm not interested in divination.

Another passage in Deuteronomy against astrology occurs in chapter 4, verse 19.

"And beware lest you raise your eyes to heaven, and when you see the sun and the moon and the stars, all the host of heaven, you be drawn away and bow down to them and serve them, things that the Lord your God has allotted to all the peoples under the whole heaven."

This verse is clearly talking about idolatry, as is evident from the examples in the previous verses where God talks about not making idols. It even says "bow down and serve them." Many cultures around the Hebrews were worshipping the heavenly bodies, and God was telling them not to do this. Astrology definitely can be an idol, and some modern day astrologers do worship the stars in some way. However, worshipping the heavens and astrology (interpreting the heavens) are at heart two very different things. One is a worship/idolatry, the other is recognizing patterns or other varied things depending on the specific subfield of astrology. It is even further written in this verse that God has allotted these things to all people. Again, this verse is not confronting astrology at all.

There is also Daniel 2:27:

"Daniel answered the king and said, "No wise men, enchanters, magicians, or astrologers can show to the king the mystery that the king has asked,"

This was in response to Nebuchadnezzar's dream. God offered the interpretation instead as we see from verse 28. Here we see that astrology does not work for knowing dreams and interpretations of dreams. I could be wrong, but I don't think any astrologer claims to be able to do that using astrology. This very well may be a condemnation of parts of astrology, but I've always looked at this verse as meaning that God will provide the knowledge, even before I got tied up in the Zodiac. What Daniel is saying here is what everyone else was saying: the king's request is impossible. No one, not even from among those professions listed, the best of the best at the time, could do such a thing. Only God could do it. Again, we already knew that Daniel was among this group of people. He was a "wise guy," which he explicitly listed first in this passage. He wasn't putting down all of those groups (though many of them are put down elsewhere in scripture), but rather just stating the obvious: that they couldn't do it, only God could. He is in front of an emotionally distraught king too, I'm sure he is choosing his words carefully.

What I would consider a better passage against astrology is Isaiah 47:13-14

"You are wearied with your many counsels; let them stand forth and save you, those who divide the heavens, who gaze at the stars, who at the new moons make known what shall come upon you. Behold, they are like stubble; the fire consumes them; they cannot deliver themselves from the power of the flame. No coal for warming oneself is this, no fire to sit before!"

I could be wrong, but I believe this is the only passage in scripture that specifically mentions astrology in a negative sense. Let's break this down a little bit. First of all, this is Isaiah talking about the Babylonians or Chaldeans which is evident from verse 1 and verse 5 in the chapter. It's well known that they practiced astrology in different forms. Isaiah first and foremost speaks of their destruction. God says He will take vengeance on them in verse 3. The reason for this is in verses 6-9. God was angry with the Israelites and gave them into the Babylonians hand. They showed them no mercy, which angered God. Then in verse 8 we hear that one of their sins is pride, that they are better than everyone in their own eyes. In verses 9 and 11 we see that their sorceries and enchantments will not save them from this. This is important: in verse 12 Isaiah taunts them telling them to keep resorting to their enchantments and sorceries to see if those will save them. He's using sarcasm here. This continues on into verse 13 – the same taunt but now it's pointed at astrology. In verse 14 he says basically that they will be unable to save themselves as well (the Babylonian astrologers, sorcerers, and enchanters).

As we see here, this is not God condemning astrology directly like He does with divination in the Deuteronomy passage we read earlier. What is specifically being said here is that astrology will not save them from the disaster(s) that are about to come on them. This is again 100% true, astrology will not save anyone. More importantly though, this is very similar to the judgement God pronounced on Egypt as well as most other nations. They all participated in idolatry to some extent, trusting in this or that, sorcery, enchantments, astrology, their own strength, their own gods, their (often despicable) acts of worship to these gods, instead of trusting in THE God. It's very plain to see that astrology was an idol to them. It is almost certainly the case that God is condemning their idolatry of astrology, as that's part of the reason for the taunt in verse 13. Isaiah here is listing all of their idols and sins, and telling them that all of these things that they trust in above God will not save them. It's not necessarily the case that this verse alone is a direct condemnation of astrology. In a literary sense, these verses aren't even a condemnation of enchantments and sorceries, though we do have other verses in scripture to condemn those. Astrology for many people today is indeed an idol, and it's an especially dangerous one in my opinion. I will get into this more in later chapters.

There is a good point to be made here that all of the other things being mentioned here are in a sense condemned elsewhere in the Bible except for astrology per the argument I laid out above. So then, shouldn't astrology be lumped in with those in the condemnation? That's a fair point. Perhaps there is some condemnation of the Babylonian astrologers intended here. Going back to the divination passage above though, I would again ask if prophecy is a sin. There are false prophets mentioned in scripture, and prophets of Baal, all of which are condemned. On the flipside, there are prophets of God who are commended. It's obvious therefore that there is good prophecy and bad prophecy. It's quite possible that whatever form of astrology the Babylonians were practicing was something that God detested. Perhaps it wasn't the astrology that God intended for mankind to use.

Again with this verse in Isaiah as well, we have to weigh that against all the evidence that we find supporting astrology in other books in the Bible, as well as the historical accounts that seem to confirm it. The takeaway that I find in all of this, the good and the bad, is that it's not biblically sound to make a blanket condemnation of all aspects of astrology, as some are pretty well established in scripture. It's quite possible that not all aspects of astrology are true, allowed, or beneficial based on some reading into the verses in Deuteronomy and Isaiah.

Most importantly, whatever your take on astrology is, it's evident that the Zodiac signs played a significant role in early Judaism. There was the necessity of telling time, the origin stories involving Enoch, Seth, Abraham, etc., and also the fact that it's engraved into their synagogues. They were all very much aware of it, which is important to keep in mind in the coming chapters.

12

Searching for Twelve

Like I said earlier, all of these thoughts were happening at the same time. While I was researching to see if the Zodiac signs actually fit people in real life, I was looking into the origins of it all, specifically for a possible scripture connection. There were twelve Zodiac signs, and the number twelve was all over the Bible. Was this a coincidence? If the Zodiac signs were real, and me personally knowing that God created everything, the only logical conclusion to me personally was that God created the Zodiac signs. Not only did I know that God existed, I knew who he was. I was absolutely convinced of it. Years ago I didn't think that would be possible, but now it would be dishonest for me to say otherwise.

Like I mentioned earlier, I knew it was a mistake to try to fit things into scripture. My method was wrong, but this was different. I knew who God was, and I'm pretty sure the Zodiac signs were real as well. If I truly believed in both of those things, then the significance of the Zodiac signs was too much to ignore. If the Bible truly is the inspired Word of God, then it really should be in there, or at least one would expect God to make mention of such an important thing.

****

I had a lot of studying to do. A quick search on the number twelve in the Bible will tell you that it mostly stems from the twelve tribes of Israel. This is mostly recorded in Genesis 29 and 30, where Jacob has twelve sons from four different women. Later on, these twelve sons became patriarchs for the twelve tribes of Israel. Most of the other instances of twelve that you find in the Bible are related to this in some way. Similarly, the Ishmaelites, Ishmael being Abraham's firstborn son, consisted of twelve tribes as we see in Genesis 17:20

"As for Ishmael, I have heard you; behold, I have blessed him greatly. He shall father twelve princes, and I will make him into a great nation."

There were twelve tribes of Israel and Ishmael. There were twelve signs of the Zodiac as well. Fitting with my hypothesis of the Zodiac being part of creation, the inference that stuck out the most was that this could be considered twelve generic "tribes" or spiritual types of people.

Looking at most other symbols of twelve, they are usually related to the twelve tribes of Israel. Here are some notable ones below. The High Priest's breastplate in Exodus 28:15; 21;29

"You shall make a breastpiece of judgement, in skilled work. In the style of the ephod you shall make it-of gold, blue, and purple and scarlet yarns, and fine twined linen shall you make

it....There shall be twelve stones with their names according to the names of the sons of Israel. They shall be like signets, each engraved with its name, for the twelve tribes......So Aaron shall bear the names of the sons of Israel in the breastpiece of judgement on his heart, when he goes into the Holy Place, to bring them to regular remembrance before the Lord."

Another important one, the bread offering for the Tabernacle in Leviticus 24:5-9

"You shall take fine flour and bake twelve loaves from it; two tenths of an ephah shall be in each loaf. And you shall set them in two piles, six in a pile, on the table of pure gold before the Lord. And you shall put pure frankincense on each pile, that it may go with the bread as a memorial portion as a food offering to the Lord. Every Sabbath day Aaron shall arrange it before the Lord regularly; it is from the people of Israel as a covenant forever. And it shall be for Aaron and his sons, and they shall eat it in a holy place, since it is for him a most holy portion out of the Lord's food offerings, a perpetual due."

In the book of Revelation, the tribes are also mentioned in Revelation 7:4

"And I heard the number of the sealed, 144,000, sealed from every tribe of the sons of Israel: 12,000 from the tribe of Judah were sealed,....."

Also in Revelation 4:4, we see this as well, but as 24 (12 x 2):

"Around the throne were twenty-four thrones, and seated on the thrones were twenty-four elders, clothed in white garments, with golden crowns on their heads."

Related to the twelve tribes, Jesus also called twelve disciples, listed in Matthew 10:2-4

"The names of the twelve apostles are these: first, Simon, who is called Peter, and Andrew his brother; James the son of Zebedee, and John his brother; Philip and Bartholomew; Thomas and Matthew the tax collector; James the son of Alphaeus, and Thaddaeus; Simon the Zealot, and Judas Iscariot, who betrayed him."

Also in Revelation 21:9-21, we see twelve written all over the New Jerusalem, which was meant to be the new dwelling place of God and man. There's a high wall with twelve gates. Each gate has the name of a different tribe of Israel on it. The wall had twelve foundations, each foundation had the name of one of the twelve apostles of the Lamb. It was a square that was 12,000 stadia in length, width, and height. The wall was 144 cubits thick. The foundations of the wall were adorned with twelve different kinds of jewels.

Another one, though this could just be "coincidentally" twelve as opposed to intentionally twelve, occurred when Jesus fed the five thousand in Matthew 14:20

"And they all ate and were satisfied. And they took up twelve baskets full of the broken pieces left over."

****

The leading theories on what the number twelve meant was that it was a sign of power, authority, perfection, or government. The terms "power" and "perfection" to me seem almost too vague to be considered of any practical use to anyone. The "authority" and "government" aspect of it were a little more specific, which is more useful. Where the government part stems from was that whenever God made a new nation, he seemed to do it in the order of twelve. He founded the nation of Israel with twelve tribes, and similarly with Ishmael. When Jesus founded Christianity, He did it with twelve disciples. You can make a similar case with the new Jerusalem in Revelation. Then, as these nations continue, twelve (tribes) seems to remain an important part of the governing of these nations.

If you were to tie that in with the Zodiac, then what you get is essentially a democracy. If the number twelve was meant to represent twelve types of people, then having representation from each tribe or sign, ultimately leads to a form of democracy, or a council. Equal representation. The Zodiac interpretation of this fell in line very well with the leading theories.

The biggest revelation for me came when I started studying some of the "hidden" or "silent" symbols in the Bible. One of the more advanced things that you learn when studying scripture and prophecy, is that God uses Israel as a microcosm of the rest of the world. For instance, take the whole story of the Israelites starting in Exodus. The Israelites became slaves to Egypt. We became slaves to sin per scripture (Romans 6:16). Only through God's judgement on the gods of Egypt, and the blood of the Lamb via Passover, were the Israelites finally set free. Similarly, only through God's judgement on the demonic forces at work (John 16:11) and the blood of Jesus are we set free from sin. The Israelites grumbled against God in the desert, and were partially destroyed because of it. We grumble against God even after Jesus, and face the consequences. The Israelites finally made it into the promised land. Eventually we will make it to the new earth. If you pay close attention in the book of Esther, you'll find a very similar parallel between the story and the fall and redemption of man. This is something a little more advanced in studying scripture, but also very crucial to understanding how God works.

The "silent symbol" I discovered, concerns the three patriarchs of Israel. A good background of this is found at the burning bush in Exodus 3:14-15:

> *"God said to Moses, "I AM WHO I AM." And he said, "Say this to the people of Israel: "I AM has sent me to you." God Also said to Moses, "Say this to the people of Israel: "The LORD, the God of your fathers, the God of Abraham, the God of Isaac, and the God of Jacob, has sent me to you."*

Here God names himself as "I AM", but also names himself as the God of Abraham, Isaac, and Jacob. In a way, he defines himself as God of the 3 patriarchs of the nation of Israel. This is further supported in the next passages we'll discuss. If you go back to the book of Genesis, you'll see that God promises Abraham and Sarah that they'll have a child, and that God will greatly bless Abraham, and that he will be the father of a great nation. God makes this promise on several occasions, but the last, and most notable time he does this is in Genesis 22:15-18, right after he was willing to sacrifice Isaac.

> *"And the angel of the Lord called to Abraham a second time from heaven and said, "By myself I have sworn, declares the Lord, because you have done this and have not withheld your son, your only son, I will surely bless you and I will surely multiply your offspring as the stars of heaven and as the sand that is on the seashore. And your offspring shall possess the gate of his enemies, and in your offspring shall all the nations of the earth be blessed, because you have obeyed my voice."*

Here God confirmed His covenant with Abraham because of his obedience to God's order to sacrifice his own son. The blessing was that Abraham would be the father of many nations. In Hebrew, the name Abraham even means "Father of a multitude." This name was not given to him at birth either (he was originally Abram, which means "high/exalted father"), but was something that God gave him in Genesis 17. Isaac had two sons, but gave Jacob the blessing of Abraham, while Esau was destined to serve his brother. Now if we skip forward to Jacob and look at Genesis 32:28, we see the rest of the symbology. This takes place right after Jacob had wrestled with a mysterious man all night, who many scholars believe to be an angel or even God himself.

"Then he said, "Your name shall no longer be called Jacob, but Israel, for you have striven with God and with men, and have prevailed."

Here we see the blessing that Jacob got was his name changed. The name "Israel", in Hebrew means "fighter of God," "God contended," "triumphant with God," or "wrestles with God." Here the symbology we see, is that the Trinity of God is present and being represented by the three patriarchs of Israel. Abraham was the father of many nations, just as God the Father is creator and Father of all things. Isaac is represented by Jesus, the Son of God that was willingly sacrificed by the Father (Abraham), as stated in John 3:16. It was only when Abraham was willing to do this that God cemented His promise to Abraham, in order to create such a connection or picture as we're seeing now with the fulfillment of the gospels. Similar to how Moses was punished for smiting the rock twice because he was messing up God's symbolism in addition to being careless, Abraham was rewarded for fulfilling God's symbolism. Jacob's new name "Israel" represents the Holy Spirit's role as counselor. He's the go-between with God and man.

So here we see the godhead Trinity woven into the three patriarchs of Israel. God could have had Isaac have a dozen children, and have it end there. Or he could even have had Abraham have several children and called it quits there, but it's the way it is in order to highlight a greater spiritual truth. It's also important to note that both Abraham and Isaac had multiple children, but only one of their children was given the blessing of Abraham. If both of their children were given the blessing God gave Abraham, then the symbolism here would not hold true. This symbolism laid out here is something that most Christian bible scholars would probably agree with. What I realized with the Zodiac and the number twelve though, is that it doesn't end there. Jacob had twelve sons who would become the twelve patriarchs of the twelve tribes of Israel. So, if the Zodiac was the reason for the number twelve, the greater spiritual truth that we see here is God the Father, God the Son, and God the Holy Spirit giving birth to twelve kinds of people, or twelve generic types of spirits/souls. It's also important to note here that now all twelve children are included in the blessing, where in the previous generations only one of the children got the blessing. Here in this symbolic setup of the Trinity as demonstrated by the lineage of the patriarchs of Israel, we're given sort of a "lineage of God" (though God is eternal so it's not quite the same), and this lineage includes twelve additional tribes. Since they're included in the "lineage" of God, there are several conclusions we can draw from this.

12: Searching for Twelve

1. Twelve tribes are included in the lineage of God.

2. Because we are in God's lineage, we are also made in the image of God (Genesis 1:27)

3. Also because we're included in the lineage of God, we're also heirs to God. (Romans 8:17)

4. Since the twelve Zodiac signs include all people, and the primary symbolism of twelve in the Bible is associated with the twelve tribes of Israel, then if the number twelve's true meaning is tied to the Zodiac, it means that twelve in the Bible represents **all people.**

5. This symbology fitted perfectly with my hypothesis of the Zodiac being how we are wired/designed to think. Here is the direct reference to it being part of our spiritual creation, a part of who we are. Just like each Israelite was born into a specific tribe (which was one of the ways that Israelites identified themselves to each other for generations to come – which tribe they belonged to), each person is born into a specific Zodiac sign.

6. Since the twelve tribes are in the lineage of God and represent all people, and we know that God creates nations in the order of twelve (12 disciples, 12 tribes, etc), it follows from this symbolism that God created **all people** in the order of twelve. This fits well with the idea of twelve referring to divine governance, and offers a more unifying reason for this interpretation. God used this repetition of twelve and governance because it's derived from how God originally created (and continues to create) people via the order of twelve Zodiac signs.

****

Now that we have what could be the true understanding of the symbology of the number twelve in the Bible as representing all people, we can take a second look at all of the other instances of the number twelve in the Bible. Remember, the number twelve primarily represents **all people**. This is our default decipher for understanding twelve. Ishmael's twelve princes is now another symbol that he would have a huge nation, sizeable to all people. It also helps further cement the Zodiac to the twelve tribes of Israel.

Similarly, look again at the breastplate of the high priest that has twelve stones fastened to it (Exodus 28:15; 21;29), one for each tribe, that the high priest was to wear while ministering for the people to God. In the New Testament, we know that Jesus is the high priest (Hebrews 4:15).With the new decoder knowledge, we see that Jesus, the High Priest, is carrying the remembrance of <u>all people</u>, not just the 12 tribes of Israel. This is something we already knew from other verses in the New Testament.

Again, look at Leviticus 24:5-9, where the twelve loaves of bread are to be offered before God.

"it is from the people of Israel as a covenant forever."

Here we even have the decoder straight up mentioned in verse 8. The people of Israel now representing all people. The offering is supposed to come from all people, not just the Israelites.

Now jump to Revelation 7:4, where the twelve thousand from each of twelve tribes are sealed and/or saved in the rapture. Here this specifically mentions the twelve tribes of Israel. With the decipher though, this is easily shown to mean that the pool is instead all people, not just the Israelites. This is a huge help. There are a few different theologies that have this being Israelites exclusively, since God's pattern has typically been to the Jew first, and then the gentile. Most theologians skirt their way around this and take it to mean all followers of Christ by using Revelation 7:9 and 1 Thessalonians 4:16-17. While I do agree with this interpretation, still Revelation 7:4 presents a little bit of an issue with that theology. With this new understanding though, the issue completely disappears using the cipher. This is a big confirmation of the Zodiac theory as it actually ties up a big loose end traditionally occurring in scripture.

We can look more into Revelation, but instead chapter 4, verse 4, talking about the twenty four elders. Here this would likely be two elders from each tribe as rulers. Using the symbol of government tied with the Zodiac, what we get here is a democracy, or representatives of all the people co-ruling.

Lastly in Revelation 21:9-21, we see the new Jerusalem being described by twelve in several different ways. The foundation was made of twelve apostles of Jesus, so the foundation was laid by all people who followed Jesus. It had twelve gates, one for each tribe. Therefore, all people are allowed to enter in, given they belong to God. The whole thing's major theme is therefore people with all of the other measurements. The heart of its purpose and construction is people.

Jesus took twelve disciples. Again this means that Jesus is calling all people to be His disciples, not just Jews.

When Jesus fed the five thousand in Matthew 14:20, there were twelve basketfuls left over. The picture we then see here is that Jesus fed everyone that was there, but there were enough leftovers for, you guessed it, all people. Jesus did this miracle to show people that he was to be their food, and that the people were to rely on Him for sustenance, just like the Israelites were fed manna from heaven in the desert. Similarly, this wasn't just meant for those present, or the Israelites, but for all people.

If you were to consider the book of Enoch to have some value as being "partially inspired by God," or something along those lines, you could consider the texts we see in section 3, notably 72:2-3:

> *"And this is the first law of the luminaries: the luminary the Sun has its rising in the eastern portals of the heaven, 3 and its setting in the western portals of the heaven. And I saw six portals in which the sun rises, and six portals in which the sun sets and the moon rises and sets in these portals, and the leaders of the stars and those whom they lead: six in the east and six in the west, and all following each other"*

Here we see the heavens being divided into twelve portals, which is kind of what we do with the Zodiac. Here "portal" in Hebrew is synonymous with "opening" or "entrance", such as in the gate of a town, though I'm not sure if that's the word used in the original texts. In many ways this is likely an allusion to the Zodiac, and if the book of Enoch possibly did come from teachings passed down from Enoch or even someway inspired from God (which is highly debatable), this could offer some insight for origins of the Zodiac. It also shows that there's portals in the sky, through which "something" can come through. If the Zodiac is meant to mean part of our spirit/soul, and represent people like I just laid out above, then it could follow from this that our spirit/soul enters into the world through one of these twelve portals, with each portal being a unique spirit-type. I'm guessing of course as to the meaning of this, but some kind of logic like that is quite possibly there.

Years later after I had initially discovered all this, God told me to research the number twelve in the Bible. I did a search for the number twelve in the Bible and exported all of the verses. I went through each verse individually. Many of them were what I would call "random" instances of the number twelve. Let's be real: sometimes twelve is just a number, no symbolism. I did pick out all of the ones that did appear to be tied to some form of symbolism. Usually you can tell when something is set apart, or perhaps might be set apart. I went through each verse, and every seemingly significant verse that included the number twelve could somehow be tied to being representative of all people or the Zodiac. This fact, even if one is opposed to the Zodiac and everything it represents, should not be taken lightly. The interpretations laid out above have more explanative power in scripture than anything else I'd ever heard for the number twelve.

****

There is one more instance of the number twelve that I have not mentioned yet. I would argue from any point of view that it is also the most important, outweighing all of the above combined. The twelve tribes of Israel may be the first time that we see the number twelve existing in scripture, but the next symbol technically speaking predates even that. It predates the creation of man, and is arguably a heavenly symbol. That is, it exists in heaven. This is found in Revelation 22:2

> *"through the middle of the street of the city; also, on either side of the river, the tree of life with its twelve kinds of fruit, yielding its fruit each month. The leaves of the tree were for the healing of the nations."*

The tree of life seems pretty important. We know it was present in Genesis at the creation of man, and that in Genesis 3:22-24 during man's fall, God said that man must be taken out of the garden so that he cannot take also of the tree of life and live forever. He also set a cherubim and a flaming sword that turned every way to guard the way to the tree of life (this is a very different topic of discussion, as God seems to be actively guarding the tree of life from man). Because this symbol is more eternal that all the rest that we've seen, it's arguably the most important. Because of that, it likely holds the key to understanding the true meaning of the symbolism of the number twelve.

This symbol here has been a major pinch point for those trying to put everything together. It just doesn't quite match up with all of the other common interpretations of the number twelve. At least it doesn't match up in quite as satisfying of a way that we would like it to.

However, when this symbology here is compared to the Zodiac, it passes with flying colors. Again, going back to my hypothesis of the Zodiac being tied to creation, this verse is probably the strongest evidence for that hypothesis in scripture.

First of all, just look at the name, "tree of life." What is life? From a biblical perspective, we define life as being tied to our spirit/soul. When we speak of eternal life, we certainly aren't speaking of our body (at least not primarily – a body without a soul/spirit is a corpse). A literal changeout of words here yields "tree of spirit/soul," though you don't have to do that to see the connection. The Hebrew and Greek translation of "life" is not much more specific, as the word can mean lifetime, lifespan, physical and spiritual existence. Again, the hypothesis is that the Zodiac is tied to the makeup of our spirit/soul. The deeper look into the Hebrew and Greek definitions here is somewhat in-line with this.

The tree of life bears twelve fruits. When "bearing fruit" is mentioned in the Bible, it is usually in reference to production. We produce good fruit when we do, think, or feel good things. Similarly we produce bad fruit by doing bad things. Also, each tree is known by its fruit. There are twelve signs of the Zodiac, or twelve kinds of spiritual/soul fruit or life. Again going with our interpretation of twelve representing all people, the fruit of the tree of life is **people**, or at least the spirit/soul that governs people.

It yields its fruit each month. This is how the twelve sun signs that are the primary focus here are defined, as happening each month. This is a perfect match with the Zodiac, not so much with astrology as a whole, but for the Zodiac yes. Not only that, if you were to include the passage from the book of Enoch as coming from God, the twelve portals matches the tree of Tree of Life fairly well. Don't forget about the cosmic clock that the Hebrews of the time were familiar with and used to tell time every day. The tie-in with a twelve-month time period here and the Zodiac very well could have been obvious to them, as it was their calendar. Remember, the Zodiac was engraved in several synagogues (Gilad & Schuster, 2020). All in all, the tree of life is a perfect match for not only the Zodiac, but also my primary hypothesis.

To recap, we can clearly see that the number twelve is symbolically tied to people and the governance of people. This is evident in just about all scriptures that involve the twelve tribes of Israel or the twelve disciples of Jesus. It's also tied to time through twelve months and the tree of life, however you want to define the word "life." Again, I'd argue that this symbol, the number twelve, is being used in a similar way that God used Passover to point to Jesus. It's a forerunner that reflects a greater truth – something that is real or tangible, something that would have weight to the common person in spreading the truth of God. What else could fit into all of these clues?

Throughout all of my research mentioned above, it became clear that if nothing else, the Zodiac combined with my hypothesis fit all the symbols of the number twelve in the Bible with near perfection. It hit everything major very well, and much of the minor stuff very well too. Where other theories had to take a bit of a stretch on a few items, this fit with outstanding grades. This fact alone, coupled with the Zodiac actually being real, logically should seal the deal as it being the correct interpretation of the symbology of the number twelve in scripture.

13

Anything Else?

At this point in my mind, the relationship between the twelve Zodiac signs and the symbology of the number twelve in the Bible was pretty cemented. With the whole Zodiac thing though, at least from a curious scientific perspective, I couldn't help but beg the question, "Is there anything else?". What else am I potentially missing?

I still (and to this day as well) was not completely sure what exactly it meant to be a Scorpio, or any other sign for that matter. I see the effects, but what is the root cause of the effects? What is the definition of each sign? Was there just twelve unique signs and that's it? Was there anything more or anything else that's related to it?

Astrology is a big field. For the most part, everything that was known about it came from people studying the sky and studying people, and arranging things in patterns according to what they saw. There are different strains of thought in it, different methods of interpretation, etc. Being a natural skeptic, I was distrustful of all of it. That, and I felt like I had a one-up on most astrologers because I believed I understood the true origin of it better. Because of that, I didn't want to take anyone's word for granted. The goal above all here was to not be deceived. That would be the worst-case scenario for me.

Ideally, I was looking for something that would simplify the Zodiac. That's typically the goal of science, to simplify the complex into more manageable parts. That's also how I typically operated in my schoolwork and learning. I wouldn't memorize a bunch of things, but I would try to understand at heart what was being taught, and that way I could derive anything else that was needed from basic principles. It was a big key to my success in math. If I could find something like that, and figure out what was the "core" of the Zodiac, if any such thing existed, it would greatly help to understand this and might possibly aid in trying to figure out if individuals actually fit into their sign and further validate it.

Again, I considered the planets and other heavenly bodies. The problem with that though was that it was expansionist, not reductionist. It made it more complicated, not simpler. I decided it was too much work, and it didn't really help me much as I think it takes it a step further than what I could find in scripture.

I looked online, and saw that people had grouped the twelve signs into certain groups. This was in the right direction, but like I said I was distrustful of it all. There were masculine/feminine signs. This seemed inventive. It wasn't that grouping things this way couldn't be done, but that it seemed more like a human invention, since we often tend to label things as masculine or feminine in culture, especially in the past. I doubted it had any actual basis in reality.

Astrologers had also grouped things into four "elements", and three "modalities." At first glance this seemed inventive as well. It didn't seem right, or at least I was distrustful of it. Another alternative was to do my own research and take a deep dive into the guts of the Zodiac signs and see what I could find, and any similarities or key differences between signs. This would be a lot of work and logging. I would have to study my family and friends a lot. This was a huge project. I didn't want to do it, but I figured that was what was needed. There were a lot of potential dead ends, and I didn't trust hardly anything. Rather than wasting time on something that might be a dead end, I figured I'd just have to do it the hard way.

****

However, before I got started and while I was pondering all of this, the idea came to me to see if there were any other Zodiac references in the Bible. If God had put twelve as a symbol in the Bible for that reason, and I was ninety-five percent sure that was it, there was a good chance that there could be other symbols in the Bible that pointed to the Zodiac. It was worth a shot. I trusted God knew what was real obviously since He created it. If any other such symbols existed in the Bible, it was worth looking into to see what insights could be ascertained from them. A quick internet search revealed a few candidates, so I took a look at them.

Most of the candidates were found in the book of Revelation. One such thing was the four horsemen of the apocalypse found in Revelation 6:1-7. The first one was rider on a white horse with a crown and a bow. This did seemingly represent Sagittarius fairly well, as the sign is often represented by a centaur with a bow – mingling of horse, rider, and bow all fit fairly well. At the same time though, this white rider is often interpreted to be Jesus, as he has a crown, and we know he is a rider on a white horse later on in Revelation 19:11-16. Some also think this could be the antichrist. The symbology was definitely there, but unsure of any meaning other than being tied to the apocalypse.

The second horse was red, and rider had a sword. No good fit there. The third horse was black and the rider had a pair of scales. Here this did fit Libra somewhat well, though the horse and rider had nothing to do with it. However it's apparent from the text that this was to symbolize economic hardships, and a scale is a common symbol of the time of the economy, so that interpretation fits well, better than Libra does. Then the fourth rider was on a pale horse and Hades was with him. Nothing good there. maybe Scorpio, but not good symbology. The only one that fit well was the first horse and Sagittarius, but even then it fit better as being Jesus or antichrist. There was nothing here worthwhile related to the Zodiac, at least concerning my hypothesis.

There was another one in Revelation 12:1. There was a woman clothed with the sun, with the moon under her feet, and on her head a crown of twelve stars. The woman herself fit with the sign of Virgo, then we have the symbol twelve again. When you read this more closely though, it becomes apparent that the woman is a symbol of Israel, as her male child is obviously the Messiah. The twelve stars again can represent Israel or all people. Here it could potentially mean either. At the end of the chapter in verse 17 it mentions the rest of her offspring who follow Jesus, but those followers are also grafted into Israel. The whole sun, moon, and twelve stars also sounds very similar to Joseph's dream in 37:9, where the sun and moon were his two parents, and the stars were his brothers. It fit better. Verse 12:1 did say that a sign appeared in heaven. This could be a reference to the Zodiac or astrology for that reason, such as what Jesus said to look for with signs in the heavens, or something similar to the star of Bethlehem. However, nothing significant here stood out in regards to my hypothesis.

There was also the four living creatures found in Revelation 4:6-8 as well as Ezekiel 1:5-21. The verses below in Revelation are shown:

"And before the throne there was as it were a sea of glass, like a crystal. And around the throne, are four living creatures, full of eyes in front and behind: the first living creature like a lion, the second living creature like an ox; the third living creature with the face of a man, and the fourth living creature like an eagle in flight. And the four living creatures, each of them with six wings, are full of eyes around and within, and day and night they never cease to say, "Holy, holy, holy, is the Lord God Almighty, who was and is and is to come!""

The biggest match here is the four faces. Both of those symbols are identical between Revelation and Ezekiel. The lion could easily be represented by Leo. The ox is also very easily tied to Taurus. The man is fairly well tied to Aquarius as well, whose symbol is typically a man carrying water. The eagle is harder, it doesn't fit any of the signs at first glance. Upon further research though, Scorpio has 4 different commonly used symbols – scorpion, snake, eagle, and phoenix. So, the face of an eagle did fit well with Scorpio.

At first glance, this was a fairly promising lead. The fact that all four faces could be matched up to any Zodiac sign at all was significant. Another thing that stuck out right away, was that there was no good explanation for the symbology offered in the text. The four horseman, and the woman with twelve stars all had pretty good explanations nearby or elsewhere in scripture. The four living creatures were mostly an enigma. What I found out next though, would take this from a promising lead, to looking like there may be something there, to where the four living creatures may actually be a purposeful symbol relating to the Zodiac signs.

The next most logical thing to do was to map out the Zodiac signs represented by the four living creatures, and by that I mean fit them into the natural order of the Zodiac (see Graphic 1 on next page). Right away, you notice that all the signs listed here are equally distanced apart. A pattern emerges. Like I said before, it was a promising lead that they matched up at all. The fact that the best matched signs create a pattern really got my attention. It could have been a bull, ram, lion, and woman, in which case Aires and Virgo would have been added into the mix, and there be no noticeable pattern. Or maybe a horse added in there for Sagittarius.

Keeping in mind that the Hebrews (and Greeks) were familiar with the Zodiac, this interpretation could quite possibly have been where their minds would have went as well. The four Zodiac constellations split the sky into 4 directions after all – in a way they would act as a compass for the night sky. With these signs being imprinted on their synagogue, whenever the passage in Ezekiel came up during their services they would see the connection if they were paying attention.

What you probably don't realize is that this pattern as it relates to the Zodiac signs also emerges elsewhere in scripture, though it's much more subtle. If you've read the first five books of the Bible, you probably missed it. It is listed in Numbers chapter 2. Here God is telling the Israelites how to camp and move as they make their way to the promised land. He puts Judah on the east, with two tribes (Zebulun and Issachar)

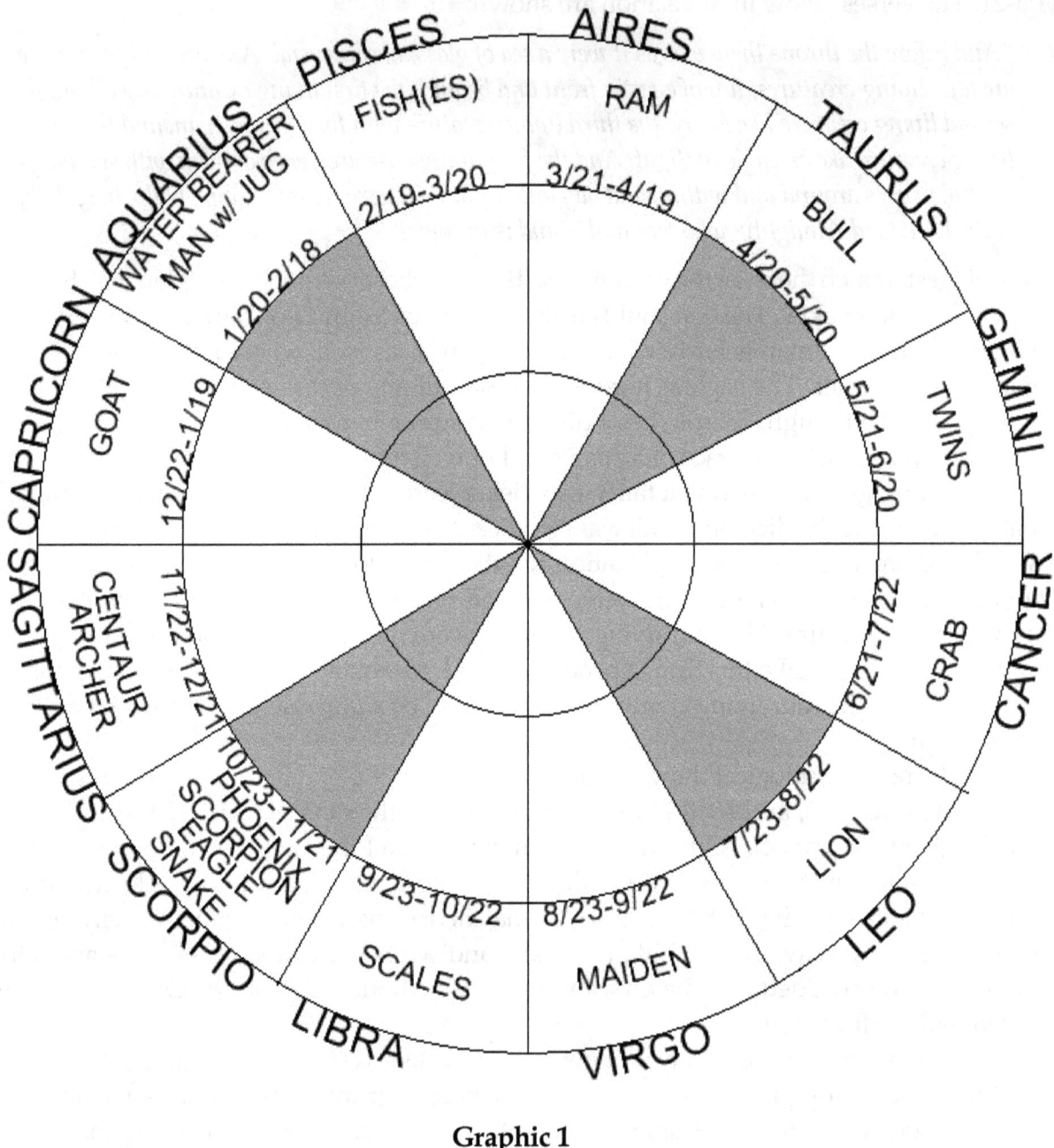

Graphic 1

next to Judah. He puts Reuben on the south side, with two tribes (Simeon and Gad) next to Reuben. The Levites are in the center. Ephraim is on the west side, with two tribes (Manasseh and Benjamin). Dan is on the north, with two tribes (Asher and Naphtali) next to Dan. Here

13: Anything Else

we can see that the twelve tribes are more or less arranged in a circle pattern, in twelve divisions (thirteenth tribe in center, or rather two half-tribes Ephraim and Manasseh on north). The pattern itself kind of resembles the Zodiac wheel.

What is the pattern though? To discern this we need to look at what each tribe is described as. This happens in a few places, but the two notable ones are Genesis 49 where Jacob blesses his sons, and in Deuteronomy 33 where Moses blesses the Israelites. In Genesis 49, Judah is compared to a lion. Reuben is compared to water. Dan is compared to a snake. Joseph (represented later by Ephraim and Manasseh) here is compared to a bough of a fruitful vine. The Hebrew words used here are very open to interpretation. In Deuteronomy 33 however though, we see that Ephraim is compared to a bull. Indeed it is commonly accepted that the symbol for Ephraim is the bull (go google it and see for yourself). So interposing those on the setup given in Numbers chapter 2, we see that the four directions (east, south, west, north) are inhabited by Judah, Reuben, Ephraim, and Dan respectively. These four tribes are represented by the symbols lion, water, bull, and snake respectively, which when translated to the Zodiac are Leo, Aquarius (water bearer), Taurus, and Scorpio respectively. Here we have the same Zodiac signs as represented by the four living creatures!

Furthermore, if you look at the four living creatures in Ezekiel chapter 1, the first face mentioned was human (Aquarius) (which if they're staring right at you, the human face and most obvious one would be on the south if you're facing north), then the one on the right (east) was a lion (Leo). The one on the left (west) was a bull (Taurus), and the last one mentioned (presumably the furthest away, the north side), was an eagle (Scorpio). The order of the four living creatures here and in Ezekiel does not match as they appear in the Zodiac, but the symbols do match.

More importantly, we can draw another solid conclusion from this by following the facts below:

1. The twelve tribes are representative of the Zodiac signs as we previously established, following the symbology laid out in Numbers, Genesis, and Deuteronomy.

2. The passage in numbers shows how the "four" tribes/signs are singled out of the "twelve".

3. This pattern from the book of numbers matches exactly what we see in the four living creatures in Ezekiel, both in symbology and order.

4. Therefore, it's a pretty solid case that the Zodiac interpretation of the four living creatures in Revelation/Ezekiel is the correct one.

5. We can proceed with digging into the significance that these four signs have in the Zodiac with confidence that we have the correct starting interpretation of the four living creatures: Leo, Aquarius, Taurus, and Scorpio.

****

What did this pattern mean though? After further research, I got taken back to something I had initially written off. The pattern seen here matched another pattern that was already commonly used in astrology: the elements. In this interpretation, each Zodiac sign was attributed to one element. There were four elements: fire, earth, air, and water. Each of the Zodiac signs corresponding to the four creatures belonged to a different element. Leo was fire, Taurus was earth, Aquarius was air, and Scorpio was water.

Similarly in this system, there were three modalities: cardinal, fixed, and mutable. All of the four signs related to the four living creatures were considered fixed signs. Also interestingly, at least in John's account in Revelation, the signs are listed in order of the elements. The Zodiac traditionally starts with Aires, a fire sign, then progresses to Taurus, Earth sign, then to Gemini, an air sign, and Cancer, a water sign, and repeats itself. The four living creatures are listed as fire, earth, air, then water, in order. Another hit, though the order isn't necessarily as important as the former two "hits." Perhaps the meaning of the four living creatures then, was to give weight to the elements of the Zodiac. Despite my first instinct to write this system off, if God was potentially saying it was accurate then it was definitely worth investigating.

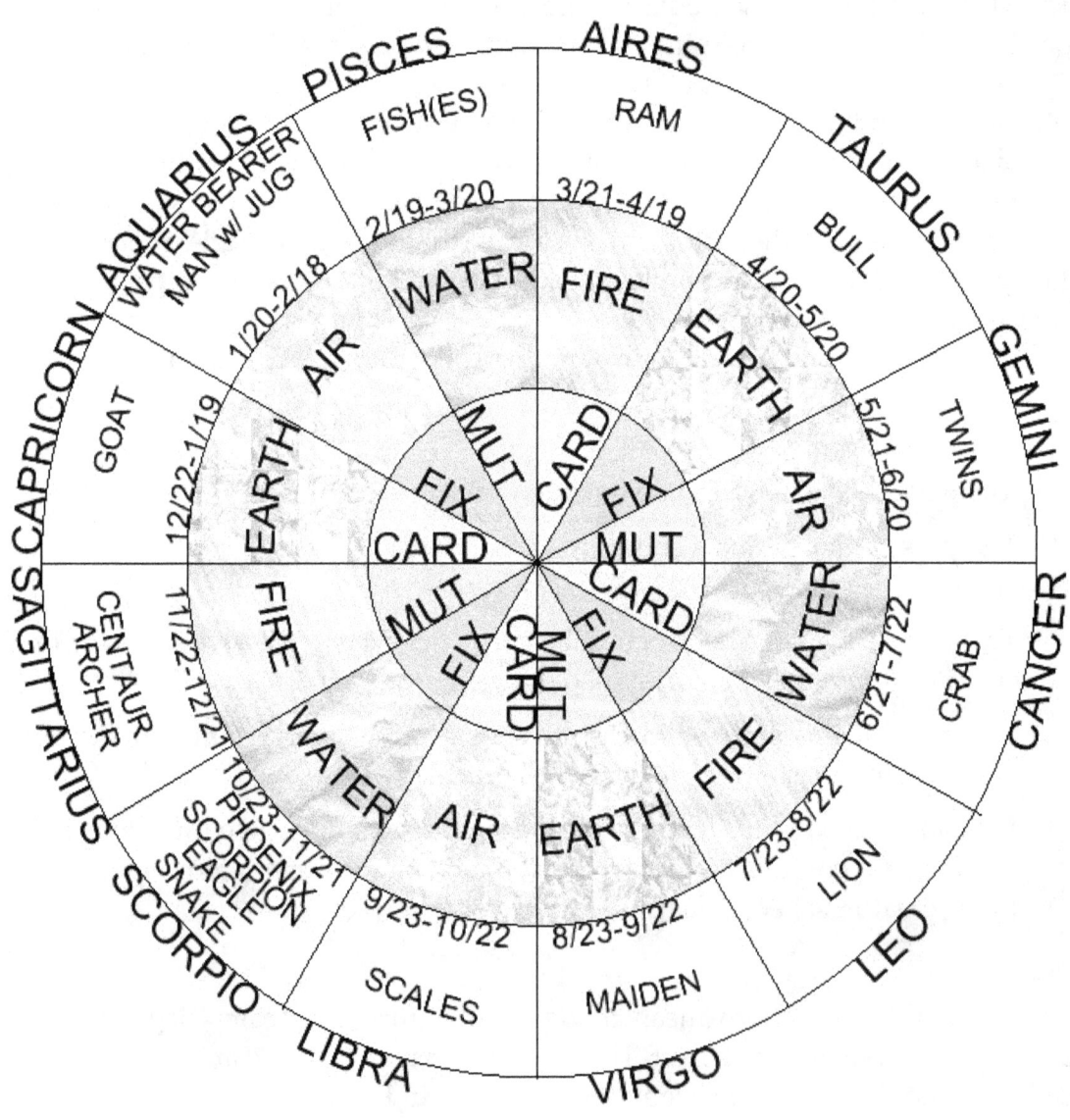

13: Anything Else

Graphic 2

After doing a little reading, I got a little bit of an idea what each of the elements were about. Fire was typically about creativity, self-assurance, fun, and what I would call "action-oriented." Earth was more about practicality, being grounded, dependability, and what I would describe as a fixation toward the material. Perhaps instead of material, it was potentially an "object-oriented" way of thinking. Air was more about logic and communication, objectivity, perhaps idealism as well. The way I best understood this was their focus is more on "ideas." Water tended to be more about emotions, nurturing, intuition, feelings.

Likewise, if the elements were supposedly real, then by relation, it was likely the modalities were real as well. So, I looked into those. Cardinal was typically all about initiation. This could be seen as starting things, or showing initiative. A constant stream of starting things, then off to the next start. Fixed tended to be about steadiness, persistence, concentration. Since I supposedly was one, I would call it a fixation on what "is", or present state. Mutable was about adaptability, flexible, change, or potentially restlessness or even diverse perspective.

Perhaps, the answer to the question, of "what else" in the Zodiac was this. Since the elements and modalities when combined each had a unique combination for each sign, then perhaps all that the twelve signs were, was just the mixing of the two. Perhaps Scorpio was just what you got when you mixed "water "and "fixed", and nothing more. Then everything that you typically see with Scorpio is just a result of water mixed with fixed, and nothing else. Then every sign was just defined by the element and modality tied to it. This, from an intuitive scientific perspective, was the most likely explanation based on how things in science typically turn out. Adding something else to the twelve signs was just another degree of complexity that didn't necessarily help or make sense.

****

I took this new knowledge of the elements and modalities and went back to the "field." I had a new way of studying people now, to see if it fit. This method of studying was also a little easier. Now I could compare fixed signs to other fixed signs, and the same with similar elements. It did make it a lot easier, made the possible connections go from one in twelve, to one in three or one in four. I found it easiest to think of it as the element being what people are primarily concerned with by default, and the modality being the way that they looked at the element.

For example, with myself being a Scorpio, I tended to primarily look at people's emotional state (water) to try to get a feel for where their heart was at as my default method for judge of character. I used this to size them up, or in most situations in general. In my pursuit of my own emotional (water) steadiness or security (fixed), I decided that hiding things was the best strategy to achieve that. I had great perseverance, which was also a fixed trait.

It took a little bit of practice to know what to look for, but to my surprise, it worked. Things that I struggled to see before now became easier to see. I had trouble seeing what stood out in Capricorn, Taurus, and Virgo. Now that it was possible that these were all earth signs, it made more sense. I didn't understand earth, probably because it was what I would call basic. But instead of looking for "earth", I could look for the modalities. Now I could see the "fixed" in Taurus, and it came out very strong. I also saw some of the earth people as being very into material things.

For example, one earth friend said to me he thought that you can tell a lot about someone by their car (material choice). I didn't really think so, but from his perspective it probably worked. While observing another cardinal friend arguing with a different friend, his method of arguing was to say, "well what about this?", and just keep doing this. He even afterwards said that was a great way to win an argument, to just keep doing it to get all perspectives. His method was to just initiate something else and repeat. On a different occasion during a class debate, a fixed friend and a cardinal friend were on different sides, and the cardinal friend did the same tactic, "what about this?". My fixed friend didn't think it was relevant, and mocked it a little. I kind of agreed with my fixed friend naturally. I was more about looking at what really mattered, and try to see the heart of the matter. To me, the "what about's" or "what if's" weren't necessarily important or essential to understanding the heart of things, though I understand that there could be good insights by thinking about things like that.

I remember going to a larger party and studying my friends. I'd watch a group of fire friends talk, and notice the theme of their conversation was about what was going on: action (fire). I saw a similar thing with fixed signs; I noticed they said things in a more "that's the way it is" kind of way. It could often be described as short, or one-liners. By focusing on the elements and modalities, I was now able to see what I was ultimately after: I was able to see the evidence of the Zodiac in everyday occurrences.

While at a friend's party, I distinctly remember getting a big grin across my face. It was there. All of a sudden, now the success rate in matching people close to me to their Zodiac signs went from hovering just above 50% using just the twelve signs, to 90-95% or more when using the elements and modalities. I could see it in pretty much everyone I knew fairly well, and at a fairly microscopic level in day-to-day occurrences. I had finally found and confirmed what I had been looking for.

14

Modalities

So far, it seemed like the elements and modalities were also true. After all, the understanding of these had spiked my success rate greatly. This sort of begged the question, "if the four living creatures are meant to represent the four elements of the Zodiac, are the three modalities also in there?" They didn't necessarily have to be, but if that's what it was supposed to represent, there's a good chance it is. So, I went back and looked at the four living creatures again. First, in Revelation 4:6-8

> "And around the throne, on each side of the throne, are four living creatures, full of eyes in front and behind: the first living creature like a lion, the second living creature like an ox, the third living creature with the face of a man, and the fourth living creature like an eagle in flight. And the four living creatures, each of them with six wings, are full of eyes all around and within, and day and night they never cease to say, "Holy, holy, holy, is the Lord God Almighty, who was and is and is to come!""

The only other things that can be picked up here is that each living creature has six wings and is full of eyes. Nothing jumped out initially, no mention of three. After thinking a while, it did dawn on me that wings always come in pairs. It wouldn't make sense to have three wings, or five wings. So, six wings was basically the same thing as three pairs of wings. Of course it would be very weird if the four creatures had three wings, there wouldn't be any symmetry. So there was a set of three on the four living creatures. It could be a potential match. There was one big issue with this though. Unlike the faces of the four living creatures which were more or less identical between the accounts in Ezekiel and Revelation, the number of wings was different. Here is the account in Ezekiel 1:4-21, with much more detail than Revelation.

> "As I looked, behold, a stormy wind came out of the north, and a great cloud, with brightness around it, and fire flashing forth continually, and in the midst of the fire, as it were gleaming metal. 5 And from the midst of it came the likeness of four living creatures. And this was their appearance: they had a human likeness, 6 but each had four faces, and each of them had four wings. 7 Their legs were straight, and the soles of their feet were like the sole of a calf's foot. And they sparkled like burnished bronze. 8 Under their wings on their four sides they had human hands. And the four had their faces and their wings thus: 9 their wings touched one another. Each one of them went straight forward, without turning as they went. 10 As for the likeness of their faces, each had a human face. The four had the face of a lion on the right side, the four had the face of an ox on the left side, and the four had the face of an eagle. 11 Such were their faces. And their wings were spread out above. Each creature had two wings, each of which

touched the wing of another, while two covered their bodies. 12 And each went straight forward. Wherever the spirit would go, they went, without turning as they went. 13 As for the likeness of the living creatures, their appearance was like burning coals of fire, like the appearance of torches moving to and fro among the living creatures. And the fire was bright, and out of the fire went forth lightning. 14 And the living creatures darted to and fro, like the appearance of a flash of lightning.

15 Now as I looked at the living creatures, I saw a wheel on the earth beside the living creatures, one for each of the four of them. 16 As for the appearance of the wheels and their construction: their appearance was like the gleaming of beryl. And the four had the same likeness, their appearance and construction being as it were a wheel within a wheel. 17 When they went, they went in any of their four directions without turning as they went. 18 And their rims were tall and awesome, and the rims of all four were full of eyes all around. 19 And when the living creatures went, the wheels went beside them; and when the living creatures rose from the earth, the wheels rose. 20 Wherever the spirit wanted to go, they went, and the wheels rose along with them, for the spirit of the living creatures was in the wheels. 21 When those went, these went; and when those stood, these stood; and when those rose from the earth, the wheels rose along with them, for the spirit of the living creatures was in the wheels."

Notably in Ezekiel, like I mentioned earlier, there were only four wings. There was also the addition of a "wheel within a wheel" which wasn't in Revelation. The "many eyes" were present in both visions, though in different locations – in the wheels in Ezekiel, but all over the creatures in Revelation. In Ezekiel, the wheels seem to be tied to the creatures, and moved with the creatures. This ate at me for a while, not being able to reconcile it.

Some time later, even up to the writing of this book, God had told me to read "The Harbinger II" by Jonathan Cahn (Cahn, 2020). At the time that happened, I luckily already had a copy of it. My aunt had stopped by for a visit and had handed out copies to friends, and she had a spare copy in her car. I said yea I'd like to read it, but I never got around to it. Now that God was telling me to read it, it was nice already having a hard copy. The book has a great message, and a timely message to demonstrate the signs of the times that we're in, notably for the United States. I highly recommend it, but that's not the primary reason why I was reading it, other than that God told me to. The book talks about many prophecies in the Bible, and how they parallel what's happening in America right now, and how many of the old prophecies and symbols matched up near perfectly with modern day symbols. I however, was more interested in the logic of prophecy. If I understood the reasoning behind the connections, then maybe that would help me understand the four living creatures better.

Eventually, it got to a point where the logic just kind of hit me on the head. Nouriel, the main character, was in a conversation with "the prophet" talking about a wall, and that the breach of the wall was a sign of judgement. The issue though, was that America didn't have a wall around it. The prophet insisted there was a wall. There was a need for protection. He then asked, "what was the ***purpose*** of the ancient wall?" The answer was defense, and in modern times America's defense was its vast network of military, intelligence, weaponry, operatives, etc. America's defense department was the Pentagon, which got attacked during 9/11/2001.

It hit me then, what was the purpose of a wing? What was the purpose of a wheel? Both things have the same purpose, they are a means of movement. In the vision in Ezekiel, there were two pairs of wings, and a pair of wheels (or a wheel within a wheel). The common theme between them was movement. Not only that, in the later verses we see the picture of the four living creatures along with the wheels *moving* all over the place, though we're not sure for what reason.

So here in Ezekiel we're able to see that there are three mechanisms for movement – 2 wings, and a set of wheels, similar to Revelation. It could still represent the three modalities. Furthermore, I saw the modalities as the way that the Zodiac sign looked at the element, but a probably even better way to describe them was how the Zodiac signs *moved*. After all, looking doesn't accomplish anything, you have to move. Movement could be in thought, or in a physical sense. It was a better, more all-inclusive way to describe the Modalities. If the two visions in Ezekiel and Revelation matched, then we wouldn't necessarily be able to see the common theme of movement.

Furthermore, if we go back to the Israelite encampment mentioned in Numbers chapter 2, we see that three tribes are grouped with each set of the four corners of the encampment. The math here supports the grouping of 3 with each set of four, much like how we see each living creature having three sets of wings, or perhaps two sets of wings and a wheel.

****

As a side note, much effort has also been put into trying to directly tie each tribe to a specific Zodiac sign, and the fruit of doing so might help to give more light on any patterns that we might see. I'm very much interested in the subject, to see if in any way some pattern arises that would give more insight that might confirm the theory put forth here, or perhaps highlight something else. However in my research of this, there are several different methodologies employed, and I don't think any of them are very conclusive. I don't necessarily agree that any of the methodologies has good grounds (biblical or otherwise), and if they do have decent grounds for their assumptions and methodologies, the results typically don't match anything significant. The only consistency that I've found, and most people agree with, is the four tribes and Zodiac signs that match up with the four living creatures.

Another thing to note is that some have theorized that the wheels in Ezekiel 1 are actually Zodiac wheels. While this does fit with the theme very well, it doesn't match up with much else. We already have part of the Zodiac mentioned with the four living creatures, why do we need the wheels? With no other details on the wheels other than they have eyes on them, it's hard to make such a connection with the wheels to the twelve Zodiac signs represented by a wheel. They're also completely missing from the account in the book of Revelation.

****

The elements and modalities worked. They worked even better than the twelve signs did. They had more explaining power than the twelve signs. Better yet, they matched up with symbols in the Bible as well, with the four living creatures. What I realized next though, would send me on an even bigger journey than what I had previously undertook with the twelve signs.

15

The Heart of the Zodiac

I did some very basic thinking. The four elements and three modalities appeared to be the heart of the Zodiac. The twelve signs are likely just what you get when you blend these two together via multiplication. In all reality then, these are more important than the twelve signs themselves. They were the "heart" or center of it all. Then it dawned on me, if there were four elements, and three modalities governing the Zodiac, then the most basic conclusion was that there were 4+3 = _seven_ governing components of the Zodiac!

This was potentially even a bigger hit than anything else. Seven was easily the most repeated number in the Bible. It was one of the most repeated symbols as well. It was God's number. Could the Zodiac be connected to the number seven in scripture as well? I needed to look into this more, but where to start? I had spent a considerable amount of time on the number twelve, but the number seven was probably twice as numerous as the number twelve, if not more so.

It was quite possible that God just used seven as a generic number in many cases just to drive home the emphasis of its importance. I had thought the same thing for the number twelve, but after more research on that, I found that pretty much every instance of the number 12 that was seemingly used in a symbolic way could be matched to the Zodiac. They could be matched to twelve signs, or twelve "spiritual tribes of people" or "all people." There were instances of the number twelve that were seemingly random, such as in Joshua 18:24 mentioning certain clans of Benjamin having twelve towns and villages – nothing that sounds significant there. Seven could fit this way, but I doubted it. There was a lot more variety, and it was hard to find a common theme.

The most common and popular meaning of the number seven in scripture today is that it symbolizes completeness. It's important to note that the literal translation of "seven" in Hebrew means "complete/full." Both the number and the word have the same spelling in Hebrew, a language that uses the same alphabet for both numbers and letters. So when the number seven is used, there's a good chance that it's a way of symbolizing completeness. The issue I have with this though is that it doesn't mean anything, especially to someone outside of the faith. Usually the symbols God uses have a significant meaning as we explored earlier with the number twelve. That being said, to investigate the significance of the Zodiac to the number seven I figured it would be best to take a similar approach to what I did with the number twelve. It's important to find the _first_ seemingly significant instance of it, look at that, and then find the seemingly _most_ significant instance of it and look at that as well. With twelve, the first instance is the twelve tribes of Israel (or perhaps Ishmael), and the most significant is arguably the tree of life because it existed before everything else.

****

The first instance is fairly easy to find, it's in the first couple chapters of the Bible in Genesis: creation week. God created light and dark on the first day. The second day we see Heaven being created, and the third was the Earth, seas, and vegetation. The fourth day God created the stars and heavenly bodies, and on the fifth he created everything in the water and the birds as well. The sixth day God created beast and man, and on the seventh day he rested. It says in Genesis 2:3 that God blessed the seventh day and made it holy. So here we have God setting apart the number seven as holy as the very first thing in scripture.

So the Zodiac doesn't seemingly match up to seven right here from first glance, but let's take a deeper look. Seven here is tied first of all to time – God blessed the seventh day. There is a strong argument that our current seven-day week is based on this scripture reference. The Zodiac is also tied to time as well, though not through a seven-day week. We also must not forget that to the ancient people, time was very much tied to the sky and stars – their clock. In a roundabout way, this ties the number seven to the Zodiac signs as well. The twelve months match up well, but not the seven day week. The common themes of time do match up though, just not as well as the twelve Zodiac signs do.

One of the other major themes here is creation. God created the heavens and the earth in a seven-day timespan (well, six days plus a vacation day, but God sets apart the number seven here, not the number six – it wasn't complete until the seventh day). This theme actually does fit very well with my hypothesis. The Zodiac is more or less part of how we're designed, or created to think or behave. The seven-day creation week encompasses pretty much all of creation as we know it, and the seven components of the Zodiac encompass all of the twelve Zodiac signs.

As an engineer, I'm familiar with that sense of pride that you get when you pull something off in a design. Oftentimes what you're most proud of is how you made it, or how you pulled it off. I would argue that God is the same way, and the number seven would represent how He created life in general. It's the crown jewel, more so than the twelve signs of the Zodiac. Just like seven was the crown jewel of creation week, seven is the crown jewel of spiritual creation. So the gist here, is that seven is tied to both time and creation in Genesis (material creation more so), and seven is tied to creation in the Zodiac (spiritual creation, which the spiritual things are typically emphasized more than the material in scripture), and more loosely tied to time through the twelve signs. It's not perfect, but it fits in a major way.

****

Now, let's look for the most important instance of the number seven. This takes a little bit more searching, but similar to the tree of life being the most important symbol of twelve, the best place to look is in heaven. It's known that God makes the earthly things reflect the things in heaven. This can be seen in several biblical studies. For instance, the temple was set up to reflect the way that we're supposed to approach God, along with a lot of the ordinances that were set up for the operations of the temple. We're looking for things that are more or less eternal, or that we know or can deduct existed way before anything else. Heaven is eternal, earth is not. Most likely, we would have to look to visions or prophecies, as that's the only way that we can have a glimpse of heavenly things.

Also, based on the context of the instance of the symbol seven, we can have an idea of how important it is which will also help us to gauge things. Creation week in this perspective is fairly eternal, since it involves what we understand to be all of creation, or at least all of our universe, and possibly more. This quite possibly could be the most important instance of seven as well, but not necessarily. A more thorough search is needed to rule everything out.

After a bit of searching, I found what I believe to be the most important instance of the number seven based on the criteria above. The most important instance is not creation week, but the seven spirits of God, which are found almost exclusively in the book of Revelation. They are first found briefly mentioned in Revelation 1:4-5

"John to the seven churches that are in Asia: Grace to you and peace from him who is and who was and who is to come, and from the seven spirits who are before his throne, and from Jesus Christ the faithful witness, the firstborn of the dead, and the ruler of kings on earth"

The only emphasis here is that the seven spirits are before the throne, and they are spoken of like they are living beings, which makes sense since that's kind of the biblical definition of a spirit.

The next instance occurs in Revelation 4:5.

"From the throne came flashes of lighting, and rumblings and peals of thunder, and before the throne were burning seven torches of fire, which are the seven spirits of God."

What we see here and in the previous verses, is that around the throne sit a rainbow, twenty-four thrones and twenty-four elders, seven torches which are the seven spirits of God, a sea of glass, and then the four living creatures also. Again, the takeaway here is that the seven spirits of God are before the throne. Not much to add from the first instance.

Now on to Revelation 5:6:

And between the throne and the four living creatures and among the elders I saw a Lamb standing, as though it had been slain, with seven horns and with seven eyes, which are the seven spirits of God sent out into all the earth."

From the language in the previous and following verses here, as well as other symbology in scripture, it is clear that the Lamb mentioned here is Jesus, no real room for debate. Jesus is depicted as having seven horns and seven eyes, which it is said right here that the seven eyes are the seven spirits of God. Now we have the seven spirits of God being linked to eyes, in addition to torches of fire. It should be noted, that seven eyes are also seen elsewhere in scripture in Zechariah 3:8-9

"Hear now, O Joshua the high priest, you and your friends who sit before you, for they are men who are a sign: behold, I will bring my servant the Branch. For behold, on the stone that I have

set before Joshua, on a single stone with seven eyes, I will engrave its inscription, declares the Lord of hosts, and I will remove the iniquity of this land in a single day."

Here again we see seven represented as the eyes, and the rock is typically used as a representation of the Messiah, as we can see in king Nebuchadnezzar's dream in the book of Daniel and in other places as well. The book of Zechariah goes on though, and mentions seven lampstands in 4:2, 4, and 10.

"And he said to me, "What do you see?" I said, "I see, and behold, a lampstand all of gold, with a bowl on the top of it, and seven lamps on it, with seven lips on each of the lamps that are on top of it."4. "And I said to the angel who talked with me, "What are these, my lord?" 10. "For whoever has despised the day of small things shall rejoice, and shall see the plumb line in the hand of Zerubbabel. "These seven are the eyes of the Lord, which range through the whole earth."

Here we have the seven lamps being called the seven eyes of the Lord, which range through the whole earth. This verse ties the lamps to the seven eyes, and we see that the seven eyes of the Lord range throughout the whole earth, just like we see in Revelation with the seven eyes on the Lamb. Zechariah also likewise has the seven eyes on the Rock, or the Messiah. In Revelation we see the seven lampstands are also the seven spirits of God, as are the seven eyes on the Lamb. So what we can put together from all of this, is that the seven spirits of God, and the seven lampstands/torches, and the seven eyes, are essentially the same thing. The fact that they are either wielded by or are a part of Jesus, the Messiah, says quite a bit. Since Jesus predates creation, it's likely that the seven spirits of God also predate creation. This alone likely sets it above creation week as the "most important instance of seven." Then when you add in that the seven spirits of God are before the throne, the most important place possible, the emphasis is just added even more. This is more than likely the most 'eternal' or 'important' symbology of seven in scripture.

Now the question comes, "does this relate at all to the Zodiac?" We see that the seven spirits are sent out into all of the earth, or that they range through the whole earth. There are a few ways to interpret this. One is that their role is to go out into all of the earth, though the purpose of that is a little unclear. Another interpretation, if this is meant to tie to the Zodiac, is that they're sent out or go into all people, or perhaps all creation.

Another thing to note here is the literal interpretation that seven is tied to *spirits*, the seven spirits of God. The Zodiac is likely part of spiritual creation like I mentioned, just like the tree of *life*, the literal interpretation of seven **spirits** fit with my hypothesis. The fact that these are seven spirits of God again goes hand in hand with the hypothesis that there are seven "spiritual" components of the Zodiac. It's part of the spiritual DNA of the Zodiac, and therefore of people, and potentially even Jesus or God himself if the symbology of the eyes on the Lamb were to mean that. We are made in the image of God after all. Perhaps seven is even tied to the image of God. We will explore this idea a little later.

Then there are the seven eyes. The word used in Zechariah chapter 4:10 and 3:9 to represent "eyes" can also mean "mental qualities" or "of mental and spiritual faculties" in Hebrew. This further confirms the importance of "spirit" in all of this, and in a way adds the "spirit" touch to the account in the Old Testament, which is important for New Testament-Old Testament agreement. The eyes therefore represent spirit at heart in this instance. This acts as big decoder for what comes next.

There is another instance where eyes are used quite a bit. Seemingly uncountable eyes to be exact. We've already been to this before, it's the symbol where the rabbit trail started: the four living creatures. In both Revelation and Ezekiel they are depicted as being full of eyes. In Revelation it seems they are completely covered all over with eyes. The account in Ezekiel has only the eyes mentioned as being part of the rims of the wheels. Ezekiel also mentions that the spirit of the living creatures was in the wheels, which are covered in eyes, so it's likely that the spirit was in the eyes which are on the wheels. So the likely interpretation here is that the four living creatures have "many spirits." The Zodiac is a characterization of "many spirits", or many Zodiac signs. It's the blueprint of spiritual, or mental diversity.

The fact that we started and ended this journey with the four living creatures helps to show how all of it could be tied together. We derived the "seven" in the Zodiac from the four living creatures – the four elements and three modalities represented as such. On the journey through scripture of the number seven, we see seven tied to creation, and then also time in creation week. Then in its most important characterization, seven is tied to spirit through the seven spirits of God, Jesus Himself, lamps or torches, and then eyes. Then through the symbology of "eyes", it all comes full circle back to the four living creatures, showing that the four living creatures are also tied to spirit, and possibly, even probably, the seven spirits of God.

****

I did do a more in-depth study of every instance of the number seven, and the best thing that I could come up with, which I even got from others, is that the number seven represents when God is doing something "by His Spirit." Think about this: if the number twelve represents all of mankind, and the number seven's primary importance represents the seven Spirits of God, then it fits with the pattern that the number seven is God's number. Read that again but slowly and literally: the number seven is literally the number of God. God's nature or His Spirit is literally sevenfold, or tied to the number seven in a similar way that twelve is tied to humanity.

The new inference and "decoder key" to understanding the number seven in the context of scripture then, is it's being used symbolically in scripture to say "all of God" instead of "all people." That seems kind of odd to say "all" of God since He is either one or a trinity depending on the situation, but I use it just to demonstrate the link and similarity to the number twelve. So the number seven would often either mean God is bringing something about, or perhaps that people are to do something *for* God or as God would do it.

Now we can take this hypothesis of God being represented by the number seven to scripture and see how well it fits. One of the common themes of the number seven includes some kind of judgement or punishment for disobedience, as in the seven seals, seven trumpet blasts, and seven bowls of God's wrath in Revelation. Here this would be "God" bringing about these judgements. Elsewhere we see Israel was captive to Babylon for seventy years, or that God would bring on sevenfold punishment if the Israelites did not follow Him.

Other places it can be seen as God's provision, such as when Jesus fed the four thousand and the five thousand (Matthew 16), or when the Israelites camped at Elim (Exodus 15:27) and there were seventy palm trees and twelve springs of water. An interesting side note here is that these two instances are one of the few, if only places where twelve and seven are mentioned together in scripture. When Jesus fed the multitudes on 2 different occasions, there were 12 and 7 basketfuls left over at different times (and Jesus specifically points out this fact). God (seven) gave provision for all people (twelve) here.

It's often also referenced in forgiveness or purification, even healing. People had to be cleansed seven times and/or wait seven days to be considered fully healed. The inference here is that the healing comes from God or is according to God. In the law you'll see blood being spattered seven times in a few places, and you'll see sacrifices in the multiples of seven, oftentimes in regards to sin offering. Here the inference is the sacrifice is for God, in accordance with God, to make oneself right with God, or that (all of) God will forgive. Jesus said we are to forgive seven times seventy times in one day, or using our decoder, we are to forgive as *God (seven)* forgives.

If you've been paying attention to scripture this is not really a surprising, new, or novel interpretation of the number seven. What I do think is new or different though is that we are potentially able to actually see what the sevenfold nature of God is through the Zodiac if this interpretation holds true. If seven is in some way part of how God is revealed via the Zodiac, then twelve (the actual Zodiac) is in a way the image of seven, or in the image of God. Since twelve represents people, then it follows that people were created in the image of God, which we already knew from scripture. This interpretation also fits well with the 3 patriarchs of Israel (God as a Trinity, also represented by "seven) creating the twelve tribes of people that we previously established from the accounts in Genesis. This was not something that I thought originally, but it comes as a consequence of what seems to me to be the best interpretation of the number seven in scripture. Similarly with the number twelve being a symbol that could bring about faith in God through a real-life connection, the Zodiac interpretation of seven does the same. Furthermore, if the real meaning behind the number seven (or twelve for that matter) is hidden from us or undiscoverable, then it has little to no practical use for us, so why even repeat the numbers at all?

One important side note to reiterate is the connection of the number seven to time found in scripture, which typically is seven days, or oftentimes seven years. This is quite extensive, not just in creation week but several other places. I've not found a good link to this like there is with the number twelve. Perhaps there is something else out there but I'm not quite sure.

****

One thing that I have received criticism on regarding this theory is adding the four elements to the three modalities to get seven, and doing such in scripture. Again, the major support for all of this, is very much a scientific question: are the elements/modalities real? If they are, then that in itself is very strong support for this interpretation of seven. I did find a few references in scripture that does offer some support for "four" being a part of "seven". The answer is in Revelation chapter 6, particularly verses 1, 3, 5, 7, 9, 12, and then chapter 8 verse 1. This is where the Lamb is opening the seven seals to the scroll. Pay attention to the pattern here. The first four seals are the four horsemen. After that, each seal represents something more unique. In this instance here, we already have four (horsemen) as a part of seven (seals), but it goes further. In verses 1, 3, 5, and 7, one of the four living creatures, a different creature each time, each says "Come!". So here we have the direct embodiment of the four elements in scripture (the four living creatures), as playing a part of the first four seals. You'll notice in the last three seals that they do not play a distinct part in unveiling the seals.

If you look at the seven trumpets in Revelation 8:6 you'll notice a similar pattern. The first four trumpets blow and their dooms follow, then there is an interlude in verse 13, a break.

"Then I looked, and I heard an eagle crying with a loud voice as it flew directly overhead, "Woe, woe, woe to those who dwell on the earth, at the blasts of the other trumpets that the three angels are about to blow!"

This creates a break and a distinction between the first four trumpets, and the last three. Perhaps it's not significant and just a coincidence that there is an interlude here, but look ahead to 9:12

"The first woe has passed; behold, two woes are still to come."

This is right before the 6th trumpet is about to sound. Notice it only mentions that one woe has passed, even though it's on the fifth trumpet. Technically speaking five unfortunate things have happened, but it only mentions one. Why? There appears to be a division made between the first four trumpets and the last three. It's possible that the separation may not be significant, but these two scripture references should show that dividing seven into four and three is not unnatural or out of line.

****

One other competing theory for the number seven that does tie to astrology and I do want to note, is that the number seven is supposed to represent the seven governing bodies of astrology at the time. This would be the Moon, Mercury, Venus, Sun, Mars, Jupiter, and Saturn. These bodies are the only ones that are visible to the naked eye and could have been seen back in biblical times, thus they would have stood out as unique. One plus to this interpretation is that this does potentially help to tie the seven days of the week to the Zodiac or astrology (which the seven-day week or period does have roots in the Bible). In our common vernacular, each day of the week is named after a planet. 'Sun' day, 'mo(o)n' day, 'satur' (n) day are three more obvious examples, but the other days of the week have planetary roots in other languages.

This interpretation of 'seven' referring to the planets at the time could have been seen as having seven be the number of god, but in a different, pagan way. Many pagan cultures worshipped the stars and heavenly bodies. Since there were seven "special" heavenly bodies there would be seven primary gods. We do see pagans use the number seven quite a bit as well, such as Nebuchadnezzar heating the furnace seven times more than normal before throwing in the three dissenters in Daniel 3:19.

I see a few major problems with this. One is that nowadays we have more planets: Uranus, Neptune, arguably Pluto, and possibly more depending on your definition of planets and astrology. Therefore, the number of planets I would argue is not specific, or open to interpretation. Second and more importantly, I can't find any justification in scripture for this; though I'm very open to being proven wrong. The days of the week in Hebrew translate to "first day", "second day", etc. so the days of the week are out. Jews were not polytheistic so the whole planets being gods is out – God even specifically states not to worship them. Third, this makes birth signs many of orders of magnitude more complicated. The theory of seven I put forth above simplifies the Zodiac, the planets make it orders of magnitude more complex. While that doesn't necessarily make it wrong, it goes against what you would intuitively expect when dealing with scientific matters. It would also make it that much harder for the common person to detect, and for us to validate as well. God tends to try to keep things simple for us in scripture.

****

Overall, the symbology ties to the number seven wasn't as exact as the Zodiac tie to the number twelve, but it was definitely there in many ways, and it did fit the major instances of the number seven in one way or another. Moreover, the four elements and three modalities appeared to be very real, and in many ways explained more than the twelve signs by themselves. If they're real, and if the number twelve was meant to represent the Zodiac, there's a high probability that the four elements and three modalities were also in scripture, and together they did fit into the number seven as the best summary of the two combined.

This interpretation also helps to tie up the big loose end as to "why are there twelve Zodiac signs and not thirteen or something mathematically easier to subdivide the sky such as eight or sixteen?" Dividing the sky into eight or sixteen after all would be easier to do as you would just keep dividing the space by two. The answer to "why twelve," is because it's derived from seven (and seven being derived from four and three). We can only speculate the reason as to why there are four and three, but the answer likely lies in the complex engineering problem of the mind, of which I think only God could answer.

16

Gravity

Up to this point, all of what you read in chapters nine to fourteen was more or less the conclusion(s) that I had drawn from my own research. As I fit the pieces together more and more, the gravity of it all slowly started to hit me. It all made too much sense with my hypothesis to be coincidence. I was 95%+ sure the Zodiac signs were real. My own personal sample of people I studied had a near perfect success rate, which statistically is beyond significant compared to a control group. I knew that God was real from my own personal encounters with Him. Others might not, and I understand where they were coming from, but I knew better. It's clear from scripture and even just basic philosophical argument (assuming God exists) that God created all things, or at least all things that are of any importance to us. Therefore, if the Zodiac signs were real, and I was very confident they were, God created them.

If God created it, and with the signs being a huge deal themselves if real, you would almost expect it to be in scripture, and it was. It fit better than any interpretations I had ever heard. The symbol twelve was a near perfect fit. The four living creatures fit better than any other interpretation I'd heard of. Not only did it explain the four faces, but also arguably the wings, wheels, and eyes. Every other explanation I'd heard of only fit the faces, and usually not in a satisfactory way at least in my way of thinking. The symbolic fit to seven was also there, though not as strong as the other ones.

Like I mentioned earlier, oftentimes symbols such as this were tied to future events, though that's not necessarily the case. The heart of biblical symbols, was that they needed to point to something tangible. The snake on a stick raised by Moses – it was something tangible that pointed to a real thing (Jesus on the cross). That's God's pattern for doing such things – tying real, tangible meaning to symbols and events. The point of doing things that way, is that people need to see tangible evidence of God to believe in Him and the person He sent (Messiah). If those symbols that God uses are not tangible, then they have near zero value in accomplishing His purpose in reaching the lost, doubtful, or questioning. Even if the Zodiac was completely false and I was self-deceived in all of my research, this point would hold true from a Christian perspective. The symbols twelve and seven in scripture most likely represent something tangible that could be used as a sign to a non-believer. The fact that the Zodiac is tangible on some level meant that it also fit this pattern that God used in scripture.

Because it was in scripture, it was not only just an argument that God exists. That's all I had been after in the first place: anything supernatural that could be used to make an argument that God existed. The logic would probably have room for error somewhere, but to the nonbeliever/atheist it would help to break down the barrier. I could accomplish that goal solely based on the Zodiac itself being real. The Zodiac itself being real is evidence that God exists. Since it was in scripture though, it went beyond that. The bulk of the evidence we get is in the book of Revelation, even though most of it is present in the Old Testament as well. The tree of life however, as well as the direct phrase "seven spirits of God", which are invaluable in the argument, are not present in the Old Testament. Since the book of Revelation was written by a New Testament believer, this was not only an argument that God exists, it was an argument for who God is. Because it proves who God is, it validates the Gospel message that Jesus delivered 2,000 years ago, that "God so loved the world, that he gave his only Son, that whoever believes in Him should not perish but have eternal life."

You could get this argument from just looking at the Old Testament scriptures as well, in the same symbology that helped me make the connection in the first place. The three patriarchs of the Jews: Abraham, Isaac, and Jacob, were symbolic of the Trinity. It's through this "lineage of God" represented by the Trinity, that we see the Zodiac (represented by twelve tribes) represents us being made in the image of God (Trinity), and that the number twelve represents "all people." If the Zodiac is true, then it means that the symbology of the three patriarchs is likely true. Since there are three patriarchs and not just one, it points to the Trinity being true. In accepting this tie to the three Patriarch's you're also accepting that the Messiah is likely represented by Isaac, who was set up to be sacrificed by his father Abraham. Then you have this symbology of Abraham and Isaac heavily hinting at God the Father sacrificing His Son, Jesus, the Messiah. Thus, you get Jesus as the Messiah from the supporting symbology for the Zodiac.

****

The result is that the evidence for God, even God's own handpicked evidence for Himself that He set in scripture, exists inside of every living person on the planet. It doesn't lie in some buried artifact or fossil that could be argued as not important, or hidden. It's not hidden in biology that requires a trained biologist to decipher. It's not hidden in the cosmos or physics that requires the masses to trust what the experts are saying. We live it all the time. It's who we are. The evidence is spiritual or of the mind.

Unlike miracles, which are typically one-off events that are often difficult to validate, this is ever-present inside of all people. Even for validated miracles, people have a hard time trusting the source of the news. Skeptics will use all kinds of arguments, some better and more justified than others, to argue against that sort of evidence. Some miracles were subjective, as in my own experience. This argument was not elusive like those were, it's inescapable! The evidence of God has to do with how we operate at a fundamental level. Even while arguing against it, you'd probably be using some aspect of your Zodiac sign while doing so! You would more than likely be proving the point as you try to disprove it.

One of the biggest complaints of critics, nonbelievers, atheists, or agnostics, is that there isn't any evidence of God. They claim biology and all of physics can be explained without God, so why include God? Probably the biggest dent in this philosophy is the fine tuning of the universe argument, but there's still ways to get around that. When asked what would possibly make them believe, they often point to needing some kind of evidence.

For example, atheist chemist Peter Atkins has been asked what evidence might persuade him that God exists, and he mentions perhaps if there was some equation in the Bible, it might persuade him. (Hugh Ross, 2018). Some have said a supernatural sign or something, but then go on to say that even that probably wouldn't convince them as they think it's more likely that they're being deceived or gone mad. Well, as it turns out, there likely is an equation in the Bible that people ages ago probably didn't completely comprehend. $X*Y = 12$. $X+Y = 7$. $X=4$. The Bible even gives clues as to what X, Y, twelve, seven, and four represent. The equation isn't one of physics though like one might prefer, it's one of spirit. The Zodiac, quite frankly, is probably the best evidence we're going to get in a traditional sense.

The evidence also leaves no room for an atheistic explanation, at least one that is compatible with "molecules to man scale" Darwinian evolution. One of the major beliefs of the day is that we are purely the product of the DNA of our parents, which has downstream effects on one's belief system. This leads to ideas such as "we're not set apart from animals," "we're not special or made in the image of God," "there is no mind-body duality," and therefore "there is no life after death." The evidence from the Zodiac suggests that there is a part of us that doesn't come from our parents. It decouples at least part of our mind from our DNA, and ties it to God. In doing so, it is suggestive that there is a mind-body duality, which gives rise to the possibility of life after death. This is a major thing that people need to realize in today's world, to understand our true place as spiritual beings – defined by our spirit, not necessarily just our DNA.

I get it though, Zodiac signs and astrology are just superstitions, old wives' tales, made up, etc.. It's laughable to even consider it. I get it, and I agree. That is exactly the point though. If it wasn't absurd inside a modern day naturalistic worldview, then it wouldn't necessarily be evidence of God would it? If there was any way to tie it to naturalism, people would and then it would be absorbed into naturalism, much like how biology (which was traditionally a powerful argument for a designer) has been explained by evolution in recent times. At the same time, if you claim to be sincerely interested in the question of God's existence and identity, and you don't consider the evidence that God is presenting to you through scripture because it's "laughable," then can you really say that you're sincerely interested in the question? If it was just myself making this claim of Zodiac signs being evidence of God, I understand that someone more established in science could laugh me out of the room and dismiss it then and there, as I would probably do the same thing. If this argument is coming from a supposedly higher authority though (God speaking through men in compiled writings we call the Bible), can you really claim that you have enough knowledge and intellectual superiority to dismiss it without consideration?

Since this was so repeatable and widespread, it's possible for this to be scientifically validated. I had done some searching for scientific studies of astrology, and most of them came up inconclusive or with no significant correlation. At the same time though, most of the studies I was able to find were testing the wrong hypotheses. The most likely hypothesis, like I mentioned earlier, is that this has to do with how we're wired to think. It's part of our spiritual or mental programming. It's not necessarily testing to see what the results are of a person's thoughts, but how they arrive to those results, or how they tend to behave or process things.

Doing something like this would be much harder to test, which is probably why to my knowledge it has never been done before. You would probably have to get a little creative. Anyone who knows about the Zodiac or the purpose of the test would be inherently biased. It's not enough to throw out the test results completely, but would make it harder to be confident of them. Testing children would probably be the most promising. They're arguably less biased, and probably would exhibit the natural tendencies of the Zodiac signs more since their mental processing abilities would be more "pure.". As we grow older we tend to grow wiser as well, and I would say probably incorporate the wisdom we learn from others and said others' signs into our ways of thinking. For that reason older people would be less preferred than younger ones. I myself also don't completely understand exactly what the Zodiac signs are, but the best test would likely incorporate the four elements and three modalities. I'd like to say I have a better grasp on "water" and "fixed" since that's my own sign, but you also need a good working definition of all of those things as well.

Another wonderful thing about all of this, is that ~29% of the United States population already believes in astrology to some extent (Gecewicz, 2018). This is true both inside and outside of the church. The twelve sun signs are the most prevalent things in astrology, so most of those people likely believe in sun signs for one reason or another. Basically, the major leg work is mostly done for a large percentage of the population who already accept the basic evidence. What if the ante was upped though, and that this evidence and argument could finally put to rest the ultimate question of importance, "does God exist?" and if so, "who or what is God?". I'd bet a lot more people would be interested.

****

Most Christians have always wanted to know when Jesus would come back. It's always been the question of the century. I was typically more interested in what would actually happen that would cause that to happen. Jesus gives several signs of what's going to happen before He comes back in Matthew 24. He says many things will happen, and that many false signs will happen as well. For that reason it gets a little confusing. "This is going to happen, but when you see things like that happening it may also not be it as well." That's the kind of vibe that I get sometimes anyways. The one thing that most people agree on though is Matthew 24:14

> "And this gospel of the kingdom will be proclaimed throughout the whole world as a testimony to all nations, and then the end will come"

The gospel must be preached for all to hear. Once you understand God's heart, you understand why this must happen. God wants all people to be saved, and He's very patient in doing so. Only when everyone should know better, and then choose Him or otherwise, would it then be acceptable to throw in the towel and intervene. Once everyone's choice was made, there would not be much point in delaying it further.

16: Gravity

    I always took this as somehow everyone is going to know who God is. The Bible says "every knee shall bow", on heaven, on earth, and under the earth. Everyone will know better, or at least should know better. The church for the most part was doing a good job of spreading the gospel. At the same time though, many people were falling away in droves as well. Europe used to be Christianity capital of the world, and now it is very devoid of religion in many aspects. Short of God doing insane miracles all over the place, which I do believe could happen, even likely to happen, I had a hard time seeing how the gospel would spread and penetrate so many of the barriers set in place in the world. Progress was being made. It was just slow, often localized, and seemed to be capped at a certain point. Yet the gospel must be spread to all before the end. So how would that ultimately happen?

    This argument had the potential to do just that in large droves of people. Like I said, the truth lies inside of each person. Some person on television or the internet might be trying to sell you lies or this religion or that religion, or that they've witnessed this or that miracle. They can easily deceive you if you're not careful. For this argument though, the evidence is inside of you. You would have to deceive yourself. People argued that Jesus was demon-possessed to discredit Him. Look inside yourself, does the Zodiac fit who you are? Surely you're not demon-possessed, are you? If so, that's just another argument that demons exist, and therefore God likely exists. Once you see the truth in the Zodiac, it's very difficult to argue around it. Like I said before, the evidence is inescapable. People could come to see the truth in the Zodiac for themselves, and then let the logical argument laid forth take it from there. They would have to really. I wouldn't buy into something that didn't work for me, like I almost did in my first peering into the Zodiac. At that point, the argument and hypothesis I laid out would take effect, and the reality of God becomes undeniable. This had real potential to bring the world to Jesus.

    The only downside to all of this was that it was considered "taboo." Not just a little taboo, a lot. This was true both inside and outside of the church. While that's often considered a bad thing, in this case it's absolutely necessary. Being taboo is exactly what makes it stand out. It's essential for the logic of the argument to work. The argument works because the Zodiac exists supernaturally. If it didn't, then people would make attempts to tie it to materialism or the natural world, perhaps with some success. Indeed, people have already done things like that, trying to tie it to planets, as if the planets as physical bodies had influence on a lump of flesh on earth (*without a supernatural basis). Being supernatural, whether for better or worse, is exactly what makes it both taboo and a strong argument for the existence of God.

17

Darkness

Like I said, the Zodiac was taboo. That was its major downfall. It was taboo inside and outside of the church. It was taboo outside of the church because it was in many ways non-materialistic. It also shouldn't work by any conventionally rational perspective. It's typically labeled as nonsense by the mainstream. I get it. I had that perspective too for most of my life up to this point. The problem is it did work. It worked very well once you know what to look for.

It was also taboo, or even shunned in general inside of the church. At best, it was labeled nonsense like most of the rest of society labeled it. It typically was grouped with new age beliefs, which at worst are seen as demonic, and in many ways rightfully so. There are many Christians whose testimony is God brought them out of that belief system of astrology. I didn't doubt it. Every good lie always has a little bit of truth to it, and people were seeing the truth in the Zodiac and it attracted them. They get too deep in it and then follow all kinds of other new age beliefs that lead them astray. Then when they turn to God, they realize that there are things in it that are leading them astray, and that it all needs to go.

I'm sure that Satan has used this to further his purposes. Much like many "personality profile systems", there is potential for every one of these to be used for good or for evil. What happens is now people get labeled this way or that way. Then you treat people worse or better because of it. When people date others, they'd look for this sign or that sign to complement their own, or write off people completely if they fell under a certain Zodiac sign. You might avoid someone because of their sign. You also might unfairly favor someone because they were this way or that way.

Another downside is it can lead to justification of excuses for people. This includes both in oneself and also for others. "I'm just the way I am. God made me that way. Therefore, I don't need to change. I'm fine the way I am." Or it could lead to other slippery slopes. "God understands my weakness, He'll forgive me." This isn't necessarily false, but it can lead to taking God's grace for granted, and becoming complacent with spiritual growth. This very thing is warned about in scripture in several places. 1 John 3:6 probably says it in the most damning way

> *"No one who abides in him keeps on sinning; no one who keeps on sinning has either seen him or known him."*

Also, Hebrews 10:26-27 will put the fear of God into you.

"For if we go on sinning deliberately after receiving the knowledge of the truth, there no longer remains a sacrifice for sins, but a fearful expectation of judgement, and a fury of fire that will consume the adversaries."

This is a very complex subject, and the answer lies somewhere in the middle of two extremes, but such "personality systems" like the Zodiac can start to justify negative behaviors and aid in complacency. At the end of the day though, the command from Jesus in Matthew 5:48 leaves little room for arguing about what we are called to be:

"You therefore must be perfect, as your heavenly Father is perfect."

The issue with labeling the Zodiac as demonic from a theological perspective though, is that it falls outside of Satan's realm of what he can do. He can create false divinations using horoscopes, and use that to manipulate people. Or he can just let humans do it themselves and manipulate circumstances to bring them about in some fashion. What I found to be true though, and I'd say what most people find to be true at first, is that their Zodiac sign describes who they are on some level. I'd say personally that it described how I was predispositioned to think or behave. That falls more within the realm of creation. It's completely outside of Satan's territory; it falls within the realm of the creator.

****

I'm very aware of the potential for harm in buying into the Zodiac and incorporating it into your belief system. I unknowingly fell into this myself for a time. In life I was all about maximizing your strengths and minimizing your weaknesses. For example, I did well enough in more social sciences such as communication, but it was also one of my weaker points. So in college I made it a point to take more English/writing/communication classes as electives, to minimize my perceived weakness. I knew my strengths were in math/science, so I took the harder classes in those to build those skills up more, and went for a minor in math. Likewise, if I was a Scorpio, I figured maybe there's a way to better myself from knowing this knowledge. I figured I should focus on some of the strengths of Scorpio and minimize the weaknesses, or in some cases ignore it.

For example, Scorpio tends to struggle with forgiveness. In my case, I was able to foresee much of the results of people's actions, even my own, to where I saw the damage coming. "Can't you see this is what's going to happen if you do this?? So why did you do it??" That was my thought process most of the time. I would usually go silent before lashing out for that reason - I tended to have good foreknowledge of the effects of my words/actions. I was trying to get the best outcome, and using my mouth was probably less helpful than remaining silent. Or I just would overthink things and miss the opportunity to say something in the process. So if I struggled with forgiveness, and it was part of how I was wired, maybe God will understand and let it slide.

This sort of thinking though, is a lie straight from hell. Jesus clearly states in Matthew 6:14-15:

"For if you forgive others their trespasses, your heavenly Father will also forgive you, but if you do not forgive others their trespasses, neither will your Father forgive your trespasses."

17: Darkness

If God doesn't forgive our trespasses, then technically we're not allowed into heaven, thus our salvation is in question. In order for God to forgive us, we need to forgive others. Forgiveness is therefore huge, and tied to our salvation.

A lot of descriptions of Scorpio made them seem powerful, independent, self-sufficient possibly. Looking back it's kind of funny now to ascribe "powerful" to any sign; it doesn't seem based in reality, but more just perception. I played up some of these aspects though – I figured knowing who I was would help me maximize my potential.

Boy was I wrong. I realized this in a sobering way in a conversation with my mom. She had called me, and I can't remember what I said but it made her cry over the phone. I know what I said stemmed from this warped mindset I got from thinking about myself as a Scorpio too much. She was my spiritual rock at the time, and I had shared all of my research with her. She was just looking for some support, disguised as trying to offer help to me, and I blew her off and pushed her away. I instantly felt terrible. She was just trying to help, as this was all kind of overwhelming to her as well.

It was at this time that I realized this way of thinking, and knowledge of the Zodiac signs, was changing who I was. I realized that I made better decisions before I knew all of this. My mind worked just fine the way it was designed, but this new level of self-awareness was clouding my judgement. It was at this point that I realized I needed to come down a little and just kind of "forget about it", at least when it came to my own personal life and interacting with people. I still did not doubt the authenticity of it. Implications of the truth do not discredit the truth itself. It worked very well, but I tried my best to just ignore it when dealing with myself and others.

Ultimately, I don't believe the Zodiac will likely make you a better person. The best benefits I can see is to realize how everyone is wired and then love them anyways, and learn to love the diversity that God has created. Perhaps you will learn to see the value instilled in others. Then for yourself, just realize that there's other ways of thinking and doing things, and don't let yourself get stuck in a rut of thinking you're right for this reason or that. Jesus tells us to come to Him and through spending time with Him and learning from Him, we will grow to be like Him, as it states in 2 Corinthians 3:8

> *"And we all, with unveiled face, beholding the glory of the Lord, are being transformed into the same image from one degree of glory to another."*

This was the most effective way that I've become a better person: through spending time with God and letting His presence and love fill your heart until all negative things leave. That and trying to walk in humility.

As for the Zodiac though, I think there's a great potential for spiritual harm when one takes it on as part of their identity, which can manifest itself in several different ways. It's probably better for a lot of people that they don't get caught up in it at all. At the same time though like I have mentioned several times before, this has great potential to show people, even all people, not just that God exists, but who God is. For that reason alone, the risk is worth the reward. The best case scenario I could imagine is that people could use this to see that there is a God, then seek after Him and find Him, then just forget about or not focus on the Zodiac for most practical purposes and needs.

18

Now What?

    I said earlier I had found what I was looking for. There was no guarantee that I would find anything in my quest for the supernatural. If I did find something I expected it to be a little mediocre. Instead what I found was a gold mine. It wasn't just my argument, it was God's argument. It's been there the whole time. Just the gravity of it all hit a lot harder. This was much bigger than myself or my simpleminded quest. Instead of trying to tell everyone about this, I got a much bigger sense of respect, or even duty.

    I was clearly not the first person to see many of the symbol-connections in the Bible. I had used online sources in my search for all of this (though it's been so many years, I couldn't tell which ones I used even if I found them). Those people must have seen part of it as well. The tree of life, the four living creatures, I do remember seeing people put those things together. Some of the other connections like "seven" and then twelve meaning "all people" I didn't find anywhere. Most of the sources that I read that showed the connections between the Zodiac signs and the Bible seemed to be more interested primarily in using the Bible, which is typically more popular, to validate their hobby of astrology. God is not interested in that though. Like I said previously, there's a lot of potential for harm in that. I don't believe God's primary interest is whether or not you believe in the Zodiac. The whole theme, and purpose of scripture, is to point the way to God. God's heart is for people to find Him, come to Him, get to know Him, and follow Him. What is more important here, and the reason that it's in scripture to begin with, is the converse of that: the opposite. The Zodiac is a means to point the way to God. If others that made some of these connections realized this, it didn't appear that they were actively pursuing that end. Otherwise I think this argument would have made bigger headlines and many people would have heard about it. After all, this is in many ways the proof and evidence of God.

****

    The big question though, is what do I do now? By the time I put it all together, it had been about a year since I had heard the call to ministry. Now I had found this. It just seemed like too much of a coincidence to be "coincidence." Was this what God was calling me to do? That was the most logical thing I could think of. I imagined this was how God led people. Things just happen all of a sudden that lead people in a certain direction. I decided that seemed to be what God was leading me to do. Rather than tell a bunch of nonbelievers though, I felt like this needed to start with the church. If people inside the church didn't believe it, why would outsiders who have limited knowledge of scriptures believe it? The potential was still there, but diminished. If this was just some pet theory by someone, the impact wouldn't be very much. If a significant number of people got behind it though, it could spread a lot more, and have better odds of reaching nonbelievers—the people that really need to hear it. Like all things, I felt like this was meant first for the Church, and then for outsiders.

What I did was write a persuasive essay about it and sent it out to a few different outlets. It was mostly big names, televangelists, but also a few somewhat local people as well. The ones I sent to the bigger outlets probably ended up in the trash, but in any case I didn't hear anything back (surprise, surprise). I did hear back from a few local people. It was nothing that I hoped; no one bought into it. I don't blame them - like I said it was taboo, shunned. I did get some good critiques though which I used to help refine the argument more.

The calling just wasn't working out the way I thought. It seemed like I was being called to spread this particular message, but it wasn't going anywhere. I had stopped doing homework in one of my classes because I figured I would be dropping out of college to pursue this. I never not did my homework. My mom luckily was adamant that I need to get my degree. I didn't get it at the time, but I still saw the wisdom in it. She helped me get back on track for the time being. Luckily, I had always been a good test taker, and exams account for about 85% of your grade, so somehow with probably 50% of the homework done I still came out with an A. I still don't quite understand how that math worked out, I was figuring on a B+.

After several failed attempts and it all going nowhere, I just gave up for the time being. I felt like God was calling me to this, but at the same time He never really told me to pursue it. It was just my reading into my circumstances that led me to come to that conclusion.

There was always the possibility that maybe I'm just seeing things that aren't there, both in real life (the Zodiac) and in the Bible. It didn't seem likely. Roughly 29% of Americans had also fell for it (Gecewicz, 2018)– that's quite a few people. I was very careful in my studying as well, inventing something that wasn't' there would have been terrible. The scripture references were arguably easier to see than the Zodiac, everything fit fairly well there.

At the same time though, I prayed very much about the whole truth of the Zodiac. Proverbs 3:5 says:

"Trust in the Lord with all your heart, and do not lean on your own understanding."

It was absolutely crucial that it wasn't just me, that it was from God as well. The argument made a lot of sense, but God would ultimately have the final say on truth. Whenever I prayed and asked God if it was real, His Spirit seemed to always confirm the truth of it, though I did often question if I was hearing correctly. If it's true, then shouldn't I be pursuing this?

****

Still yet, I could not let it go. It all made way too much sense. Something that I picked up on sooner than probably most people was to not take arguments or science at face value just because some established person(s) said so. I didn't accept arguments from authority of this person or that person, etc. I was of the caliber of intellect of people that come up with

18: Now What?

this or that argument, so things had to make sense from basic principles for me to accept things. This was true of my study of the Bible as well. I know God's ultimate reason isn't "because I said so". He has reasons for why He tells us this or that, and I'd try my best to find out why. I actually gained a lot of insights in studying scripture this way. I would argue it's this same deep questioning of scripture and trying to make sense of it all that led Martin Luther to rediscover the gospel of grace in scripture, leading to the protestant revolution. He was trying to reconcile many different scriptures that seemingly contradicted each other when they all played out to their ultimate end, and realized the only way it all made sense was if we were saved because of God's own goodness, and not of our own efforts.

The only way to talk me off of it was to succinctly refute the argument, or offer a better alternative for the numbers and symbols we see in scripture. Some people did help point out a few fallacies or gaps in some of my reasoning, and I did agree with some of their assessment (such "gaps" are not included in the book obviously, they didn't make the cut, though probably the biggest one had to do with matching specific stones on the 12 foundations of the new Jerusalem to the birthstones in the Zodiac). The critique I got was not enough to discredit the argument as a whole though. Other than that probably only God Himself could have talked me out of it.

Anyways, for the time being, with all of that considered, I decided to just push it to the side. It wasn't going anywhere, and I didn't know how to make it go anywhere with my failings. Then there was the negative aspects of the Zodiac. I thought perhaps someday God will tell me to do something with it, but for now the only logical thing left to do seemed to be to drop it.

19

Life Goes On

College came to an end, and thus it came time for me to figure out what to do with my life. I had heard the call to ministry years before and made a promise to God more or less. I was afraid that if I didn't do it now, I would just push it aside and never get involved in it, at least in the way that I thought God would want me to. It made me very uneasy. I did do a few interviews for engineering positions, though nothing seemed to work out. To be fair though, I didn't try super hard – I only actively pursued that for about a month or so.

My dad did really need help with some construction projects he had. He was trying to get out of his self-employed business and build up for retirement, and had bought a bunch of nearly-junk houses very cheap to fix up. He planned to rent them out for steady retirement income. He also did a few odd jobs here and there. He had a good reputation as a carpenter so didn't have trouble finding work if he needed to. For the meantime helping him seemed like a good plan. My dad of course wanted me to get a real job in engineering since I went to school for it, but at the same time he wanted the help, so he was perfectly fine with it. He didn't have the money to pay me though, so I got paid in "I owe you's". I didn't need much money though. I lived in their house with all meals paid for, rent free. I got paid a little here and there for things that popped up. I quit drinking and smoking pot right after college, which would have probably been my biggest expense otherwise, so money wasn't really needed all that bad.

****

Shortly after graduation, while trying to figure out the whole ministry thing, my older sister Sheryl and I drove to a Benny Hinn conference a few hours away. I went looking for an answer, hoping God would do or show me something. At some point during the service, we were all instructed to hold hands before we prayed "The Lord's Prayer." Not holding hands wasn't an option, Benny said it could stop the anointing, and wouldn't proceed until we all did as told. I didn't have a problem with that and did it anyways, but it was a good thing to know. While we were holding hands though, with God's presence pretty thick, I prayed silently that God would just bless the people's who's hands I was holding and transfer what God had given me to them. What I meant when I prayed that was the "tingling" sensation or the "fire" He had given me all those years ago and felt all the time. It had been such a blessing to me and I wanted to share that with others.

I prayed for a few minutes, waited, and then just began to praise God silently. I didn't speak a word or sound. It didn't seem to be happening, but I was just like "God, even if you don't do it, you're still good." I didn't let it get to me. Less than five minutes after that point the woman next to me, a complete stranger probably my parents' age, while still holding hands, took my hand and put it to her face. For a little context for those who haven't been to things like this, that's not something you typically do even in a setting like that. At that point I knew that God had answered my prayer – I had never had a prayer answered that quickly as far as I could tell. She continued to hold my hand and pray for the rest of the service, long after everyone had already stopped holding hands.

At the end of the service, she finally spoke to me, and confirmed everything that I had prayed about. She felt the tingling, and said it was coming from me. She then went on to say something like "God's going to use you to preach His word," or something along those lines. My jaw dropped quite a bit. I had went looking for an answer, and that seemed to be it. She saw my face change and then kind of reneged on them or said something like "or maybe it could just be stuff like this, etc." I don't think that's what she meant though, or at least that's probably what God meant for me to hear: the first thing she had said. The takeaway from it was I felt a renewed call to ministry, I guess in a more conventional means.

This story holds a lot more significance to me besides just the call to ministry. I mentioned before that sometimes I questioned if the "tingling" sensation was really from God, or perhaps I just have some medical condition. This kind of put the latter explanation to rest. The whole scenario could in a way be treated like a blind experiment, as I didn't say or do anything out of the ordinary and the person was a perfect stranger. The woman didn't know that I was praying for that to happen, or for anything to happen for that matter. She didn't know that I had that gifting either. That throws out any argument for coercion or confirmation bias, unlike other times when it got transferred to people and they knew about it. It proved that it was outside of myself; that was the only logical explanation. After this I never questioned it again.

Another instance, though I can't remember when, happened while I was praying with my mother who could interpret tongues. For those unfamiliar, that basically means she can prophesy, or God can speak through her in a more literal way. While praying, she told me that this specific word was for me. It sounded like "Kay-hua-nay" from what I remember. It was a word in tongue, so neither one of us knew what it meant. She repeated it several times, "Kay-hua-nay".

If God wanted that word to mean something to me, it made sense that he would provide a way to translate it. For that reason, my first assumption was that it was a Hebrew word. I had done some very minor studying in Hebrew prior to that, and what I knew from that was that only consonants are written for the most part, and vowels are left out. That made it a lot easier. My best guess was that it was "K-H-N". H can tend to be silent when spoken, but there were too many vowel sounds in the middle, so I figured there was an H there. I found the best Hebrew literal translation to be "Khaf"-"He"-"Nun". I looked that up, and was a little surprised to see it actually was a word. Not only that, the best interpretation I could find for that word was "priest" or "to serve as priest." The English translation for priest is typically "Kohen." I guess that was about as good as it could get for a sign. After that I quit doubting if my mom was really hearing from God.

****

19: Life Goes On

Shortly after graduating, I started attending church after not going to church hardly at all during college. The local Assemblies of God was where my mom's family went, so I started going there. I figured if I was going to go into ministry I needed to get plugged in. It was nice getting back to church. Taking time out each week to be with God and fellow believers was rewarding.

After talking with my pastor, I started taking online classes for ministry. If I was supposed to go into ministry, schooling just seemed to be the next logical step. The bookwork was easy. I've never struggled with things like that. Each lesson required a "ministry activity" though. That was much harder for me. I was bad at sharing my faith. I didn't know how you would weave it into a conversation without sounding pushy. If no one asked about it first, then trying to bring it up just seemed weird, like you have an agenda. I suppose that's not too far from the truth, but I didn't know how to do stuff like that. Most people didn't want to talk about it, so I typically didn't unless asked. This was to the point that many of my friends in college probably couldn't tell if I believed in God or not. It wasn't something that I typically publicized. One of my (atheist) roommates even offhand asked me if I believed in God. I guess he couldn't figure it out.

I did get through one ministry activity. I went to hang out with my friends at one of the bars we frequented. I had quit drinking, and they knew why, so this time was a lot different than usual, at least for me. They had a lot of questions for me, ranging from questions about God or religion, to even why I was doing what I was doing. To my surprise, most of the questions were more on what I would call "moral" grounds, or deeper theological questions. I was expecting more existential questions, such as the intelligent design vs. evolution debate, which I was probably better rehearsed in. What I took from that, was that most people's hang-ups about God are probably more on moral grounds. Everyone understands how intelligent design could explain life on earth, whether they believe in it or not. After all, life does heavily look like it was designed from just first glance. I tried to answer a lot of their questions as best as I could during that time, though I could have done better. They kept me so busy that I didn't have time to share my testimony beyond a few short sentences.

After that, I went on to my next class, but the required ministry activities just kind of started to fall behind. There were other things I could do for ministry activities, like teach a class, but I also didn't want to take the easy way out. At least that's how it seemed to me at the time. If I couldn't share my faith effectively I felt like I had no business jumping forward in classes, so I slowly just stopped doing the classes altogether. The ministry path in general was just kind of falling to the wayside, like I had feared. I was still working for my dad for "I owe you's"; he still needed the help. I couldn't help but think, "what am I doing with my life?" I was supposed to be pursuing ministry, but I wasn't. I wasn't making any money. I wasn't applying for "real" jobs.

****

Two or three years later after college, my mom was diagnosed with stage 4 kidney cancer. After some mild research, it appeared that this particular type of cancer had the second worse survival rate after pancreatic cancer. We were all naturally sad or concerned.

One of her kidneys had to be removed because of a large mass on it, and when they removed it, it was found that the cancer cells were not kidney cells, but something resembling the GI tract, though they couldn't pin which organ exactly. That was a little bit better news. At least it wasn't kidney cancer. Being Pentecostal, we believed in God for healing naturally, and prayed for it a lot. She started on chemo immediately of course and all that.

Eventually, my dad ran out of work, so I did start looking for a "real job", and found one working as an engineering technologist. During college, I had asked God where my first real job would be, thinking it would help me to narrow down my job search. I had a map open of the U.S. and asked God to point to me where it would be. He took me to what I thought was probably close to Greensburg, IN, which was not far from home. I was in school for nuclear engineering, and I knew very well there was nothing in that area related to that degree, the closest ones were probably Illinois, Pennsylvania, or the Carolinas. I figured I had just heard wrong, but kept it in mind. As it turned out though, my first job was in Greensburg, IN just like God had told me years ago. It had nothing to do with nuclear engineering naturally, but there I was. I didn't even really apply for any jobs there either; I just put my application on the job search websites and a headhunter had set me up with an interview.

About that same time my mom started to not feel so well. The second week of work I got up and got ready to leave. Usually my mom would still have strength to get up and do a little bit of chores in the morning, such as dishes. She instead just kind of took it easy. I went ahead and did the dishes, a little annoyed but she did need to rest I guess. My mom called me later that morning and went to doctor, saying she had the flu. She said they were going to try to admit her to a hospital room to monitor her, since her immune system was weakened from the chemotherapy. She was very peaceful and happy about it and just wanted to fill me in. Little did I know that would be the last time I ever spoke to her. An hour or so later my dad called me with panic in his voice. Mom had passed out in the bathtub, and was being rushed to the hospital. Several minutes later I got the call that they confirmed her death. Of course we were all heartbroken, but life goes on. I didn't blame God or anything.

All of those years staying at home, not doing anything, started to make sense now. I felt like I was wasting time, but if I hadn't stayed home and not worked, I'd probably be two states away chasing a dollar and using my degree. Instead, I got to spend the last days that my mom was on earth at home with her. I wouldn't have traded that for anything.

****

Staying at home had other advantages as well. I started dating a girl I met at church. A few years later we ended up getting married about a year after my mom passed away. We built a house, and started a family. We ended up with three kids. I was doing well at my job, and through many odd circumstances (I call it God) as well as performing very well, I got promoted as high as I wanted to go. By all conventional means I was happy and successful. I had finally arrived to everything I had hoped for in life.

There was just one thing wrong. I had promised my life to God, and in my mind I wasn't living up to it, at least in what I thought that meant. I thought about God all the time,

19: Life Goes On

and I thought about ministry all the time. Almost daily. I taught Sunday School at our church, but I just felt like God had called me to more. It just ate at me continually. I felt like I was successful in everyone's eyes except for the one person who mattered most, God.

Of course, along those lines, I thought about the Zodiac. It just seemed like God had called me to that. It seemed like it had to be. It was in scripture, therefore it was a part of God's plan as a whole. No one else seemed to get it though, or if they did, it wasn't advertised well enough. I certainly hadn't heard of it. At the same time, I was overly cautious about telling people about it. If I was wrong about it, I'd essentially be teaching witchcraft. The damage to God's Kingdom could be large. If God wanted me to do that, I needed to be absolutely sure of it- both in the truth of it, as well as His calling to it. It made too much sense, but there was that 5% chance I had gotten it all wrong somehow.

I got to the point where I told God if He wanted me to pursue teaching the Zodiac stuff, he would have to give me some external heavenly experience, or have someone not familiar with the situation tell me to do it (via prophecy). Preferably it would be someone I didn't know at all, that way I'd know they didn't accidently find out about it and try to feed me things. I'd be more suspicious that they were hearing from God if the person knew me.

I always imagined if I ever met God face to face, the Zodiac would probably be the first question I would ask Him about. I even had a dream about being told those things once. I thought about what such an instance might look like. Obviously, the person probably wouldn't know the subject, but they could say some generic things about it, and I would know what it meant if it was coming from God. In the dream, I was standing in the audience of some big church service, and like you'll sometimes see, the speaker on stage would call people out and prophesy over them. That person who was being prophesied over was me. I can't remember exactly what was said in the dream but it was stuff like, "that thing that you want to do for God that you hold close and don't tell anyone about", "that thing that you're not sure about", or "the mystery in scripture you know about". After that it seemingly started to get a little too specific. I thought at that point that maybe I was starting to influence the dream on some level and wishing things into existence, as one is often able to do in a typical dream. Like I said I couldn't remember what exactly was said in the dream, but it gave me a little bit of an idea of what could possibly happen.

20

2019

This thought pattern just continued on for several years. There was a lot not going the way I thought it should in my call to ministry. Eventually, I just stopped telling people that I had the call for the most part. It became embarrassing after so long. It all just kind of came to a point in 2019 where I just really needed to get some direction from God. During a church service, one of the ladies on the worship team had a "word of knowledge" for me on her way back to her seat. She said something along the lines of "God hears all of your prayers, and is answering them."

I decided then that I should pursue God more to get some answers. Some time after that I started doing another "Daniel fast". For those unfamiliar with that, it's basically a vegan diet but stricter – no unnatural ingredients. You try not to snack as well since you're fasting. There was also a men's conference coming up that our church was going to attend. I decided I wanted to go to that. I've found God usually tends to speak more during things like that, or He can anyways with so many people praying over these events and expecting God to move. Maybe that would help with my pursuit of getting more information from Him.

One night, while I was fasting and praying, God's presence came on me strongly. I decided to just ask God, hopefully once and for all, "do you want me to do anything with the Zodiac?" With His presence so strong, I would be more trusting of any answer I may have got. By this time, I had heard a few bigger named people say that God had told them certain secrets that they shared, and later found out that they weren't supposed to share them. I heard that God sometimes just wants to tell us things like you would want to tell your best friend, just because you're friends. Maybe that was it. I went looking for evidence, and maybe God just led me down that path because I was asking or looking. Maybe I wasn't supposed to do anything with it. It was potentially so big, that perhaps it wasn't meant for me to share, but for God to do.

I kept praying. "Is this real?"

Answer: "yes", or maybe "you know it is".

"Ok God, then what do you want me to do with it, if anything? If the answer is nothing, that's fine. If the answer is "wait", I can do that as well." The whole thing was just really messing me up though. I felt like I couldn't get past it. It was holding me back. It consumed my life and ate at me. I kept on praying, asking, and waiting. Eventually, what I heard from God, was "I'll take care of it when I come back." I took that as God would take care of it, and I didn't have to worry about it, so I let it go. I quit worrying about it. That took such a huge load off of me. It was so freeing. If that was the only thing I got from fasting, it would have been worth it.

Also during this time of fasting, I had gotten up early to feed and rock our second child who was an infant at the time. I asked God what He wanted me to do. God told me, "I'll tell you what to do in a song." Well that's not very helpful, I thought. How will I know which song it is? I prayed more, and what I got from God was that he gave me a clue to the what the song was. I did not find the clue super helpful at the time, and didn't know how it could possibly help me. To me it was a very generic clue. It seemed hopeless to me, but I went on and kept that in the back of my mind.

****

The night before the men's conference was the last night I would fast; the next day I broke it. As with many fasts, if you've ever done one, at some point you may begin to wonder if God will do anything. I was there at that point. While praying that night, God told me, "I will surely speak to you tomorrow." In all my years I don't think I'd ever heard God use the word "surely" when He spoke to me. So I went to the conference in anticipation of whatever God had for me.

The next day at the conference, God did speak to me. While worshipping, His presence was so thick that I was very sure of the words He spoke. What He told me, was:

"I'm coming back very soon. You will see it in this lifetime."

He repeated it again, maybe two or three times, more for clarity for myself. He also told me to tell everyone. I had heard people say that very thing, several times. Many of those people were very in-tune with God as well, many probably more than myself. Many of those people were dead now, so obviously they probably missed it. It went against my better judgement, but like I said, I was very sure I heard God correctly. Even today it doesn't feel real, but I don't let my judgement of things when I'm not as close to God cloud what I was confident in when I was very near to Him. I felt like God was wanting me to start telling people at the conference, but between having cold feet and just not finding a good opportunity, I didn't do it that night.

The next day at the conference, I continued to look for opportunities, but at the same time kept waiting. During the later service while worshipping, by judging how many songs had been played, I felt like worship may have been ending soon. A song was starting to come to an end. At this, I started to actively remember what God had told me about telling me what to do in a song. It was in the back of my mind the whole conference, but now it came to the front.

As a side note here, the more you walk with God and learn about Him, the more you begin to realize that not all thoughts are your own. Sometimes God, or other spiritual beings, even demons, inject thoughts into your mind. It's one of the ways God talks to people. It's hard to know for sure if it's your thought or if it came from somewhere else. Hearing evil things doesn't mean that you're demon possessed, but you need to know that a lot of those thoughts don't originate with you, and reject them.

Anyways, the thought came to the front of my mind. I was expecting worship to end any moment, maybe one more song. The next song was starting to come on. I cannot say what it was, but I remembered what God had told me about the song. The very first line of the song spoke to that clue God had given me and matched exactly what God had said.

Between that and actively remembering it (probably not me who began the thought, but God who interjected it into my head), I knew this was the song. At that point I was just hoping something in the song would hit home to confirm it and speak something that made sense to me. The first line didn't mean anything to me other than an identifier. The song went on.

Eventually something did hit me hard. God had shown me that I had a lot of apprehension. It was a big motivator in my life. God was telling me to stop letting this doubt cripple me. If God's truly sending, then you have all strength and all authority behind you to see it done, no matter what the end is. If you're truly saved and God's Spirit is living inside of you, then you have the most powerful being in existence working with you, granted that you are in line with His will.

More than just that. God said He would tell me what I need to *do* in a song. The more important thing was that God was saying that what I needed to "do" was to just "be.". Jesus calls us to "be perfect." There's a whole sermon in itself on this subject, but ultimately, what that means, is that most of the Christian walk is to simply just exist in a state of being like God. We are called to be made into the image of Jesus. Perfect in love, righteousness, justice, mercy, humility. This is largely accomplished by just spending time with God, and as you spend time with Him, you'll become like Him. Being in that state is then contagious, and people will see the fruit of your life, and it rubs off on them as well. They'll see the joy, peace, happiness, and love you exhibit, and it will brighten their life as well. As you then grow to be like God, God will naturally push you into doing this or that, and everything you do will flow from your relationship, and you being like God. Once you're in this state of being, you're always in God's will, even if things aren't going the way you think they should be. God was telling me that the Christian life is more about "being", not "doing." If you're doing the "being" right, then the "doing" should just naturally take care of itself.

This was the boost I needed. They played one more song then did a sermon. A few other people went up on stage during the service(s) throughout the previous sessions and shared a word of knowledge God had given them. I knew what I had to do. God was telling me to do it, therefore I had every right to do so. I went up at the end of service, full of confidence in God, and shared what God had told me: that He was coming back very soon, and that we would see it in this lifetime.

****

In the following months I shared what God had told me with several people. I felt like God was telling me to even "shout it from the mountains", which was fairly uncomfortable, basically making a scene in public places. I shared it with friends and strangers alike. Reactions varied from belief, to being intrigued, even to mean looks.

While sharing it in this season, I did come across a lot of things that personally helped to confirm the message God told me. For example, while sharing it with an acquaintance, to my surprise she said something like "yea I believe it, my uncle just had a dream or vision two weeks ago where God told him pretty much the same thing."

I had also started reading Howard Storm's book, "My Descent into Death" (Storm, 2005). In the book, Howard gives his testimony of having a near death experience (NDE), where he reportedly died an atheist, saw the other side, spoke with Jesus, and woke back up a Christian more or less. While on the other side he had the opportunity to ask Jesus lots of questions, and was shown the "new earth" spoken of in Revelation. He asked when that would come about, and Jesus and the angels told Him "In two hundred years". That was in 1985. I had not expected the topic to come up at all in the book, but there it was, and it is arguably in the ballpark of what God had told me, considering the new earth is later on in the end-times timeline.

Another instance, I was watching Sid Roth's show "It's Supernatural." I was a longtime fan of the show. I believe strongly in sharing our personal testimony of our walk with God. I believe it's a big primary means of building faith in others and bringing people to Jesus. God seems to think so too, as he states the same thing in Revelation 12:11
"And they overcame him by the blood of the Lamb, and by the word of their testimony; and they loved not their lives unto the death."
Sid seemed to think this was the best way to build a program as well, as he had guests on from all walks of life share their testimony on the show, not just the big mainstream televangelists. He tried to get them to focus on the supernatural things that God was doing in their lives. Again, this is something that I was extremely interested in as that's how God brought me into a relationship with Him, and also how I go deeper with Him as well. It was the best methodology of any televangelism program I'd ever seen, and for a long time I looked forward to watching the program every week. I still do like to check in every now and then.

Anyways, on this particular episode that I saw just a few weeks after God had told me all that at the conference, he had on a guest who said he wanted to specialize in raising the dead. David Hogan, (Hogan, 2019) had seen over 500 people raised from the dead under his ministry. Halfway through the episode, Sid asked him,

"You were telling me, that not all, but many people that have been dead and then come back, and they report what they've observed are saying the same thing. What is that same thing?"

"Jesus is sending messages to us that he's coming back soon," he replied. And then went on to share one such incident.

Those were all just nice little confirmations that God had placed in my path to help confirm to me that I had heard correctly. I had also planned on giving a testimony at our church about all of it in the following weeks. I felt God was telling me to do so as well. What I didn't expect was the short notice. Sunday morning a week or two later, I had woken up early to feed our second child, and I heard God tell me to share it that service. It happened to be Pentecost Sunday as well. I hadn't prepared at all, so I wrote it all down that morning. Luckily it was all forming in my mind already so I just had to put it on paper to keep me on track. It was my first time speaking in front of the congregation as well. It went surprisingly well considering that.

****

As time went on, the message felt less real. After all, people have been saying that for centuries, and here we are. Life keeps going on as normal. I stopped sharing it as liberally as I had initially. It started to feel weird, and I felt like I was not being effective with the bottom line of getting people ready for it. If people asked I shared it, or if I felt it was appropriate. I'm still convinced I heard correctly, despite not always feeling like it was "real" during whatever mood I was in at the moment.

21

Waiting

God had taken the Zodiac off of me as far as I could tell. I was very relieved to have it taken off. I quit being obsessed with it. I quit thinking about it. I kind of just forgot about it really. There was just one issue: now I had no idea what to do with ministry. I still promised my life to God, and just had to figure that out. I suppose ministry was probably more open-ended than what I had imagined. I took things one day at a time, and just tried to listen to God more. I do believe that's how God wants us to walk, just one day at a time. It was definitely more effective. I got more from God and heard more from Him.

Shortly after the conference, our associate pastor and men's ministry coordinator at church was offered a lead pastor position at a church in Illinois, and took it. He prayed about who to pass the men's ministry off to, and told me he felt like God was telling him to pass it to me. I figured this might be God leading me further, so I accepted. It was a good learning experience. It was very open-ended and kind of whatever you make of it.

One of the things I did do was just share devotionals or scripture verses a couple times a week, and keep the channels of communication open. I would share different things that God would lead me to. Quite frankly, if God wasn't leading, then I typically didn't have much to share. I always wanted to have the intention of rather than me finding good generic verses to share, to just let God pick what to share. I would rather God speak volumes to one person than something "eh" or "ok" to everyone. It worked out pretty well for the most part. Since my "normal" supernatural experience with God involved much mechanical control with my hands, I would just pray and let God move my hands to different verses on bible apps on my phone. I knew most of the subjects in the Bible, but I couldn't tell you where exactly they were at. I've always been bad at that type of memorization—I don't see the point. Most people remember the day they got saved or other big milestones. I do not. To me the important thing is the content, not how they're filed away. Through this gifting though I take it as a point of pride, so that I didn't know what verse or passage God was leading me to, and thus suffer from possible confirmation bias.

Sometimes I got gold, other times, I didn't know what God was doing, or if I was even hearing right. Other times I got sent to passages that were kind of downers that I didn't really want to share. If God was confirming it though through other means, then I would send it out anyways. I felt kind of lazy in doing this; it took a lot of work out of trying to find good devotional verses. At the same time though, Jesus said, "My yoke is easy, and my burden is light." Why does it necessarily need to be hard or require extra effort?

****

After my mom passed away, my older sister Sheryl started church hopping quite a bit, trying to find a place to call home. Five years or so later, still searching and trying, she went to a Vineyard church in Cincinnati. At the first service she attended, the speaker on stage had a word of knowledge and said,

"Someone has this thought right now, thinking "I don't belong" and God's saying you do belong here."

This really hit home with her after attending several different places. Needless to say, she started going there, and her spiritual walk with God really started to take off. I was very happy for her. It was nice to see the "sparkle" in her eyes again, and a new hunger and pursuit of God that she had been trying for a while with mixed results. It seemed like it was finally starting to stick. I myself was probably more in a spiritual slump. I was getting by and going through the routine, trying my best with mixed results. I wasn't sure what to do with the whole ministry thing that God had called me to. I wasn't seeing an open door anywhere, and wasn't sure how a door could possibly even open at this point.

The church she attended was heavily involved in prophetic ministry. I hadn't heard much about things like that. It wasn't super common in a formal church setting anyways. Periodically, they would do what they call "prophecy tents." What that basically was, was they would have 3-4 "prophetic listeners" on one side (many of whom are prophets), and then have 3-4 guests on the other side, and the prophets would just listen to God, and give words of knowledge or "prophecies" to the guests. This would go on for about 20 minutes.

My sister really liked the prophecy tents. She was getting personalized words from God and confirmation through that, and was getting a better ear for hearing God through some classes she was taking there. She had always had more dreams, and those "dreams from God" were starting to pick up as well. She had tried to get me to go to the prophecy tents a few times. I wasn't sure I could go with my schedule. I did pray about it, and I felt like God was telling me to not go at the moment.

****

During the spring of 2023, my sister told me about a prophecy conference that her church was planning at the end of May, right before Pentecost Sunday. She invited me again. I said I'd play it by ear. She must have heard from God because she went ahead and signed me up for everything ahead of time, including the prophecy tents, and paid for my ticket. I couldn't say no. After all, it was her forcing me out of my bed all those years ago that caused me to encounter God in the first place, and changed my life. After the conference, she explained to me that God told her I'd attend the conference, so she went ahead and bought my ticket.

About this same time, my sister shared a dream she had about me. She was starting to get a lot more into dreams like I had mentioned. Like many dreams, it was a little weird. She said she saw me holding a newborn baby that was "fresh" with all the slimy afterbirth, and that she knew it was mine. Then I had handed the baby over to her shortly after birth while I got cleaned up from the mess. She explained to me that babies symbolize something new, like maybe a new ministry, or it could be something else. I just listened and put it in the back of my head. I had no idea what could come about that was new. Nothing significant seemed within reach at the moment.

Sometime during this time I believe I also had a dream. In the dream, it felt like it might be a "god" dream. I have had "god" dreams before, and they just feel different, it's a little hard to explain. I was standing in a parking lot next to a building, and there was a busy street nearby. It was the type of street where you just drive and there's shops all over the place on both sides. Somehow, I perceived that I had been there before, like it was an actual location in Cincinnati. My best guess was Colerain Ave, it was a place I had been frequently. I think at some point there was an angel possibly, or someone standing next to me in my peripherals five feet away. I didn't turn to look at them. My attention turned to a person across the street on what I thought to be a park bench. It was a black man with what I would describe as a Jamaican hairstyle possibly. It looked kind of like a mop-style, afro hairdo with dreads that went down to just above the shoulders maybe, or at least that's what came to mind. He appeared to be in mental or emotional distress. Somehow, I perceived that this person was gay. It may have been the person next to me telling me, I don't remember. My initial thought was, "well, if he's gay it's probably for the better. Perhaps in his distress he'll get right with God." Then he started acting even stranger. He started talking to someone, but no one was there. I believe he even acted like he was touching someone next to him, maybe slapped them. At that point I perceived that he wasn't crazy (he looked crazy by his behavior), he was seeing things, even into the "supernatural" realm. If that was true, I felt like he had been gifted with more than I had. At that point my thought was, "well, maybe I shouldn't judge." At that point the person standing next to me may have told me something else, but I don't remember it.

I woke up after that, or it ended. It was so weird, I kind of just forgot about it for most part. It seemed like it may be a God dream, but I hadn't prayed for anything, and none of it made any sense at all. What did that have to do to me? Maybe it was just some random dream like people have, like I had had before. If it hadn't seemed like a "god dream" I'm sure I would have forgotten it altogether.

****

During this same season, I was looking for something in my sisters' barn, and I stumbled upon a brown envelope laying on top of something. Years ago, I had written a paper about the Zodiac and put it in such envelopes when giving it out to a few select people. If this was one of those copies, why would it be laying out instead of in some storage tote? I figured it was something else, but I'm a curious person so I pulled it out about two or three inches to see what it was. It was my paper on the Zodiac. It probably belonged to one of my sisters. I believe they each had a copy, but I wasn't sure.

Some emotions came rushing back. Quite frankly I was tired of it. I had closed that chapter in my life for the most part. A dream deferred. A big part of me wanted to just throw it away. Roughly 3 years had passed since I had given it up for good. It was a bad reminder of everything I had went through, the ups and downs. It wasn't mine though, I had given it to my sister, so I couldn't do that.

I tried to slide the paper back into the envelope, but to my surprise I could not do that without crinkling the paper and forcing it in. The friction was very strong. I did not understand how that much resistance was possible, but it wouldn't budge at all. Not one millimeter would go back into the envelope. I was in a semi-rush, and since the whole thing was now too long to neatly fit on the pile it was on, I just pulled the whole thing out and put it on top of the envelope and moved on.

22

Prophecy Conference

May 2023 finally came around, and my schedule became relatively free so I was able to make it to a lot more of the sessions at the prophecy conference than I had initially thought. It was a three-day ordeal, Thursday through Friday. I was able to go Thursday, and then again on Saturday morning. God was moving, which is always great. If nothing else, it was good to just stay and exist in a very thick presence of God.

At the end of the Saturday morning service, while everyone was praying and seeking God, the speaker asked everyone to start praying for God to speak to them and give them a people group to reach. So, I started praying for that. I still didn't know where that could possibly go, but you won't know until you ask. What I felt like I heard back was, "wait", and maybe "and see." It was an answer that I was used to, though it was always unsatisfactory. It was better than nothing though. Maybe I just wasn't hearing right. I prayed again and got either, "whoever comes to you" or "whoever I send to you", or something along those lines. That was a little better, but at the same time it was pretty generic. I feel like that applies to every person. Maybe that was it, and was just another call to walk out the typical marching orders. I did think God said to wait though, which also makes sense. So I just kind of let it go for the time being.

Right after the morning service ended, they started doing the prophecy tents. My sister had signed me up for the earliest session, so I was up right away in the first group. My sister explained to me that it helps to go ahead and record everything using my phone and showed me how to do that. I hadn't used it before, so that was helpful. From her own experience she found she sometimes couldn't remember everything that was said while it was happening, so it helps to record it. I had been in that situation before and agreed, so I got it all ready to record. They had about a half dozen tents set up it seemed like, which were just portable shade canopies. There were four "prophetic listeners" or prophets set up on one side of each tent, and four chairs for the people they were going to prophesy over.

I wasn't sure why, since I had more or less gotten over it, but during the short time between the service being over and the prophecy tents starting, I couldn't help but think to myself,

"God, if you've ever wanted me to pursue all the Zodiac stuff, now would be a great time to tell me one way or the other."

I always knew I'd never trust I was hearing right if God's answer came from within me. If others I knew told me to pursue it, I'd probably suspect that they had somehow found out, and might be encouraging me from a place of knowing about it. If that's the case, how could I trust that they were hearing correctly from God, as they're just as flawed as I was?

They may have some personal investment in it as well and be biased like myself. The best way for me to trust it was to hear it from strangers. I had always admired king Nebuchadnezzar in the book of Daniel when he had his dream. He was smart enough to realize that if he told people what his dream was, then he couldn't trust that they were interpreting it right. At that point they could make something up that sounded good enough, and he may or may not buy into their interpretation. Nevertheless, he couldn't logically trust their interpretation to be accurate or divinely inspired in such a scenario. Since I knew no one here, and it was their job to prophesy over people, all of my prerequisites were met. Still though, I was hoping I wouldn't hear anything about the Zodiac, and wasn't expecting to. I was done with it, and my life was easier without worrying about it. God said he would take care of it, and I figured I wouldn't have to worry about it. Throughout the conference though, it kept coming into my mind.

****

I went over and sat down in my tent. I sat down on the far right. There were three other guests with me, all women, and all to my left. Three of the prophets were also women, two younger ones about my age were on my far left, one a brunette and one a blond. The other was an older black woman I would guess to be at least sixty years old. The last was a younger white man about my age, I believe with a few tattoos. The brunette explained how things would work. They all were listening to God, and would share what God was telling or showing them as they heard things. They would kind of just "popcorn" back and forth between each other and each guest, delivering what God was telling them. The guests were asked to not speak until the end to keep the flow going and not cause interruptions. I turned my iPhone recorder on as they started. They started talking to the other people first. One prophet would speak, then maybe another would chime in afterwards. Then there'd be a little bit of silence, then one of the prophets would bounce to a different person. Eventually, they came to me. The brunette was the first to speak to me:

"Greg I felt like I heard the Lord say you're a builder, and I don't know if that's like how, I almost feel like you're a builder in the spirit, maybe not in real life. But just like you take things and you see pieces of things and you just understand where they can fit together or how they can fit together and it's like you just understand it, you get it, you get how to build with the Lord, so I just bless you with that."

There were a few things running through my mind as she said this. I was an engineer, so I was a builder in that sense. I had a decent carpenter background through working with my dad as well, so that part did fit. While all of that was true, I felt like the "spiritual builder" was more applicable. Sometimes prophets will tell people things that were already true in order to convince them that they were hearing from God. If what she said had to do with that kind of tactic, it would quite honestly annoy or irritate me immensely, and God would have known that. I've already been to the point where I trust that people can hear from God, and I expected these people to all have that capability to some extent since they were putting it into practice in a public setting. I don't want to hear things I already know for sure, that

22: Prophecy Conference

has no value to me. Not only that, but there's nothing spiritually helpful in that interpretation.

Because of that, the "spiritual builder" made more sense. Since that was what made the most sense though, honestly the first thing that came to mind was the Zodiac. Just like how she said I see pieces of things and how they fit together, and "get it", that's exactly how I've always felt about the Zodiac. I saw how it fit into "kingdom building" for God, how it could be used as a means to build God's kingdom, to show people that God was real and who He is. I just "got it", when to my knowledge I'm not sure anyone else quite did. I hadn't heard about it in quite the same way from anywhere else. Still though, I had buried the subject, and wasn't too excited to hear it possibly coming back up.

The older black lady spoke next, it was to me again:

"I see you working crossword puzzles, like you said, you like to put things together, you try to figure out the answers, that seems like that's just who you are, use that for God's glory."

In my mind this was similar to the first prophecy, but if that was like a seven out of ten on the Zodiac likelihood scale, this was like a nine. To me, the whole process of figuring out all of the Zodiac ties with the Bible was just like a puzzle, so the whole puzzle thing really stuck out to me. Personally, I don't like crossword puzzles. I prefer Sudoku; I'm not a word person. Later on after thinking about this more, I realized that a crossword puzzle is actually a pretty good analogy. In a crossword puzzle, you're looking for words that fit certain criteria. First, usually there is a clue given for the word, like a sentence or definition. The Zodiac had to fit the clues given in the Bible. Second, the word has to fit in a certain number of spaces. With the Zodiac, this is the matching of the biblical numbers to those found in the Zodiac. Then number three, the answers have to agree with everything else that intersects with them. An example of this is twelve representing "all people" as well, to give that interpretation purpose in the context it's written in, such as twelve basketfuls of bread and fish being collected afterwards in Jesus's feeding of the five thousand. Outside of the Zodiac, I don't know what else this prophecy could possibly mean in the context of God or spirituality.

The younger blonde spoke next, again directed at me:

"bouncing off of those words, I see the anointing of Noah, Noah's ark over you, just the willingness to go forth and to do what God tells you to do regardless of what people say. I don't know if that's something that you have felt in the past or that you carry now or that you may birth within the future, so I bless you in that; it's rare to see that in people, the willingness to go against the tide."

Again, the first thing that came to mind was the Zodiac, especially after the first two prophecies. I always knew it would be controversial, a relatively unwelcome message in many ways, both inside and outside of the church. I had run into that already. Still, I believed it had great potential to bring people to know who God was. Because of that, I always wanted to do it, despite what people might say or think. I just needed to be 200% sure that God was in it.

To be fair there were a few other things that could go along with this. Like I mentioned before, I believe God told me that He was coming back very soon, and that we would see it in this lifetime, and to share that word with everyone. That was kind of out there too. I had shared some other words from God with our men's group that may not have been very popular. All of those things would probably be more well received than the Zodiac though. They also were a lot easier to deliver though because I was mentally prepared to go forward with the Zodiac, which was a lot worse. The other issue with that interpretation though was that it was more focused on the past. Like I said, things like that would probably have annoyed me. Perhaps, it could have been to tell me to once again be more vocal about Jesus's coming, as I had become less vocal about that. After the previous two messages though, the Zodiac interpretation was still the better fit.

The prophets moved on and talked to other people for a while. Eventually they bounced back to me, with the brunette talking first again:

"Greg, I also felt like I heard the Lord say you bless His heart. Everything about who you are blesses Him and He sees the deepest parts of your heart that have not been opened for a really long time, and He says, "I am here, you can trust me with those places, you can trust Me your king, your friend, with those places."

After she said this, I did get a little visibly emotional. I constantly questioned if I was doing what God wanted me to do. I felt like I wasn't living up to what He expected of me, both in ministry and oftentimes my personal life. Hearing that "everything about me blesses Him," was just something I desperately wanted to hear.

The second part of that initially was not making much sense. God knows everything about me, more than I do, and I know that. Therefore hiding things from Him doesn't make much sense to me. I felt like I was pretty honest with God about everything. Not being honest with God seemed pointless. If God was talking about the Zodiac here though, since the last three prophecies heavily had to do with that, it would kind of make sense. I had shoved the Zodiac stuff far away from me, at least for the last three years. I was tired of thinking about it, obsessing over it, even talking to God about it. I'd talked to Him about it countless times with no good answer on what to do with it. It gave me anxiety, thrill, passion, as well as a lot of uncertainty in several ways, and I was just tired of the emotional rollercoaster. It still stayed in the back of my mind, but I was done, and for the time it felt like God had taken it off of me.

Anyways, the older black lady saw my visibly emotional response, and she chimed in,

"You know, I just felt your reaction to those words like it touched a soft spot in you; like there's things that she said that you never revealed to anybody else, like this is who I am, this is how I feel about things. I'm kind of sensitive and it takes a lot to get in there, and when she said I just saw there was a reaction to you, so you can go ahead and be you."

I'm not sure she interpreted that correctly, my visibly emotional response. I was emotional because of the first thing that I had heard, not about the second. What she said was true for me in many ways. I'd even go as far to say it's a more common characteristic of

Scorpio, though I don't think there was any tie to the Zodiac here. I did hide the whole Zodiac thing from pretty much everyone except a few immediate family members. I had gotten a lot better at being open and I feel also more vulnerable, mostly because I believe that's what God wants us to do. It's a big part of how he shows his strength and character, through our weakness. Overall though, I think she kind of misinterpreted things here, spoke out of turn, or fed off of the wrong thing.

They "popcorned" to other people for a bit, and then finally came back to me. The man in the group spoke next.

"Greg I got, I get these weird analogies, hopefully this will make sense. I feel, I feel that you have this hunger for God, but you want to, you want to make sure you choose the right thing, and God's just saying no. No this is like, this is like cheesecake factory. The menu is like a novel, and you get to choose which meal you want. He's going to, he's going to provide you like, the you know it's going to be better than cheesecake factory food, but it'll be the best meal, it will satisfy, it will, it will nourish you. Uhh But, but yea, it's just the that you know umm paralysis of analysis type thing where you're just like I just want to choose the right thing. And he's saying there isn't a right thing to choose, you can choose anything you want."

This seemed more personal than anything. I did have a hunger for God, a hunger to please Him, but I didn't know how to translate that very well into ministry or His call on my life. I was just more trying to think of what is the right thing to do, and more importantly, how to accomplish that. I was very much paralyzed by analysis in this aspect. It's still in many ways how I live. I think this whole thing just helped me more to get an understanding of how God works, and the concept of "destiny" perhaps. I had heard in a few people's sharing of their "near death experiences," where they die, see the other side, and come back, that God often gives them some kind of choice. I always felt like sharing how the Zodiac is evidence of God was my life's calling, as the ripple effects could be huge. This could be God's way of telling me that I do have a choice in everything. Perhaps it also meant more to just walk with Him and be obedient in what is thrown in my path, and not think that I have to do this specific thing or that to be walking in His will.

The older black woman spoke next to me.

"And I was thinking sort of along the same lines, that there's something hidden in your heart that you really want to do, or something for, for Jesus, and like you said you're not sure it's the right thing. You want to be sure, that's, that's your um, your thought. But like He said, God says you don't have to worry about that. Go ahead and step out and what your desire is, you have a heart's desire that you're just not sure about. The Lord says, go ahead and step out and He's' going to embrace that. Whatever that is in you, that longing, there's a longing for something, and I don't think you ever told anybody what that is. It's just something that you keep to yourself. But the Lord knows, He sees, He hears, He knows all about you and your desires so just step out."

As she was saying this, my jaw dropped a little. It was one of those moments where you ask someone to pinch you to make sure you're still in reality. *"Something hidden in my heart that I want to do for Jesus."* There are a few things that qualify, but the Zodiac argument is definitely and easily the biggest. Many of the other things I didn't really want to do either, but was maybe willing to do if I heard clearly. *"I'm not sure it's the right thing. I want to be sure, that's my thought."* That is exactly my thought about the Zodiac. In general, I'm not sure about a lot of things in ministry, but the Zodiac was again, easily the biggest. I don't know what I would do in the moment if I ever met God face to face, but once I came to and remembered things, that would definitely be top of the list, if not the number one thing I'd ask Him at the time. That was true for the last thirteen years as well. *"There's a longing."* Only the Zodiac argument fit that description. *"I don't think you ever told anybody what that is."* I did tell a few people, but that list was very, very short. I don't know how much it spread past those people, if at all, but it was something I didn't share at all after I had tried initially once I figured it all out thirteen years ago. *"Go ahead and step out, and He's going to embrace that."* The other prophecies danced around it, but here the direction on what to do was finally given.

I had waited thirteen years to hear something like this, and it was hard to believe what I was hearing at the moment. Furthermore, what she said was very similar to the dream I had years ago. I knew no one would be able to say exactly what it was, but many of the things that were said were just like what I heard in the dream. The thing I wanted to do for God that I wasn't sure about. I hadn't told hardly anyone about it. Some of the other prophecies I had heard before were also potentially related to the clues I had seen in the dream. I couldn't be sure because the memory was foggy, but it was just an eerie sense of deja vu. The only difference was that instead of being called out in a church service, it was in a backroom tent kind of deal.

I believe the brunette spoke next, though I honestly don't remember paying attention too much after what I just heard that really shocked me.

"I'm really hearing that there's a possibility that there's a fear of stepping forward, out of reluctance and just thinking, what if I mess up God's plan for me. And like I was saying earlier, God spent countless hours crafting you and crafting your future and your plan and just umm, sorry I'm trying to find the words, umm, I hear God saying that you're not going to mess up or disappoint him, if you're listening to Him. And oftentimes people are thinking what if I'm not hearing God, and that just lines up so well with the doubt and the box that Micah's been preaching about all weekend. So, I just I encourage you to work through prayer with God, like journaling or reading the bible and just saying God I'm going to trust you no matter what you tell me to do. And just remembering that God wants to partner with you, not stand in front of you and cover the light that he created you to have."

There was a fear of stepping forward with the Zodiac argument. It wasn't so much messing up God's plan for me, but messing up God's plan in general. It seemed like it was too big, way bigger than myself. I didn't want to mess it up for God and everything that was at stake. If some part of the argument was wrong in a critical way, I would be spreading false teaching, or potentially leading people astray. God's Word for teachers who lead people astray is potentially very terrifying. *"I wouldn't mess up or disappoint God as long as I'm listening to Him."* Yes, I already believed this, but one of the hard parts is trusting your ability to listen. *"What if I'm not hearing from God… the box Micah's been preaching about."* It's hard to remember now, but I believe what he had been preaching about was doubt, and to stop doubting, to have eyes of faith.

The black woman chimed in again.

"Micah said on Thursday night, to punch a hole in the box, punch a hole in the box."

Yes, the box of doubt. Punch a hole in it, and break through the doubt. I suppose it was true for me in many ways. I had stepped out in faith several times, but there was still doubt in many cases, especially with the Zodiac argument. It seemed like God was telling me to quit doubting, and believe His words. After everything I had heard it was becoming hard to doubt it at the moment. Still there were many thoughts running through my head. I needed time to sort them all out. With those last words, the timer was up and they had to move on to the next group. They asked for feedback briefly, if anything they said rang true. I kept it short and just said, "yea, pretty much all of it." I wasn't about to divulge more details while still processing things.

****

My sister naturally asked how things went right after it was over. I just told her I had to think about it more, but heard some things I didn't really want to hear. I'd talk with her more later.

I had a few hours to myself after that for lunch, and to do a few other chores around home. I thought about it some more. All of the major things I had heard with the exception of a few could all be tied to the message of the Zodiac. No doubt, the best fit for all of them was the Zodiac message. I knew I was partial to it, but it was the most logical conclusion I could draw from all of that. To be truthful, the only sign I ever asked for from God was the latter thing the older black woman had said. The fact that the others heavily pointed to the Zodiac as well just seemed like the cup was flowing over. These people had no idea what they were telling me other than what they were shown, but I did. It all flowed together so well, more than what I had ever asked for from God. If it was not meant to be the Zodiac, then I had no idea what any of it meant.

Logically, at this point, it seemed to be almost willful ignorance to not pursue it. I had a choice, just like at the cheesecake factory, but I wanted to do this. I want to see the world come to God; I want to see His kingdom come. This argument had the potential to do just that in a way that nothing before it ever had. I don't know what God's backup plan for all of this was, but I know that plan A usually works out better than plan B, so I wanted to be a part of plan A if that's what God was calling me to.

Still, despite all of this, I wanted more confirmation. The anxiety I had for years concerning all of this was starting to come back. If I went forward with this, I fully expected to be put through the wringer. It would likely not come easily. I expected much opposition, possibly from friends and family, all well intentioned of course. Opposition would also likely come from within the Church and also outside of it. I asked God to just give me some kind of confirmation at the evening service that night, just to help cement the words I heard earlier. Perhaps I'm letting my own bias cloud my judgement or something. It didn't seem likely; I really tried my best to not deceive myself, but everyone who's ever blinded themselves probably thinks that. Once you reach a place where you're unteachable, I believe you need to be concerned.

****

Service that night was great. God's presence was very thick again. Micah Turnbo was the main speaker and coordinator of the event. By his own description, he was a "seer prophet". What that basically is, is he can often see into the "supernatural realm," and did so quite often. He shared some of his encounters with God (the Father, Son, and Holy Spirit), seeing angels, and visiting God's throne room. The goal for the service seemed to be to get people to enter into God's throne room, so at the end of the service, he had us all spend time in quiet prayer, and to enter the throne room through the eyes of faith. We were all standing at our seats, no one went up front to the altar like what often happens at such services. While we were all praying, Micah started going around the room laying hands on people.

I was just standing there, praying with my eyes closed in God's presence. Suddenly, I felt a hand on my head. I assumed it was Micah's. Later on, my sister confirmed it was. He had stayed there for a few minutes it seemed like before moving on. Based on his pattern, I figured he had probably only done that to maybe a dozen people in a room of probably 150 to 300 people, though I wasn't tracking his movements too much, I was more focused on God. I hadn't visibly seen the throne room like we were trying to, but it kind of felt like it otherwise with how thick God's presence was.

It wasn't exactly the confirmation I had expected, but to have someone who sees into the spirit realm on a regular basis lay hands on me, was great confirmation that God had something bigger going on here. I didn't do anything to stand out such as go forward, but I assumed Micah had seen something to direct his steps. It wasn't just my thinking God had bigger things in store; through this act I knew he did. It wasn't all in my head, or some horrible misinterpretation. I wasn't looking for validation so much for myself, but in God's leading of it all. It was a big thing, so I expected that God would act according to how important it was.

Later on after reviewing the video, I was able to get the facts down a little better. He laid hands on my sister and myself at the same time and stayed there for 25-30 seconds, which was on the longer end. Laying hands on two people at a time was a common pattern for him during the service. My sister and I were around numbers 8 and 9 chronologically. After number ten, Micah went back to the stage and did more of a "leading" role again for almost four minutes. For this first group of people that he laid hands on he tended to stay there with them a little longer. Then he went back out and started laying hands on more people, this time moving more quickly through the audience, just a few seconds for each person typically. Micah ended up laying hands on about three dozen people, though for many the duration was very short –just a few seconds. Immediately after he let go of my sister and I he said, "I feel the fire of God again, I'm just blessing what he's doing."

It also matched up with my dream in that regard. I didn't hear anything being said now, but in the dream I was singled out in a church service, then words spoken to me. I had heard the words earlier, and now I was being singled out. It wasn't quite the same, but everything that happened in the dream more or less had happened at the conference; it was just a little mixed up.

    The service ended, and I chatted with my sister for a bit. I told her I'd probably share with her later what I heard from prophecy tents. I went home and had trouble sleeping that night. I was concerned with everything I had just heard. The anxiety had come back, and hard. I knew what I had to do now, it was just a matter of doing it. The best part about all of it though, was that I had evidence of God's leading. I had what was spoken at the prophecy tents all on audio recording. I had witnesses at the church service, and it may have even been recorded on video. If I had a visitation or something from God about the Zodiac where He told me to pursue it, people would say I was lying, and I wouldn't blame them for thinking that. None of it came from within me, only the interpretation, as I knew what it likely meant. That essential aspect of it would help whatever was to come next so much easier. I didn't expect people to take the Zodiac argument at face value, especially without looking into it for themselves which takes time. However, spirit-led people should be able to see God's leading through the testimony he had just given me, and then at least give it a more serious look.

23

Onward

The next morning I got up and went to church as usual. Like I said, I didn't sleep well. The anxiety had come back. At that point I was just praying for God to give me peace about everything so I could get back to some sense of normality. During worship, the lyrics of one of the songs that was played helped to just calm my nerves. The sermon subject that day was "David vs. Goliath." I don't remember all of it, but a lot of it spoke to me. This did seem like the Goliath in my life. One of the things that I do remember hearing was something about a mountain being removed, and I felt like God was saying that the mountain that was in place preventing this before was going to be taken down. Later on, our pastor's wife came up and shared a scripture passage that God put on her heart to share, which wasn't super common but also not unheard of. She shared a passage out of Isaiah 43. Verses 1-4 specifically hit me, mainly verse 2.

> *"But now thus says the Lord, he who created you, O Jacob, he who formed you, O Israel: Fear not, for I have redeemed you; I have called you by name, you are mine. 2 When you pass through the waters, I will be with you; and through the rivers, they shall not overwhelm you; when you walk through the fire you shall not be burned, and the flame shall not consume you."*

I just really needed to hear that. God would protect me and be with me through it all. It wouldn't be the end of me; I wouldn't be overwhelmed by it. By the time I left the service, with everything that happened, the anxiety was gone, and I was at peace.

The next day on Monday, I shared what I heard at the prophecy tents with my sister Sheryl, and what I thought it meant. I had told her about the Zodiac stuff years before, and I think she either agreed with my interpretation or was nice about it and just played along. She went back home though and later sent me the following text:

"I dunno if this means something..but I walked in the barn to get a tool and I saw this thick packet of paper sitting on top of my stuff which I thought huh that's odd I am not the kind of person to leave paper out bc it gets dusty and crinkly. I walk over to it & pick it up and realize it's the 1 copy of your paper you gave me in college and it wasn't dusty or dirty. It looks like it hadn't been sitting out long. I'm really in shock and believe it's another sign. You pray on it of course but phew shock lol"

This was the first of many signs I got after this confirming I was on the right path. What she probably found was the copy that I pulled out of the envelope and left it on top when I was in the barn a few months ago, but it was still an "odd coincidence" that she found it just hours after I had shared everything with her.

****

After the conference was over, my sister had bought a second copy of Micah Turnbo's book "The Invitation" (Turnbo, 2022) for me. It was mostly about his testimony of things he saw and experienced in his gifting as a seer prophet. I read it pretty quickly (for me) in a couple of weeks as I enjoy reading people's testimonies. There were a few passages that helped me out in just putting everything into perspective, which I'll share briefly.

In the first passage, he spoke about the steps to becoming a prophet. I don't really consider myself a prophet, but in my want of validation of what God was doing in my life, this passage stood out to me. What caught my attention was the steps he outlined. He mentions there is a calling, a commissioning, and an anointing. I had the calling to ministry when I was 19, and then I felt like I had figured out what that was almost a year later when I found all the Zodiac stuff. God had never told me to do anything with it though until the prophecy tents just a few weeks earlier (the commissioning). Then, I would argue that I got the anointing when Micah laid hands on me later that day.

Along those same lines, the other passage that really spoke to me was one that otherwise probably wouldn't have been noteworthy to me. Micah was going through a hard time, and an angel named Samuel came up and visited him. While talking to the angel, he eventually kind of burst out in anger, and slapped the angel's leg. While reading this, I got a sense of déjà vu, like I had seen this before. It was at that moment, I remembered my dream about the gay black man in distress, who was talking to the air. Micah openly admits that he used to define himself as gay until God set him free of it. He was the man who laid hands on me. Those few months ago, God had shown me in a dream the person who would lay hands on me and in doing so confirm everything He had told me. None of it made sense, until now.

****

At some point after this I realized something else. I was thirty-three years old when I heard all of this. I remembered back all of those years when I first heard God's calling at age 19, when I was under continuous demonic attack. My best guess was that God had told me it would all happen when I was thirty-three years old, or possibly thirty four, though in my mind I left it at 31-35 since the second part of God moving my mouth could have possibly been mistaken for 34 or 31. If I just had more trust in God and of my hearing God's voice accurately, I could have spent those 14 years worry-free.

Also related to that, as well as dreams, my sister Sheryl's (weird) dream of me having a baby was coming true, with babies representing something new. Something new was definitely happening!

I figured the best way to spread the message was to go and preach a service at local churches, so I made up a condensed sermon on it all and started reaching out to pastors. After I had written the sermon up though, I felt like God was telling me to write a book. I wasn't sure I had heard right, so I asked God to please give me confirmation if that's what I was supposed to do, and I just didn't worry about it after that. Writing a book would be a lot of work, and then you have to try to get it published, advertising, and everything else. I didn't want to waste time on something so extensive if it wasn't God's plan. God sent me

23: Onward

confirmation in less than a week, maybe as soon as one or two days later. I received a text from my sister, who had shared it with some of her friends at church to try to get a feel for how to look into sharing the message at her church.

"Also as I was sharing your story, specifically when I did about prophecy tents, Sally (fake name) said wait show me a picture of your brother – I think I was in his tent praying. And you were! She said she actually had another word for you but she held back bc she wasn't sure if she was to share it then – I believe she said she saw pages of writing & that you were a writer / would be writing"

Well, there was confirmation that God wanted me to write a book. I hadn't told anyone I thought God was telling me that. I hadn't had a chance to, though I likely wouldn't have told anyone that anyways in order to help myself believe any confirmation I may have gotten. Sheryl said after she mentioned the prophecy on puzzles that Sally was like "I know him!", and she remembered specifically because of the word on writing that she didn't share and tucked away.

****

My sister's church had more prophecy tents in September later that year. I decided to go again, though I didn't think I needed much direction at the moment. Who knows though, it's always good to hear from God. This time it was three on three and indoors, so the audio quality was a little better. I didn't recognize any of the prophets from last time, so it was all new people. There was a black lady about my age in the middle who spoke to me first.

"I got something for you, Greg. I saw um, I don't know if it's a kayak, or if it's a canoe, but it's a boat leaning against the wall. and so and asking the Lord about that, it's the boat is only out because it's about to be used, so in a sense this is a season of getting ready for some adventures, and it was the boat and the oars for it as well. So, I think that is representing that you'll have what you need, and God is going to give you the guidance for whatever is coming up next."

I was hoping to start the adventure sooner, but I guess I had to write the book first and convince pastors and influencers to let me have an audience. I had started that process already, but I knew it would take time for leaders to consider it and see it. It was definitely a big ask I was putting on them. Right after her, an older white woman on my right spoke next.

"Greg I saw for you, as you were walking here, wherever you put your feet would bring a light, I just sensed he was saying he has places for you to step and take place, and just pay attention to where you're going, because He has you bringing light into situations and just walk where he has you walk"

Well that was cool to hear, and decent confirmation that I was on the right path. Next, an older man on my left spoke.

"Greg What I'm hearing and seeing is that the Lord is wildly enthusiastic about you, and he may be bringing you into some uncomfortable situations uh that you're not super excited about. But He is, and he's right there with you. I think that's some of that light cause you're carrying Jesus with you wherever you go and it's evident and obvious to a lot of people around you. Um but he is wildly enthusiastic about every time you take a step, every time you go forward and

reach out and start some level of adventure. He's with you and he wants to encourage you to just kind of be a little wild when it comes to that, so sort of a wild man attitude, even though you don't portray that in any way when looking at you now, but he is wildly enthusiastic about you."

I would think God would be very enthusiastic about this if unveiling this was part of his bigger plan. I had already started those "uncomfortable" situations – talking to a few people about it. Pastors and church leaders tended to be loving, but at the same time I went into the few talks I had expecting the worst. It's not something that most people in the church would be warm and welcoming to. There's almost no way they'd leave being convinced of it – it's truly something you have to see for yourself. They then went on to the other two people for a while. The middle black lady came back to me next several minutes later.

"For you Greg um I was seeing like a river and there are like these different pieces of rock, so I was seeing like a river, and there was just layers of rock, and no matter how strong a rock is, water can kind of wear it away. I believe he's saying you have the power of water, and it's like a process, but he's blessing you with endurance or patience to see some things change, just like water changes rock over time"

The older woman spoke next right after her, which was the last thing that was spoken to me.

"I'm getting from the Lord that you're steadfast like a stable, there's a lot of stability in you, and that's something that he really likes about you, that you're almost like that rock too, you're not easily moved or swayed, you're firm. I sense that's going to have an impact into other people's lives."

Pretty much everything I heard this time I already knew or could have guessed. Months later, someone from a major school of supernatural ministry told me that he saw zeroes and ones, or new codes on me, perhaps especially my fingers. He also mentioned something about spiritual innovation in relation to me somehow. Yes, the message God put on me was very innovative, at least I thought so. The message in a way also had to do with how we are "coded." More of the same, but good confirmation still.

The argument for God from the Zodiac is something that I knew would not catch on too quickly. After all, it took me 2-5 months of intensive studying to see it in everyone around me and know what to look for. Then, depending on where you stand on God, it would likely take more time to accept the biblical part of that. I had a rough idea of what I had to do. It would just take time, effort, persistence, and a lot of help from God and others. Like water on rock, slowly withering it away — that was my course.

Appendix

For the benefit of the reader for this to be a more "all inclusive" book on the Zodiac signs, I included this appendix to help get a basic idea on what the twelve Zodiac signs are, as well as the four elements and three modalities in the Zodiac. A brief History of the Zodiac signs is also included here. To be perfectly honest, I have no intention of trying to write such things as Zodiac sign profiles and take on such a research project at the time, so what you'll find here concerning the twelve signs, elements, and modalities is mostly written by artificial intelligence with some editing on my part. With that though, I think you'll find that the descriptions are fairly accurate, though there are a lot more in-depth studies from other writers.

A Brief Historical Account of the Zodiac Considerations

The history of how the Zodiac came to be in its present state is a very natural question, and is important to cover. That being said though, especially when dealing with things of God, I would argue it is not as critical or important as one might think. Ultimately, the validity of the Zodiac profiles stands or falls on its ability to accurately describe the reality that we see today. It's more a question of science, than of history. Just like physics or chemistry, the fact that we didn't understand these things thousands of years ago does not mean that our scientific inquiry into how the universe works was fruitless or without a good foundation.

Much of what we know about Zodiac signs and astrology was discovered using scientific principles in a way that resembles alchemy. Alchemy was of course the pursuit of trying to transform matter, mostly to convert metals into gold. What I mean by this, is that it's mostly trying to figure out patterns in nature without understanding the fundamental principles of nature. Once chemistry came around and we realized that making things into gold couldn't be easily or realistically done, we gave up on alchemy. Similarly in astrology, all of the vast amount of understanding is basically "guess and check, then adjust", and repeat. All of this is done without knowing what the underlying causes could be, if any such cause exists. Because the foundational cause of such studies is more or less non-existent, all of the research is on shaky grounds until it can be more rigorously tested and confirmed, and even then ideally you would want to find what the underlying cause is.

Like what I laid out in this book, I'm not sure what the underlying cause is or could be. I do know that a naturalistic cause is completely insufficient though, and that a supernatural one is the only likely one. Similarly, the answer is likely tied to our creation. I would also argue that much of the history of astrology and the Zodiac signs, especially in modern days, is full of skeptics like myself who take a peek, and then have trouble rationalizing the results against what you would expect to find if all of it was fabricated.

Prophecy

Another point that comes up is the history of the Zodiac symbols, as well as the history of the symbols in the Bible. Which one came first? The potential consequences would be that it's arguable that the writers of the Bible stole the symbols from the Zodiac, or vice-versa, that astrologers assimilated the symbols of the Bible and made it fit into their interpretations. This is the "conspiracy theory" argument against everything. At the end of the day though, I'd argue it doesn't matter too much.

For example, consider the prophecy about Cyrus, who is mentioned specifically in Isaiah 45:1, years before he was born. This same Cyrus was the grandson of Queen Esther in the Bible, and is therefore also 25% Jewish. There is a conceivable chance that Esther passed on knowledge of scriptures to her son, the king, who then named his son Cyrus, knowing the scriptures. Still though, the prophecy came to fruition, whether it was conspired or not.

Likewise with the Zodiac, whether the chicken came first or the egg, it works. Ultimately, it's a question of whether or not the Zodiac signs work. The "why" comes later. Since the symbols twelve and seven in scripture happen in Genesis, they do pre-date our earliest records of the Zodiac. Moreover, the symbol twelve could not have been planned by any human as it originates through the twelve sons of Jacob.

Appendix

Gentile History

The history of the Zodiac and/or astrology largely originates in ancient Babylonia, with "experts" or "scholars" called *ummanu*. The idea was that there was a connection between the divine and the natural. These experts would look for signs in nature, and then compare them to the events that followed, in order to come up with a system for interpreting omens. Signs could be the flight path of birds, reading entrails, and notably the movement of the heavenly bodies. Mesopotamian tradition speaks of divine teachers who dwelled on earth in the past and taught men many different kinds of knowledge and wisdom. This Babylonian tradition seems to agree with what we find from the book of Enoch where the Watchers (angelic beings) interbreed with humans and taught them several things, including astrology. You could also take a different perspective that Enoch or Seth's descendants may have been taught astrology during the time by angels. So if you were to buy into this tradition as well as a Jewish perspective, it's likely that the principles originated with either good or fallen angels..

Sometime before 1000 BC, the path of the sun was subdivided into twelve parts. Between 600 BC and 400 BC these twelve zones became marked by a constellation that lies within each division. The origins of the Zodiac figures (Leo, Virgo, Taurus, etc.) is largely a mystery, though it is often assumed that they go with the constellations inside of their sign. The division of twelve came from their twelve-month calendar.

It is also worth noting that the four seasons were mapped out into the four corners of the sky early on, which would correspond to Leo, Taurus, Scorpio, and Aquarius, the same connection that we draw from the four living creatures, though the signs themselves likely came afterwards.

The earliest evidence that we have of the idea that a person's date of birth could correspond to their character comes from a statement from the Greek historian Herodotus while visiting Egypt around 450 BC. He mentions that they (Egyptians) assign each month and each day to some god, and that they can tell what fortune, what end, and what disposition a man should have according to their date of birth. It is somewhat accepted that the Egyptians likely got it from the Chaldeans though.

The earliest reference I could find in relation to the four elements as well as the three qualities was from Marcus Manilus and dates to around 10-15 AD (Roman Empire), though it is believed that he built a lot of his work on top of that of the Greeks, but that their work did not survive. Marcus's book, "Astronomicon" mentions dividing signs by squares, triangles, hexagon, and opposite. The triangle would represent elements, as you can draw four triangles in the Zodiac signs (three signs per element), and the square would represent qualities (four signs per quality).

Astrology had died out quite a bit around and after the scientific revolution, and gained a reputation of superstitious nonsense more or less in the general population. There was enough interest in it to keep it alive, but it was very much a shadow of its former self, whatever that was considered to be.

The emphasis of the position of the sun particularly at the birth time of someone came more from the twentieth century. The sun signs are what we typically think of when we hear

Zodiac signs mentioned today. A modern Astrologer, Alan Leo, started a magazine "Modern Astrology" in 1895. He used a quick method of horoscopes that just had "sun in Virgo", etc. to group people into larger groups for purpose of magazine astrology and horoscopes. Classical astrology took all kinds of different planets and aspects into account.

Another important distinction between modern astrology and classical astrology of the past, was the intellectual basis of all of it. Classical astrology was heavily tied to religion, potentially science, maybe philosophy. In modern astrology, there was no tie to anything. The scientific revolution and turn to a more material nature had no place for astrology. In modern Judeo-Christian eyes, astrology was also widely rejected, though in times past it did have an obscure place in these religions, though I'm not sure what the scriptural basis would have been, if any. One such justification could come from Genesis 1:14 where God says the stars were for signs and seasons. There are a few other verses that allude to that, probably the best example being the three wise men who followed a star that led them to the baby Jesus. It is also important to note that to most, if not all, ancient cultures, the sky played a huge part – if nothing else just to tell what time, day, and time of year it was. God even mentions that in Genesis. For that reason it was an essential part of life to them, and they were likely at least familiar with the Zodiac signs/constellations for that reason alone, even if they did not practice astrology. I would argue it's more of a foreign concept to us today than it was to them as we have digital timekeepers, and even before that we had mechanical clocks for a few hundred years.

The intellectual basis that modern astrology ended up with came from psychology. Psychiatrist and psychoanalyst Carl Gustav Jung had done a lot of work in modern astrology-psychology connection, but was elusive to state the causal connection between the two. He did notice significant patterns did recur. Onward from here, astrology largely moved away from fortune-telling focus to character analysis, which brings us to what we see in modern day astrology. It's through this lens that astrology became popular in today's world, regaining a fairly broad following. (Whitfield, 2001)

Appendix

Condensed Timeline

Event Date	Document Date	Author/Book	Civilization	Event Details
6000 BC??	1500-1300 BC	Bible	Jewish	God creates stars for Signs and Seasons (Genesis 1)
3382-3019 BC	300-200 BC	Book of Enoch	Jewish	Watchers taught astrology to men. Enoch is taught astronomy and "twelve portals" by angel Uriel
3382-3019 BC	100-200 BC	Pseudo-Eupolemus	Samaritan	Enoch was among the first to learn astrology
3382-3019 BC	93-94 AD	Josephus	Jewish	Possible allusion of descendents of Seth inventing astrology
2100-1900 BC	1500-1300 BC	Bible	Jewish	Abraham walks the earth (12 tribes of Ishmael, later on 12 tribes of Israel) (Genesis)
2100-1900 BC	100-200 BC	Pseudo-Eupolemus	Samaritan	Describes Abraham as an astrologer. Learned it from Chaldeans & taught to Egyptians & Phoenicians
2100-1900 BC	93-94 AD	Josephus	Jewish	Cites source "Berosus" that mentions Abraham was an astronomer and/or astrologer. Josephus also references Abraham alluding to astrology while arguing against planets being gods.
2100-1900 BC	93-94 AD	Josephus	Jewish	Claims Abraham taught astronomy to Egyptians
1446-1225 BC	1446-1225 BC	Bible	Jewish	Numbers 2 - first hint of 'four tribes' pattern corresponding to four elements
?? - 1000 BC	?? - 1000 BC	3 Stars Each tablets	Babylon	Origins of division by 12 by Babylonians (prior to 1000 BC)
700-300 BC	700-300 BC	Bible	Jewish	God's reference to constellations/Astrology in Job 38:31-33
600 BC	600 BC	Mul. Apin.	Babylon	Division of sky into 4 corners/4 seasons
600-400 BC	600-400 BC		Babylon	Addition of constellations to the 12 months
620-538 BC	620-538 BC	Bible	Jewish	Daniel was made chief prefect over wise men, who were known to practice astrology
592-570 BC	592-570 BC	Bible	Jewish	Ezekiel's four living creatures (four elements of zodiac)
520-470 BC	520-470 BC	Bible	Jewish	Book of Zechariah talks about seven lampstands, and rock with seven eyes
6-4 BC	40-90 AD	Bible	Christian	Three wise men follow star to find Jewish King Jesus.
10-15 AD	10-15 AD	Astronomicon	Greek	Early beginnings of four elements & three modalities in astrology
134 AD	134 AD	Emperor Hadrian	Roman	Emperor Hadrian states all chiefs of Jewish, Samaritan, or Christian groups are either astrologers, soothsayers, or anointers
68-96 AD	68-96 AD	Bible	Christian	Book of Revelation written (four living creatures, seven spirits, twelve fruits of tree of life, plus more)
200-300 AD	200-300 AD	Synagogues	Jewish	At least 7 synagogues uncovered with zodiac mosaics

Graphic 3

The Four Elements

The way that I always thought of the four elements, was that it was the primary thing that the sign was concerned with. When someone is thrust into an unknown situation, what is the default thing that they are concerned with in trying to process what they are witnessing? Yes everyone is likely capable of seeing or doing every aspect of something if given enough time, but the elements are the "what" of how they interpret things by default. If possible, it helps to think of all of this in terms of "computer programming." Whether you think the Zodiac is part of that, there exists a method to all of the madness of the human mind no doubt, it's just a matter of finding it. The "what" in terms of computer programming, represents different ways to gather information or process things around us.

I share my thoughts and my take on what a lot of these things actually are below, but I'm human and prone to error. I could be significantly off on many of these, but it's one way that I interpreted the signs, elements, and modalities that helped me see things a little better.

Appendix

Fire

Zodiac Signs: Aires, Leo, Sagittarius

Common Characteristics:

Fire signs are known for their high energy levels and enthusiastic nature. They often possess a passion and drive that fuels their actions and pursuits. These people are naturally inclined to seek adventure and explore new horizons, and have an optimistic outlook and believe in their ability to overcome obstacles. Fire signs are also known for their courage and willingness to take risks. They are not afraid to step outside of their comfort zones and embrace new challenges.

One way this "fire" can manifest negatively is through quick-temperedness and impulsivity. This same quality and focus that allows for greater enthusiasm and spontaneity can also lead to impatience and a quick temper. Those with this tendency may have to work on managing their anger and impulsive reactions. Fire can also manifest itself as selfish and/or aggressive, and want to be the center of attention.

Those influenced by the fire element tend to display leadership qualities. They are confident, assertive, and have natural charisma that attracts others to follow their lead. Fire signs are often creative and have a strong imagination. They are often inspired by new ideas and are quick to take action to bring those ideas to life. They also value their independence and have a strong sense of individuality. They are often self-reliant and prefer to take charge of their own lives.

My Thoughts:

The way I've typically interpreted the Fire element, is that it is raw "action." These are action-oriented people. When observing fire people, the topic of conversation is often "what are you up to", or the subject matter has to do with activities, what they see others "doing." In the explanation above, many of these qualities can all likely be explained as a result of action-oriented thinking lived out. Their independence could be interpreted as not wanting to give up their right to "action." Their leadership qualities could also be explained as people just jumping on the bandwagon of their "action" and following their lead, or as the desire of the fire sign for others to come along with their "action."

Earth

Zodiac Signs: Capricorn, Taurus, Virgo

Common Characteristics:
Earth signs are known for their practical and down-to-earth nature; they have a grounded approach to life and tend to prioritize stability and security. They are patient and tend to have a steadfast and reliable nature, making them good at providing support and maintaining consistency. Earth people are sensible and responsible with a strong sense of duty and can be relied upon to get things done. They are loyal and tend to be there if the need is warranted.

One way this can manifest negatively is through stubbornness or inflexibility – the practical way is the way to go. Sometimes laziness can be an issue as well. I'm not sure how that is possible as earth signs tend to be some of the hardest working people out there, but I have observed it in a few individuals. It seems this may be two sides of the same coin that is part of the earth element, laziness and hardworking. We see the same pattern in other elements where a focus in one area leads to two highly related, yet opposite characteristics. I just find it hard to pin down what exactly that "coin" is for the earth element.

Earth signs place importance on the physical realm, including material possessions, finances, and physical comfort. They have a natural ability to handle practical matters and are often skilled at managing resources. Earth signs often have a strong connection to their senses and enjoy indulging in physical experiences. They appreciate the pleasures of life, such as good food, comfort, and physical touch. The love of material things may lead to overindulgence though, and in some cases they may go into debt in pursuit of these things. Because of a focus on physical things, hoarding can be an issue for earth signs as well.

My Thoughts:
The element of Earth is one that I've probably struggled with the most in understanding. I believe this is because it appears to be very basic in nature, nothing really stands out about it to me. Quite frankly, that's probably the point. In both of my high school and college classes, I will say that the two topped ranked people in both cases were Taurus and Virgo. I don't necessarily think they were smarter than everyone else in many ways, but I knew for a fact that they worked harder than the next people in line. The grounded, tried and true approach seems to work best. My best guess as to what "Earth" actually is, is a sense of materialism, or perhaps object-oriented thinking. They're concerned with "things", or "objects." Sometimes, objects could be thoughts too perhaps.

Appendix

Air

Zodiac Signs: Libra, Aquarius, Gemini

Common Characteristics:

Air signs are known for their sharp intellect and analytical skills. They have a natural ability to analyze situations and think critically. They are skilled at seeing multiple perspectives and finding logical solutions to problems. The focus here is on a logical and rational perspective as opposed to an emotional one. The downside to this is that at their worst they may come off as "cold" in their assessment and behavior, missing the emotional impact of their words, demeanor, or course of action.

Another bigger theme here is their excellent communication skills. They are quick-minded and enjoy engaging in stimulating conversations. They tend to be social butterflies who enjoy being around others and thrive in a social setting, often being the life of the party. Talking politics or sports is often a hobby. On a bad day they can be a bit aloof though, kind of distant, which is easier to pick up on in contrast to their normal, more positive social interactions.

Air signs are often full of innovative ideas and possess a creative flair. They tend to enjoy exploring different intellectual pursuits and may excel in fields that require creative thinking. They are also typically adaptable and versatile, and can quickly adjust to new situations and enjoy change and variety in their lives. The downside to this is they can come off as fickle, bouncing around perhaps too much. The focus on ideas and logic can also lead these signs to come off as superficial if such ideas lack sufficient roots in reality.

My Thoughts:

My best guess here is that this is pure "logic." Related to that, "idea-oriented" is another way to look at it. Tying the logic together between ideas as well, giving the bridge. Much of the thinking takes place in the metaphysical. Perhaps the mastery over logic and ideas allows for much easier communication, and provides a wide-array of topics of discussion or things to ponder, since ideas can vary quite a bit. Another possible reason for this proclivity for communication is that logic and ideas are not easily spread nonverbally, and must be transmitted through language. Other elements' main themes can in many cases be spread and picked up nonverbally. In the realm of ideas an logic though, that may be more difficult to do without language and communication, so this proclivity may come as almost a necessary side effect rather than a main feature.

Water

Zodiac Signs: Cancer, Scorpio, Pisces

Common Characteristics:
Water signs are highly attuned to their emotions and the emotions of others. They tend to live through "feeling" the world around them. Because of this, they have a natural inclination towards nurturing and caring for others. They are empathetic and compassionate, often putting the needs of others before their own. This proclivity for emotional attachment can lead to a very loyal individual. The downside to this is they can be easily hurt, or take things too personally

They are also known for their depth and introspective nature. They have a rich inner world and are comfortable exploring their own emotions and the deeper aspects of life. Water signs have a natural inclination towards intuition and what you might call "psychic" abilities. They often rely on their gut feelings and can easily pick up on subtle "energies", vibes, or emotions people are putting off. The pitfall here is their inner world of emotions can make them more prone to be moody if things go negative. Their intuition and sensitivity to others' emotions can also lead them to be more suspicious of others, perhaps picking up on false scents that aren't really there (or they interpret these "scents" incorrectly).

Water signs can also adapt easily to different situations and environments. Just like water can take the shape of its container, water signs have a flexible and adaptable nature. They can pick up on vibes and adjust their demeanor accordingly.

My Thoughts:
The common theme that is picked up from all of this is pretty easy to see: emotions. What is emotion though? I would say it partly has to do with personal investment in matters, or a part of the psyche. Feelings perhaps. It adds a more "personal" touch to thoughts and actions, and helps to explain the "why" behind things. "Emotion", "purpose" or "why" - oriented is what I would probably go with here as the best summary. I know for me personally falling into this category, I tend to size people up by trying to see their heart or intentions, which could also be interpreted as their purpose. This is in contrast to for example a fire sign which might instinctively look more at someone's actions to judge them, or an air sign who might form an opinion on them based more on their logic and ideas put forth.

Appendix

The Three Modalities

If the four elements represented the "what" that each sign is primarily concerned with, I would argue that the three modalities were the "how." What I mean, is that the modalities represent how the sign typically looks or behaves at the element, or how the element is expressed. If the "movement" theme mentioned in the four living creatures is accurate in representing the three modalities, that's also probably a better way of looking them. The modalities are how the sign "moves" or "operates" within the element.

Cardinal

Zodiac Signs: Aires, Capricorn, Libra, Cancer

Common Characteristics:
Cardinal signs have a strong desire to initiate new projects and take the necessary actions to achieve their goals. This is often expressed via making quick decisions and taking decisive action. They are motivated, ambitious, and enthusiastic about starting new endeavors, and have the determination to see their plans through. They are often assertive, confident, and proactive in taking charge of situations. All of these tendencies make them good natural leaders. The downside to making quick decisions like this is that they may come off as bossy or domineering, with the potential to forget certain aspects or dismiss things when they are focused on one thing.

This quick dismissal is not how the modality operates on a good day though. When given time to think things through, Cardinal people process things by looking at them from many different angles and aspects, starting a new "initiation" and repeating. From looking at things from many different angles, they start to find a good, balanced solution to things. This side of the modality also helps to make them adaptable and comfortable with change. They are open-minded and willing to embrace new experiences and challenges.

Cardinal signs also tend to have a vibrant and dynamic energy. All of that initiation can come off as being fairly active. They are often restless and driven individuals who are always seeking new opportunities and experiences. Because of this, Cardinal signs value their independence and self-reliance. They are often self-starters, preferring to take on tasks and projects on their own rather than relying on others.

My Thoughts:
Initiation is the theme here. You are decisive by initiating something. Same thing with leadership and making decisions. Make one initiation, then do another initiation. The cycle repeats. You adapt by taking another initiative. Starting new things takes energy.

Another way to think of this (and the other 2 modalities) is in terms of "programming language". Cardinal is the 'start' of the program. It's the initiation of the process of accomplishing anything. Something has to be started before it can come to fruition. When coming up on the "what to do now?" question, cardinal starts something.

Fixed

Zodiac Signs: Leo, Taurus, Aquarius, Scorpio

Common Characteristics:
Fixed signs are known for their strong determination and the ability to endure challenges and setbacks. They are stable and resolute in whatever course they put their mind to. Where Cardinal or Mutable might be more susceptible to getting off track, Fixed is not and tend to have more endurance. They will continue the persisting in something steadily, which is typically works well at getting results. The downside to this is these signs can exhibit stubbornness and resistance to change, preferring to maintain the status quo or stick to familiar patterns when perhaps change may be the best way to proceed.

Fixed signs have a strong sense of identity and can be unwavering in their beliefs and values. This unwillingness to change their opinions or ways of doing things can lead them to believe they're always right, and can be either a strength or weakness depending on the situation. In relationships and duty, these people often manifest themselves as being very loyal and reliable, sticking to their commitments and maintaining a sense of consistency.

As far as processing and acting in the world around them, fixed signs will tend to try to figure out a way to do something, and then once they find that, will try to maximize it and build on that rather than try something new. This can result in deeper understanding and excelling in things, yet at the same time it can create tunnel vision and hinder their ability to see other solutions.

My Thoughts:
Perseverance is a big theme here, which can manifest as stubbornness and determination as well. Myself being a fixed sign, I think a big theme here is a focus on what "is" – the now and present. The focus is on how things are, which helps in establishing the strong sense of self and identity. Perseverance could come as a result of what "is" – the focus of thought is narrowed down to something more manageable.

Building on the "programming language" analogy, fixed would be the continuation of what was initiated. The movement here is to steady the course, and see the job done. When coming to the "what to do now" question, the answer is to continue the course, often based on what is known to work, and just perfect it.

Appendix

Mutable

Zodiac Signs: Sagittarius, Virgo, Gemini, Pisces

Common Characteristics:

Mutable signs are known for their ability to easily adapt to different situations and environments. They are versatile in their approach and can adjust their plans and ideas as needed. When it comes to problem solving they can be very resourceful, able to think on their feet and find creative solutions to challenges or obstacles they face.

Mutable signs are also generally open to new ideas and perspectives. They are curious and enjoy exploring different options and possibilities. This helps them to be more agreeable with others and thus they often excel in communication and networking. This natural ability to connect with others helps them to be skilled negotiators and mediators. In many ways they can be like chameleons, adapting to fit in with their environment and thus often unpredictable in nature. The downside to this is they can have a tendency to flip-flop back and forth between things, or come off as inconsistent, lacking boldness, or even two-faced.

These signs are comfortable with change. They have a flexible nature and can easily adjust their plans and routines to accommodate new circumstances or opportunities. However, due to their adaptability and desire for change, mutable signs can sometimes struggle with restlessness or scattered energy. They may have a tendency to start multiple projects or change their direction frequently.

My Thoughts:

The major themes picked up on here are change, versatility, adaptability. This is one I struggle with understanding better as well, as I'm not sure how exactly this differs from Cardinal. There is a different nuance here, but at first glance it seemed similar to Cardinal to me the way it's typically pitched, or it could be similar. Cardinal tends to be more of a decisive nuance, where mutable is more suggestive in nuance. I would also say this tends to be more "future-oriented" thinking, which "change" fits in with well. "What could happen in the future?" is a big thought here. Or it often manifests as changing one's mind based on new information.

I think the "programming language" analogy here helps a lot to differentiate this from cardinal. If cardinal is 'start', and fixed is 'continue', then what's left is 'stop'. Mutable becomes the end of the process. In a computer loop that doesn't end though, such as a learning algorithm, 'stop' is not exactly just stop and end, it's more of a feedback step. It's an evaluate and change step. This is where the adaptability, flexibility, and problem solving come into play. It's taking a diverse perspective and changing how things are viewed, which also could result in putting a 'stop' to things that fail the test.

The Twelve Zodiac Signs

As you read through these signs, an important thing to remember is it's not necessarily that a certain sign is this way or that way, as many of the characteristics overlap, even with unrelated signs. Pay attention to the how or why a certain sign is this way. For example, many signs are attributed as "intellectual," but they're typically intellectual in a different way. The reasoning behind the attribute is different. I've included many aspects here to try to help get a better grasp of what each sign is, and also to help you see it better in yourself and others.

Also keep in mind that for those whose birthday falls right on the border or cusp between two signs, they could potentially go either way. I doubt that we quite have this down to an exact science, so keep that in mind as you read through these. This is all mostly people's best guess on what the signs actually are. It's hard to know at a fundamental "programming-based" level what these actually are – we just see the patterns in how they are manifested.

Appendix

Aires ♈

Generic Sign Dates: March 21st thru April 19th
Element: Fire
Modality: Cardinal
Common Symbol(s):   Ram

General Description:

    As a fire sign, Aries are known for their passionate nature. They approach everything in life with intensity and dedication. Whether it's their career, relationships, or hobbies, Aries give their all and expect the same level of commitment from others. This can sometimes make them appear impatient and impulsive, as they are always ready to move on to the next exciting thing, which comes from the cardinal modality (initiation) mixed with the fire element.

    One of the most prominent traits of an Aries is their incredible energy and enthusiasm. They possess an unstoppable drive and a zest for life that can be contagious to those around them. Aries individuals are always on the go, seeking new adventures and challenges. They dive headfirst into any opportunity that comes their way, displaying a great deal of courage and fearlessness.

    Aries individuals are natural-born leaders who thrive in positions of power and authority. They possess strong leadership qualities and excel in situations where they can take charge and make decisions. Aries individuals have a natural ability to inspire and motivate others, making them great team leaders. However, their assertiveness can sometimes come across as overly domineering or aggressive, often leaving little room for compromise.

    Another characteristic that defines Aries is their independent and self-reliant nature. They have a strong sense of individuality and rarely rely on others for support or guidance. Aries prefer to carve their own path and make their own decisions, which often leads them to be trailblazers in various aspects of life.

    While Aries are known for their energetic and assertive nature, they can also display a fiercely competitive streak. They have a strong desire to be the best and will stop at nothing to achieve their goals. Aries thrive in competitive environments and excel in situations where they can showcase their skills and abilities. However, this competitiveness can sometimes lead to conflicts and confrontations, as Aries individuals can become easily frustrated when faced with obstacles.

    Underneath their strong and confident exterior, Aries individuals also possess a deeply affectionate and loyal nature. They form strong emotional bonds with those they care about and are always ready to lend a helping hand. Aries are fiercely protective of their loved ones and will do anything to ensure their happiness and well-being.

    However, Aries individuals also have a tendency to be hot-headed and quick-tempered. Their fiery nature can sometimes lead to impulsive actions and outbursts of anger.

It is important for Aries to learn how to channel their energy in a positive way and control their temper to maintain harmonious relationships.

Overall, Aries individuals bring a sense of energy and excitement to everything they do and inspire those around them to reach their full potential.

Typical Positive Traits:

Aries individuals have a reputation for being blunt and straightforward. They value honesty and transparency, always speaking their mind without sugar-coating their thoughts or intentions. Their direct communication style allows for open and authentic interactions. They are not afraid to voice their opinions or stand up for what they believe in. Their assertiveness allows them to initiate action and take risks, making them natural-born leaders.

Aries are also fearless and confident, always willing to take the lead and embrace challenges. These individuals are known for their high levels of passion and enthusiasm. They approach life with zeal and excitement, infusing energy into their relationships and endeavors. Aries individuals have an innate optimism, always seeing the glass as half full. They have an unwavering belief in their abilities and constantly strive to achieve their goals. This unabated drive and positive outlook can inspire others around them, bring a sense of optimism to any situation, and encourages others to follow their lead.

Aries individuals value their independence. They are capable of making quick decisions and taking charge of their own lives without relying heavily on others. Their resilient nature allows them to navigate challenges with confidence and determination. Aries thrives on excitement and loves to explore new experiences. This adventurous spirit makes them engaging and seeks to create memorable experiences for themselves and their loved ones. They are fiercely loyal to the people they care about. They are protective of their loved ones and will go to great lengths to ensure their safety and happiness. Their loyalty forms the foundation of trust in their relationships, making them reliable and steadfast partners.

Appendix

Common Potential Negative Traits:

Aries individuals are known for their impulsive nature and tendency to act quickly without considering the consequences. They can be impatient and prefer immediate results, which can lead to hasty decisions or impulsive actions that they may later regret. This impatience can carry over into communication, sometimes making it difficult to actively listen to others. They may be quick to interrupt or jump to conclusions, which can lead to misunderstandings and difficulties in effective communication.

Aries have a strong and fiery energy which can make them prone to anger and quick-tempered reactions. They may display an aggressive or confrontational attitude when faced with challenges or conflicts, which can be overwhelming for those around them.

They can also sometimes be overly focused on their own needs and desires, which can make them appear selfish or inconsiderate of others. They may prioritize their own goals and ambitions above everything else, leading to potential conflicts or misunderstandings in relationships.

Typical Relationships:

Aries individuals are passionate and intense when it comes to love. They are known for their fiery and adventurous nature, always seeking excitement and novelty in their relationships.

They are fiercely loyal and protective of their partners. They are known for their intense devotion and willingness to fight for their loved ones. However, they may also have a tendency to become possessive or jealous, due to their strong need for control and dominance.

They value their personal freedom and may sometimes struggle with compromise in relationships. They have a strong desire for individuality and can be quite stubborn when it comes to their own needs and desires.

Aries people are bold, confident, and direct in expressing their feelings. Because of this, communication can sometimes be a challenge for Aires in relationships. They can be direct and straightforward, which can come across as blunt or insensitive to their partners. It is important for them to learn to temper their assertiveness and consider their partner's feelings.

Overall, Aires are passionate, adventurous, and fiercely loyal partners. They bring a lot of energy and excitement into relationships and thrive on challenges. However, it's important for them to balance their independence and need for control with a willingness to compromise and communicate effectively with their partner.

Taurus ♉

Generic Sign Dates:	April 20th thru May 20th
Element:	Earth
Modality:	Fixed
Common Symbol(s):	Bull

General Description:

Taureans are known for their strong-willed and reliable nature. One of the most notable traits of a Taurus individual is their unwavering determination, which is a common theme in fixed signs. Once they set their sights on a goal, they will go to great lengths to achieve it. This sense of purpose and persistence makes them excellent at completing tasks and following through with commitments. Taurus individuals possess an incredible work ethic, ensuring that they can handle even the most challenging projects with composure and efficiency. The combination of earth (practicality), and fixed (perseverance), creates a sign that is very good at persisting in getting things done.

Taureans are also known for their practical and down-to-earth nature. They have a deep appreciation for the physical world and value stability and security. As a result, they tend to make decisions based on logic and practicality rather than emotions. This grounded approach to life often leads them to excel in careers related to finance, real estate, and entrepreneurship.

Another defining trait of a Taurus is their strong sense of loyalty. Once they establish connections with other people, be it friends, family, or partners, they are fiercely devoted and will stand by their loved ones through thick and thin. Taureans value trust and reliability, and they expect the same level of commitment in return. They make for supportive and dependable friends, always willing to lend a helping hand or offer a listening ear.

Taureans are also known for their love of beauty and sensory pleasures, material things. They have a deep appreciation for art, music, and all things visually pleasing. Many Taureans have a talent for creating or appreciating art forms such as painting, sculpting, or music. They also have a keen eye for fashion and design, often showcasing their impeccable sense of style.

However, this love for luxury and material pleasures can sometimes result in a tendency to be possessive and stubborn. While Taureans are known for their stability and reliability, they can become quite resistant to change. Their fixed nature often makes it challenging for them to embrace new ideas or adapt to unfamiliar situations. This can lead to occasional clashes with others, especially those who have a more flexible approach to life.

Despite their sometimes stubborn demeanor, Taureans are generally warm-hearted and compassionate individuals. They possess a nurturing side that makes them not only great caretakers but also excellent listeners. Many Taureans have a calming presence, and they often find themselves playing the role of the peacemaker in conflicts. They are also known to have a great sense of humor, bringing laughter and joy into the lives of those around them.

Whether it's in their professional pursuits or personal relationships, Taureans tackle life with unwavering commitment and an appreciation for the sensual pleasures that make existence worthwhile.

Typical Positive Traits:

Taurus individuals are known for their incredible patience and determination. They have the ability to stay focused and work steadily towards their goals, no matter how long it takes. Their perseverance allows them to overcome obstacles and achieve success. When it comes to getting things done, they are extremely reliable and responsible. They take their commitments seriously and can always be counted on to fulfill their obligations.

Taurus people are highly devoted and loyal to the people they care about. Once they commit to a relationship or friendship, they remain steadfast and supportive. Their loyalty creates a sense of security and trust in their relationships, whether it be partners, friends, or employees.

They have a practical approach to life. They make decisions based on practicality and long-term stability rather than impulsiveness. Their sensible nature helps them make wise choices and create a stable foundation in various aspects of life.

Taurus individuals have a deep appreciation for beauty and comfort. They often have an eye for aesthetics and enjoy creating a harmonious and cozy environment. They find joy in indulging their senses and surround themselves with things that bring them pleasure.

Common Potential Negative Traits:

Taurus individuals have a strong tendency to be stubborn, resisting change or new ideas potentially even if they're necessary or beneficial. They prefer stability and familiar routines, and they may have difficulty adapting to unexpected or unfamiliar situations.

Taurus individuals can be possessive, especially when it comes to their relationships and material possessions. They have a strong attachment to people and things they value, and they may struggle with sharing or letting go.

Taurus individuals have a penchant for the finer things in life. While it's not inherently negative, this can sometimes lead to materialistic tendencies, where they prioritize possessions and material wealth over other aspects of life. This can also manifest as over-indulgence such as overeating, overspending, or other forms of excess. They may struggle with moderation and self-discipline in certain areas of their life.

Typical Relationships:

Taurus individuals are known for their loyalty, reliability, and commitment in relationships. They value the emotional and physical connection in a relationship. Taurus individuals are patient and take time to build trust and a strong foundation with their partner. They enjoy the comforts and security of a stable and harmonious relationship, and are adverse to sudden changes. Taurus individuals tend to be grounded and practical, making them dependable partners. They are also sensuous and appreciate the finer things in life, often enjoying creating a comfortable and nurturing environment for their loved ones. Taureans are highly affectionate and attentive to their partners' needs, making them romantic and reliable companions.

However, they can also be possessive or stubborn at times, as they value their relationships and can be protective of their loved ones. Overall, Taurus individuals make devoted and steadfast partners.

Appendix

Gemini ♊

Generic Sign Dates: May 21st thru June 20th
Element: Air
Modality: Mutable
Common Symbol(s): Twins

General Description:

Known for their dual nature, Geminis have a multifaceted personality that sets them apart from other signs. The mixing of air (idea-oriented) and mutable (changing, adaptability) leads them to being able to see a wide view of things, giving rise to the common dual-nature tag (or more accurately, multi-faceted nature)

One of the defining characteristics of Gemini is their remarkable communication skills. Geminis are natural conversationalists who excel at expressing themselves verbally. They possess a sharp wit and intelligence that allows them to engage in stimulating and thought-provoking discussions. Their ability to adapt to different environments and social situations allows them to connect with people from various walks of life. Geminis have a natural charm and charisma, making them captivating individuals to interact with.

Another prominent trait of Geminis is their curiosity and thirst for knowledge. They have a deep desire to explore different subjects and broaden their horizons. Geminis are highly intellectual and love to engage in intellectual debates and discussions. They possess a quick and agile mind that enables them to grasp concepts rapidly. This thirst for knowledge often makes them lifelong learners, constantly seeking new ideas, experiences, and insights.

Geminis are known for their versatility and adaptability. They have an innate ability to easily switch between different roles and tasks, making them highly versatile individuals. This adaptability allows them to thrive in various environments and excel in different professions. Geminis can handle multitasking exceptionally well, effortlessly juggling multiple projects simultaneously. Their multitasking skills enable them to excel in careers that require quick thinking, adaptability, and versatility, such as journalism, teaching, sales, and public relations.

Though Geminis are often seen as extroverted and social beings, they also possess an introspective and contemplative side. Geminis have a deep need for solitude and introspection to make sense of their thoughts and emotions. This duality within their personality is what gives them a unique perspective on life. Geminis can be both outgoing and sociable, enjoying the company of others, but also value their alone time to recharge and reflect.

One of the challenges Geminis face is their tendency to be indecisive. With their dual nature, Geminis often find themselves torn between different options and struggle to commit to decisions. This can sometimes lead to a flip-flopping and unpredictable nature, making it difficult for others to anticipate their actions. However, this indecisiveness can also be seen as a reflection of their open-mindedness and willingness to consider multiple perspectives before settling on a course of action.

In conclusion, Geminis possess a vibrant and dynamic personality. Their exceptional communication skills, intellectual curiosity, versatility, and adaptability make them fascinating individuals to be around. While they may struggle with indecisiveness at times, their duality and open-mindedness bring a unique perspective to life. Whether engaging in intellectual discussions or pursuing diverse career paths, Geminis have the ability to thrive and make a positive impact on the world around them.

Typical Positive Traits:

Gemini individuals are known for their sharp intellect and insatiable curiosity. They enjoy learning and exploring a wide range of subjects and are incredibly adaptable and versatile in their interests, skills, and personalities. They can easily adjust their plans and ideas to accommodate new circumstances, making them resilient and able to navigate various challenges. They are adept at navigating different social settings and excel in various areas of life, thanks to their ability to quickly grasp new concepts and adapt to different situations.

Geminis have a natural flair for communication. They are gifted with words and can articulate their thoughts and ideas with ease. This skill helps them connect with others, express themselves effectively, and engage in meaningful conversations. Geminis are sociable beings who enjoy being around people. They have a friendly and approachable demeanor, making them easily likable. Geminis thrive in social settings and are adept at building and maintaining relationships.

Gemini individuals possess a sharp wit and a great sense of humor. They have a knack for finding the humor in everyday situations and can effortlessly lighten the mood with their clever jokes and playful banter.

Common Potential Negative Traits:

Gemini individuals are known for their dual nature, which can lead to inconsistency and indecisiveness. They often have multiple interests, ideas, and perspectives, making it challenging for them to settle on one path or make firm decisions. This can create confusion and frustration for both themselves and those around them. Geminis may sometimes struggle with depth and staying committed. They can be easily distracted, frequently jumping from one topic or relationship to another without fully exploring or investing in them. This can give the impression of superficiality or a lack of genuine depth in their interactions and commitments.

Gemini individuals thrive on mental stimulation and excitement. When they feel confined or bored, they may become restless and seek constant change and novelty. This can manifest as a need for constant stimulation or a tendency to become easily bored with routines and commitments. Similarly, their sharp intellect and active minds can sometimes lead them to overthink and create anxiety. Their dual nature may also lead to internal conflicts and contradictory thoughts, which can increase their levels of stress and worry.

Typical Relationships:

Gemini individuals are known for their lively and adaptable nature in relationships. They are highly social and enjoy engaging in intellectually stimulating conversations with their partner. They are skilled communicators and can express their thoughts and feelings articulately. Gemini individuals are curious and constantly seek new experiences, which can bring excitement and a sense of adventure to their relationships. They value mental connection and need a partner who shares their thirst for knowledge and adventure.

Gemini individuals are playful, expressive, and communicative in love. They enjoy mental stimulation, and their quick wit and charming personality can make them captivating partners. However, they may also have a tendency to be indecisive or easily bored, so maintaining their interest and keeping the relationship dynamic is important. Geminis can be inconsistent in their affections and may struggle with commitment, as their desires and interests may change rapidly. However, when deeply in love, they are loyal and devoted partners.

Cancer ♋

Generic Sign Dates: June 21st thru July 22nd
Element: Water
Modality: Cardinal
Common Symbol(s): Crab

General Description:

Cancer is Cardinal (initiation) mixed with Water (emotion). When you mix emotional sensitivity with initiation, what you typically get is someone who will initiate things to bring about good emotional outcomes. Because of this, they are known for their emotional depth, empathy, and nurturing nature.

One of the key traits of a Cancer is their deep emotional sensitivity. They are highly attuned to their own emotions as well as the emotions of those around them. Cancers have a natural ability to empathize with others, making them great listeners and supportive friends. They tend to connect with people on a deeper level and are often seen as the "emotional anchor" within their circle of friends and family.

Another prominent characteristic of Cancer is their natural inclination towards protectiveness. Just like the Crab, Cancers have a strong urge to safeguard their loved ones. They are fiercely loyal and dedicated individuals who will go to great lengths to ensure the well-being and happiness of their family and close friends. This protective nature extends to their own emotions as well, as they tend to guard their vulnerable side from potential harm.

Cancer individuals are known for their intuitive nature. They possess a strong gut instinct and can often accurately sense the underlying currents in a situation or the emotions of the people they interact with. This intuitive ability allows them to provide valuable insights and guidance, making them reliable advisors. They are also known for their vivid imagination and creative streak, often expressing themselves through various artistic or imaginative outlets.

Cancers have a natural inclination towards nurturing and caregiving. They find joy and fulfillment in taking care of others and creating a nurturing environment. Whether it is their family, friends, or even pets, Cancers have an instinctive desire to provide love, support, and comfort to those in need. They are seen as the dependable shoulders to lean on during tough times, and their compassionate nature makes them excellent caregivers and healers.

Home and family hold great importance in the life of a Cancer. They cherish the sense of security and comfort that their home provides and often invest their time and efforts in creating a cozy and welcoming space. Cancerians are deeply rooted in their family connections and prioritize spending quality time with their loved ones. They value traditions and family bonds, and find solace in the familiarity of their roots.

Despite their gentle and nurturing nature, Cancerians are known to possess a resilient and tenacious spirit. When faced with challenges or obstacles, they have the ability to gather their inner strength and face them head-on. Their determination and perseverance help them overcome adversity, making them highly resilient individuals who can bounce back from setbacks.

Cancer is inclined towards introspection and self-reflection. They have a natural curiosity about the world around them and enjoy delving deep into their own thoughts and emotions. This introspective nature enables them to gain a deeper understanding of themselves and others, leading to personal growth and self-awareness.

In professional settings, Cancer excels in professions that allow them to utilize their nurturing and empathetic skills. They are often drawn to careers in healthcare, counseling, teaching, and social work, where they can make a positive impact in people's lives.

In summary, Cancers are typically characterized by emotional sensitivity, protectiveness, intuition, nurturing tendencies, and resilience. Their dedication to their loved ones, strong intuition, and compassionate nature make them invaluable friends and confidants.

Typical Positive Traits:

Cancer individuals possess a heightened intuitive sense and acute sensitivity. They have an innate understanding of emotions and can easily pick up on the subtlest changes in mood or behavior. This sensitivity allows them to provide emotional support and create a safe space for open communication. This results in individuals that are renowned for their exceptional empathy and compassion.

Cancers are incredibly loyal and devoted in their relationships. Once they form a bond with someone, they remain steadfastly committed and dedicated. Cancers have a natural instinct to nurture and protect their loved ones, often going above and beyond to ensure their comfort and security. Whether it's offering a listening ear, providing practical assistance, or offering emotional guidance, Cancers are known for their unwavering supportiveness and willingness to lend a helping hand.

They are often blessed with a rich imagination and incredible creativity. Cancers can bring forth unique and innovative ideas, whether it's in artistic pursuits or problem-solving. Their imaginative nature adds a touch of magic and depth to their relationships, making them great storytellers and dreamers.

Common Potential Negative Traits:

Cancer individuals can sometimes be overly emotional and sensitive, which can lead to mood swings and a tendency to take things personally. They can easily become overwhelmed by their own emotions or the emotions of others. When faced with stress or conflict, Cancer individuals have a tendency to withdraw and retreat into their protective shell. While this may be a coping mechanism to protect themselves from emotional harm, it can also hinder effective communication and problem-solving in relationships, resulting in a lack of objectivity and difficulties in navigating conflicts rationally. Learning to find a balance between self-care and actively engaging in resolving issues is important for personal and relational growth.

Cancers tend to avoid direct confrontation and may resort to passive-aggressive behavior or manipulation to express their needs or discontent. They may expect their loved ones to understand their unspoken feelings, which can create misunderstandings and unresolved issues within relationships. Learning to express their thoughts and emotions directly and assertively can help mitigate this negative trait.

Cancer individuals value emotional security and attachment, which can sometimes lead to clingy behavior. They may have a fear of abandonment, causing them to seek constant reassurance and closeness in their relationships. This clinginess can occasionally suffocate their partners or lead to a dependency that hinders personal growth and independence.

Typical Relationships:

Cancer individuals are known for their nurturing and empathetic nature in relationships. They are highly sensitive and deeply connected to their emotions and the emotions of others. Cancer individuals value emotional intimacy and seek deep connections with their partner. They are caring, supportive, and devoted.

Cancer individuals seek a sense of security and stability in love. They value trust and loyalty, and are committed and devoted partners. Cancers are highly intuitive, empathetic, and caring, often putting their loved ones' needs before their own. They have a nurturing nature and enjoy creating a loving and nurturing home environment. They can be protective of their loved ones and may have a tendency to be cautious when it comes to opening up in relationships. Overall, Cancer individuals are loving, loyal, and deeply committed to their partners.

Appendix

Leo ♌

Generic Sign Dates:	July 23rd thru August 22nd
Element:	Fire
Modality:	Fixed
Common Symbol(s):	Lion

General Description:

Known for their charismatic and confident nature, Leos possess a magnetic personality that captivates those around them. Leos are natural-born leaders, and have a radiant energy and their desire to shine in all aspects of life. Leo is the mixing of fire (action-oriented) and fixed (perseverance, narrowed focus, or in-the-now), further fueling their passionate and enthusiastic nature.

One of the key traits of the Leo personality is their self-confidence. Leos have a strong belief in themselves and their abilities, which often translates into success in their endeavors. They have a natural flair for the dramatic and love to be in the spotlight. They are not afraid to take risks and are often seen as daring individuals who are willing to pursue their dreams wholeheartedly.

Another prominent trait of Leos is their generosity and warmth. They have big hearts and are known for their incredible capacity to love and care for others. Leos make loyal and dependable friends who will always be there to support their loved ones. They have a natural talent for making people feel special and appreciated, often going out of their way to ensure the happiness and well-being of those around them.

Leos are natural leaders and have a commanding presence. They easily take charge of situations and inspire those around them to be their best selves. They possess excellent leadership qualities such as confidence, decisiveness, and the ability to motivate others. Leos thrive in positions of authority and are often drawn to careers where they can showcase their leadership skills.

Despite their strong personalities, Leos also have a sensitive side. They can be deeply affected by criticism or rejection, as they place great value on their self-worth. They crave validation and appreciate compliments. However, when they receive negative feedback, they can become defensive or even revert to seeking reassurance from others. It is important for Leos to learn to balance their need for validation with self-assurance and trust in their own abilities.

Leos have a natural creative streak and are often drawn to artistic pursuits. They have a flair for the dramatic and enjoy expressing themselves through various forms of art such as acting, writing, painting, or performing. Their creative endeavors allow them to channel their passion and bring their unique perspective to the world.

In conclusion, Leos possess a captivating and confident personality that draws others towards them. With their natural leadership abilities, warmth, and generosity, they leave a lasting impact on those they encounter. Their creative talents and passion for life make them stand out, and their loyalty ensures that they build strong and lasting relationships.

Typical Positive Traits:

Leos exude confidence and charisma. They have a magnetic personality that attracts others towards them. They are comfortable in their own skin and have a natural ability to shine and captivate the attention of those around them. Because of this, they have a natural inclination towards leadership. They have a strong sense of self-confidence and take charge of situations with authority. They inspire others and are often looked up to for guidance and direction.

Leos have a natural flair for creativity and self-expression. They possess a strong sense of artistic ability and are often drawn to fields such as acting, music, or visual arts. They have a captivating presence and know how to showcase their talents.

Leos are also known for their warm-hearted and generous nature. They are always willing to lend a helping hand and support those around them. They have a big heart and genuinely care about the well-being of others. Leos are fiercely loyal to their loved ones. They value their relationships deeply and are willing to go to great lengths to protect and defend those they care about. They are dependable and trustworthy friends and partners.

Common Potential Negative Traits:

Leo individuals can sometimes exhibit a tendency to be overly confident and self-centered. They may have a high opinion of themselves and seek constant attention, affirmation, and admiration from others. This need for external validation can make them susceptible to seeking attention and approval at all costs, sometimes resorting to attention-seeking behaviors that may come across as self-centered or egotistical. This can lead to a sense of superiority and an inflated ego, making it difficult for them to consider the perspectives and needs of others.

Leos tend to be very strong-willed and can be stubborn in their beliefs and opinions. They may find it challenging to consider alternative viewpoints or change their stance even in the face of new evidence. This can lead to conflicts and difficulties in finding compromises in relationships or decision-making processes.

Leos have a strong desire for control and may exhibit domineering behavior. They can be assertive to the point of being bossy, expecting others to follow their lead and may become frustrated or impatient when things don't go their way. This can lead to strained relationships and a lack of collaboration in group settings.

Typical Relationships:

Leos are loyal, confidant, and passionate partners, and are known for their bold and charismatic nature in relationships. They love being in the spotlight and enjoy bringing excitement and passion into their partnerships. Leo individuals have a strong sense of self and often take on a leadership role in their relationships.

Leos are romantics at heart. They enjoy the thrill of romance and love being the center of attention in their relationships. They love being in love and enjoy the grand gestures and excitement that come with it. Leo individuals are generous and affectionate partners, always willing to go above and beyond to make their loved ones feel special and appreciated. They thrive on compliments and admiration, and they tend to be very loyal and committed in their relationships. However, they also have a strong need for independence and freedom, so they appreciate a partner who respects their individuality and gives them space when needed. Overall, Leo individuals bring a lot of energy, warmth, and love to their romantic relationships.

Virgo ♍

Generic Sign Dates:	August 23rd thru September 22nd
Element:	Earth
Modality:	Mutable
Common Symbol(s):	Virgin

General Description:

Virgos are known for their practicality, analytical thinking, and attention to detail. This is the mixing of Earth (practicality, grounded nature, possibly materialism) with Mutable (adaptability, changing, diverse). The result is a person who is able to see the many aspects of things through a practical lens and act accordingly.

One of the key traits of a Virgo is their meticulous and methodical nature. They have a keen eye for detail and strive for perfection in all aspects of their life. Their analytical mindset allows them to break down complex problems into smaller, manageable tasks, making them exceptional problem solvers. Virgos are known to have a knack for organizing and planning, making them great planners and administrators.

Virgos are also known for their reliability and dependability. They take their commitments seriously and fulfill their responsibilities with utmost dedication. Whether it's professional or personal matters, Virgos can be counted on to be the ones who get things done. They have a strong work ethic and thrive in roles that require precision, efficiency, and reliability.

Another defining trait of a Virgo is their practicality. They are down-to-earth individuals who prefer to focus on tangible and realistic goals. They value practicality over idealism and are driven by the desire to create tangible results. This practical mindset often translates into a strong sense of responsibility, as Virgos take their duties seriously and ensure everything is done to the best of their abilities.

Virgos possess a sharp intellect and an analytical mind. They have a love for knowledge and enjoy diving deep into research and learning new things. Their attention to detail and ability to see patterns make them excellent problem solvers and critical thinkers. They are often the ones who notice the small details that others might overlook.

While known for their practicality, Virgos also have a sensitive and compassionate side. They may come across as reserved or shy at first, but once you gain their trust, they are fiercely loyal and supportive. Virgos have a deep sense of empathy and genuinely care about the well-being of others. They will go out of their way to help those in need and provide a listening ear to anyone who needs it.

Virgo individuals can be perfectionists, with high standards for themselves as well as others. They are constantly striving for self-improvement and may get caught up in self-criticism. This can sometimes lead to them being overly critical of others as well. It is important for Virgos to learn to balance their drive for excellence with self-acceptance and understanding.

In terms of career choices, Virgos excel in roles that require attention to detail, analysis, and problem-solving. They make excellent researchers, accountants, analysts, doctors, writers, editors, and administrators. Their practical mindset, reliability, and strong work ethic make them valuable assets to any organization.

Overall, Virgos are practical, analytical, and conscientious individuals. They have a sharp intellect, a strong work ethic, and a caring nature. While their perfectionistic tendencies may require some self-reflection and balance, their attention to detail and reliability make them valuable teammates and partners.

Typical Positive Traits:

Virgo individuals have a remarkable attention to detail. They have a knack for noticing even the smallest discrepancies and errors in their surroundings or work. This meticulousness allows them to excel in tasks that require precision and accuracy. Virgos also excel in organization and efficiency. They have a strong need for order in their environment and can create structured systems to streamline tasks. Their ability to prioritize and manage their time effectively enables them to be highly productive.

Virgos have a natural inclination towards analytical thinking. They possess a logical and practical mindset, which helps them solve problems efficiently. They enjoy breaking down complex situations into more manageable components and finding practical solutions. They have a pragmatic approach to life, focusing on the tangible and factual aspects of situations and making decisions based on realism rather than idealism. This grounded mindset allows them to make rational choices that yield practical outcomes.

Virgos are known for their reliability and dependability. They take their commitments seriously and strive to fulfill them to the best of their abilities. They have a strong work ethic, willing to put in the extra effort required to achieve their goals. They take pride in their work and consistently strive for excellence. Whether it's a personal or professional obligation, they can be counted on to be punctual and responsible.

Common Potential Negative Traits:

Virgos have a tendency to be perfectionists, which can lead to excessive self-criticism and an unattainable pursuit of flawlessness. They might become overly focused on minor details and struggle to accept anything less than perfection. This perfectionistic mindset can create stress and unrealistic expectations for themselves and others. They might find themselves pointing out flaws and shortcomings, sometimes without realizing how their words or actions can impact others. This critical nature can strain relationships and hinder their ability to appreciate the positive aspects of a situation.

Virgos are known for their analytical minds, but this can sometimes lead to overthinking and excessive worrying. They have a tendency to analyze situations and potential outcomes extensively, which can result in anxiety and indecisiveness. Virgos might find it challenging to let go of their worry and trust in the process.

Virgos have a strong desire for control and often feel that they are the most capable of completing tasks to their desired standards. As a result, they might struggle with delegating tasks or relying on others, as they fear that things will not be done well enough. This can lead to burnout and an unnecessary burden on themselves.

Typical Relationships:
Virgo individuals are known for their practicality, reliability, and attention to detail in relationships. They are highly analytical and often strive for perfection in their partnerships. However, their perfectionistic tendencies can also make them expect high standards from their partners, which may lead to frustration if their expectations are not met. It is important for Virgos to learn to be more forgiving and understanding in relationships.

Virgo individuals approach love with a practical and analytical mindset. They value stability, loyalty, and commitment in their relationships. They have a tendency to overthink and can be reserved in expressing their emotions, but once they feel secure, they show deep love and dedication. Virgos also have a strong desire for mutual growth and intellectual connection in their romantic relationships.

Virgo individuals are loyal, committed, and take their commitments seriously. They are attentive and observant, often noticing and appreciating the small things that others may overlook. They are thoughtful and strive to make their loved ones feel supported and cared for. Virgo individuals value loyalty, trust, open communication, and are willing to work hard to maintain a harmonious and balanced relationship.

Appendix

Libra ♎

Generic Sign Dates:	September 23rd thru October 22nd
Element:	Air
Modality:	Cardinal
Common Symbol(s):	Set of Balancing Scales

General Description:

Libras are known for their harmonious and diplomatic nature. They strive for balance, justice, and peace in all aspects of their lives. This sign is the mixing of "Air" (ideas, logic, communication) with "Cardinal" (initiation). The mixing of this results in looking at ideas and the ideal from many different angles and trying to find balance in all of these.

One of the prominent traits of a Libra is their strong sense of fairness and justice. They have an innate ability to see all sides of a situation, making them excellent mediators and problem solvers. Librans are known for their tactful and diplomatic approach, always seeking to find a middle ground and promote harmony in their relationships.

Libras are natural peacekeepers who dislike conflict and confrontation. They have an aversion to disharmony and will go to great lengths to maintain a peaceful and harmonious environment. They have excellent communication skills and can effectively express their thoughts and opinions in a calm and composed manner.

Another key trait of Libras is their love for beauty and aesthetics. Librans are often drawn to art, fashion, and design. They have a keen eye for aesthetics and appreciate the finer things in life. Libras have a natural ability to create a visually pleasing and balanced atmosphere around them.

Libras also have a strong sense of social justice and equality. They champion causes and fight for the rights of the oppressed. They believe in fairness and equality for all and are often found advocating for justice on various fronts. Libras have a strong moral compass and strive to do what is right.

One of the challenges that Libras may face is their indecisiveness. Their desire for balance and harmonious relationships can sometimes lead to difficulty in making choices. They can get caught up in weighing every option, seeking the perfect solution. This can cause delays and indecisiveness, which can be frustrating for both themselves and others.

Career-wise, Libras excel in professions that require diplomacy, negotiation, and a keen eye for aesthetics. They make great mediators, lawyers, diplomats, and counselors. Their ability to see various perspectives and find common ground makes them excellent team players and leaders.

Libras are also known for their good taste and artistic abilities. Many Libras have successful careers in fields such as fashion, interior design, graphic design, or any creative industry where their eye for aesthetics can shine.

Overall, Libras are graceful, diplomatic, and fair-minded individuals. They strive for balance, harmony, and justice in all aspects of their lives. With their natural charm, good communication skills, and diplomatic approach, they are often admired and respected by others

Typical Positive Traits:
Libras are known for their diplomacy and ability to mediate conflicts. They have a natural talent for finding common ground and fostering harmony in relationships and group settings. Their ability to see multiple perspectives helps them navigate complex situations with grace and tact. Libras have a strong sense of justice and fairness, striving to make decisions that are equitable and considerate of all parties involved. Their unbiased approach in conflicts or decision-making processes can be highly valued and trusted by others.

Libras possess an undeniable charm and charisma that draws people to them. They have a natural ability to engage in conversation, make others feel comfortable, and create a positive and enjoyable social atmosphere. Their sociability and ability to get along with different personality types make them great connectors and influencers.

Libras thrive in collaborative environments and value teamwork. They are skilled at bringing people together towards a common goal and creating a harmonious working dynamic. Their cooperative nature and willingness to compromise make them excellent team players who can foster a sense of unity and cohesion among group members.

Libras have a deep appreciation for beauty, both in art and in their surroundings. They have a keen eye for aesthetics and often display artistic talents themselves. Their appreciation for art, design, and symmetry can inspire them to create visually appealing environments and experiences.

Common Potential Negative Traits:
Libras can struggle with making decisions, especially when faced with multiple options or conflicting perspectives. They tend to weigh the pros and cons excessively, fearing making the wrong choice. This indecisiveness can lead to delays or missed opportunities.

Libras often avoid confrontations and conflicts, preferring to maintain peace and harmony in their relationships. While this trait is generally positive, it can lead to repressed anger and pent-up emotions if issues are not addressed and resolved. Libras have a strong desire for harmony which can lead them to become people-pleasers, putting the needs and desires of others ahead of their own. This can lead to feelings of resentment or being taken advantage of, as their own needs are often ignored or suppressed to maintain peace.

Libras have a natural attraction to beauty and aesthetics, which can sometimes make them appear superficial. They may prioritize appearance or material possessions over substance or deeper connections, causing them to be perceived as shallow.

Typical Relationships:
Libra individuals are known for their charm, diplomacy, and desire for harmony in relationships. They value fairness and strive to create a balanced and harmonious dynamic with their partner. Libra individuals are romantic and enjoy the pleasures of love, often seeking a deep emotional connection in their relationships. They are excellent listeners and communicators and are skilled at finding compromises and resolving conflicts in a peaceful manner. Libras also appreciate beauty, elegance, and the finer things in life, and they often strive to create a beautiful and aesthetically pleasing environment for their relationship.

Appendix

Libras are also known for their loyalty and commitment. They make devoted and attentive partners, always striving to create a peaceful and loving bond.

Scorpio ♏

Generic Sign Dates: October 23rd thru November 21st
Element: Water
Modality: Fixed
Common Symbol(s): Scorpion, Snake, Eagle, Phoenix

General Description:

Scorpio results from the mixing of water (emotion) and fixed (perseverance, steadfast, narrow focus, in-the-now). The result is a person who seeks emotional stability, often through keeping emotions hidden. Known for their deep emotions and powerful presence, Scorpios often leave a lasting impression on those they meet.

One of the defining traits of Scorpios is their determination and ambition. Once they set their sights on a goal, they will stop at nothing to achieve it. Their competitive nature drives them to excel in whatever they do. Scorpios possess a relentless drive and never settle for mediocrity. Whether it's in their personal or professional life, they strive for greatness.

Scorpios are highly intuitive individuals. They possess an uncanny ability to read people and situations accurately. This makes them excellent judges of character and helps them navigate through life's challenges with ease. This natural insight allows them to see beyond the surface and understand the underlying motives and emotions of those around them.

Another prominent trait of Scorpios is their intense passion. They invest their heart and soul into everything they do, including relationships. Once committed, Scorpios are fiercely loyal and protective of their loved ones. They value honesty and expect the same level of commitment in return. However, crossing a Scorpio's loyalty can result in a powerful backlash, as they do not take betrayal lightly.

Scorpios are known for their mysterious nature. They tend to be secretive and guarded, preferring to keep their thoughts and emotions to themselves. This enigmatic quality often makes them intriguing to others, as they constantly leave an air of mystery around them. Scorpios are careful about who they let into their inner circle, and trust is earned through time and consistency.

Despite their reputation for being intense, Scorpios possess a remarkable sense of humor. They often have a dark and sarcastic wit that can catch people off guard. Their humor is both intelligent and quick, leaving others amused and entertained. This playful side of the Scorpio personality is often hidden beneath their serious exterior.

Scorpios also have a strong, magnetic presence that draws people towards them. Whether in a social gathering or in the workplace, they effortlessly command attention and respect. Their charisma and determination make them natural leaders. However, Scorpios can sometimes come off as intimidating due to their strong personalities.

In conclusion, Scorpios possess a unique combination of traits that make them stand out from the crowd. Their determination, intuition, passion, and magnetic presence make them natural leaders and intriguing companions. While they can be intense and secretive, beneath their complex exterior lies a witty and playful personality. Scorpios approach life with unmatched intensity, leaving a lasting impression on everyone they encounter.

Typical Positive Traits:

Scorpios are known for their deep passion and intensity in every aspect of their lives. Whether it's their relationships, career, or hobbies, Scorpios dedicate themselves wholeheartedly. This passion drives them to pursue their goals with unwavering determination, making them incredibly focused and dedicated individuals. Because of this, Scorpios have an innate ability to bounce back from setbacks and challenges. They have a remarkable inner strength and determination that allows them to rise above difficult circumstances. They are not easily discouraged and can handle adversity with grace and poise, making them highly resilient individuals.

Scorpios have a strong sense of intuition. They are deeply attuned to their surroundings and have a keen ability to pick up on the emotions and underlying motivations of others. This intuition helps them navigate complex social situations and allows them to understand others on a deep level.

Scorpios have a remarkable ability to be resourceful in any situation. They possess strong problem-solving skills and can find creative solutions to challenging problems. Their sharp perception allows them to see things from different angles, enabling them to find the best course of action, even in difficult circumstances.

Scorpios are fiercely loyal to those they care about. Once they form a deep connection or bond, they will fiercely defend and protect their loved ones. Scorpios are known to go to great lengths to support and safeguard the people they cherish, making them reliable and trustworthy allies.

Common Potential Negative Traits:

Scorpios have a tendency to feel intense jealousy and possessiveness. This stems from their desire for control and their fear of being betrayed or abandoned. They can become possessive of their loved ones, sometimes leading to controlling behaviors and a lack of trust. Scorpios also have a tendency to hold grudges and can be quite resentful. If they feel wronged or betrayed, they may find it challenging to let go of negative emotions and forgive. Their intense nature amplifies these negative feelings, creating lingering resentment and potentially damaging relationships.

Scorpios have a knack for manipulation. They possess a deep understanding of human psychology and can use this knowledge to their advantage. They may engage in manipulative tactics to achieve their goals or to protect themselves from perceived threats. This behavior can undermine trust and strain relationships.

Scorpios are known for being secretive and guarded about their personal lives and emotions. While they value their privacy and self-protection, this behavior may lead to a lack of transparency and hindrance in open communication. It can be challenging for others to truly understand a Scorpio's intentions and emotions, which can create misunderstandings and strain relationships.

Typical Relationships:
    Scorpio individuals are known for their intense and passionate nature in relationships. They are deeply loyal and committed to their partners, and they seek depth, authenticity, and intimacy in all aspects of their love life. Scorpios are highly perceptive and intuitive, often picking up on subtle cues and underlying emotions which allows them to understand their partner's needs and desires on a profound level. They value honesty and expect the same level of loyalty and dedication from their partners. Scorpios can be intense, possessive, and jealous at times, which stems from a desire to preserve the bond they have, but they also have a loving and protective nature. Overall, when a Scorpio falls in love, they do so with their whole heart and are willing to invest their energy and passion into building a lasting and transformative connection.

Appendix

Sagittarius ♐

Generic Sign Dates: November 22nd thru December 21st
Element: Fire
Modality: Mutable
Common Symbol(s): Archer, Centaur, Bow and Arrow, Centaur with Bow

General Description:

Sagittarius are known for their adventurous spirit, optimism, and love for freedom. This sign comes from the mixing of fire (action-oriented) and mutable (adaptability, changing, diverse). The result is a sign that is very much on-the-move from one thing to the next.

One of the prominent traits of a Sagittarius is their adventurous spirit. They have a strong desire to explore the world and experience new things. They are always seeking new adventures and are not afraid to take risks. Whether it's embarking on a spontaneous road trip or traveling to distant lands, Sagittarians have a passion for exploration that is hard to match.

Optimism is another key characteristic of a Sagittarius. They have a positive outlook on life and tend to see the best in people and situations. This innate positivity allows them to overcome challenges with ease and maintain a hopeful attitude. Their optimism often inspires those around them and helps create an uplifting atmosphere.

Independence is highly valued by Sagittarians. They have a strong need for freedom and dislike feeling tied down or restricted. This independent streak allows them to pursue their passions and interests without feeling constrained. Sagittarians thrive when they have the freedom to make their own choices and follow their own path.

Sagittarius individuals also possess an intellectual curiosity. They have a thirst for knowledge and enjoy exploring a wide range of topics. They are constantly seeking new information and are not afraid to ask questions. This curious nature often leads them to become lifelong learners, always expanding their knowledge and understanding of the world.

A Sagittarius has a natural talent for communication and is often the life of the party. They are charismatic and have a way with words that draws people towards them. They have a knack for storytelling and can captivate an audience with their entertaining tales. Their sense of humor is infectious, and their wit often leaves people laughing in their presence.

Sagittarians are known for their honesty and bluntness. They have no qualms about speaking their mind and value authenticity in their relationships. While their straightforward nature can sometimes be misunderstood, they appreciate open and honest communication. They believe in saying what needs to be said, even if it's not always what others want to hear.

An optimistic and enthusiastic outlook on life often leads Sagittarians to be quite lucky in many aspects. They tend to attract opportunities and good fortune, which can bring success in various areas of their lives. This good luck, combined with their proactive nature, opens many doors for them to achieve their goals.

Career-wise, Sagittarians thrive in professions that allow them to exercise their adventurous and curious nature. They excel in fields such as travel, journalism, teaching, and exploration. Their natural charisma and communication skills make them great motivational speakers, consultants, or salespeople. They are always on the lookout for roles that align with their values of freedom and personal growth.

In summary, Sagittarius individuals possess an adventurous spirit, optimism, and a love for freedom. They are natural explorers who crave knowledge and thrive on new experiences. Their optimism and charisma make them natural leaders and storytellers, while their honesty and independence make them valuable friends and partners. With their enthusiastic approach to life, Sagittarians bring a sense of joy and adventure to everything they do.

Typical Positive Traits:

Sagittarius are known for their love of adventure and exploration. They have a deep desire to expand their horizons and seek out new experiences. This trait makes them open-minded and willing to embrace change and new opportunities. They are often the ones to suggest spontaneous trips or try out new activities, as they thrive in the unknown and the thrill of the journey. Likewise, they are intellectually curious and have a thirst for knowledge. They are constantly seeking to expand their understanding of the world and engage in stimulating conversations and debates. They have a broad range of interests and are often well-informed about various subjects. This trait makes them engaging company and lifelong learners, always seeking new perspectives and insights.

Sagittarius individuals tend to have a positive outlook on life. They have an infectious enthusiasm that can uplift those around them. They possess a strong belief in the power of optimism and tend to approach challenges with a hopeful attitude. This optimism helps them to find silver linings even in difficult situations and maintain an overall sense of joy and excitement.

Sagittarius value their independence and freedom. They have a strong sense of self and march to the beat of their own drum. They are often drawn to activities and pursuits that allow them to maintain their autonomy and explore their personal interests. This independent nature gives them the courage to take risks and follow their passions without being overly influenced by societal expectations.

Sagittarius individuals are known for their honesty. They value straightforwardness and have a deep respect for truth and transparency, while at the same time disliking sugar-coating or dishonesty. They appreciate authentic connections and believe in expressing their thoughts and feelings openly.

Common Potential Negative Traits:

Their natural inclination towards freedom and adventure can sometimes make them feel restless or impatient when they are confined in a routine or stagnant situation. They may constantly seek new experiences and opportunities, making it challenging for them to settle or commit to long-term commitments.

Sagittarius individuals are prone to acting impulsively, driven by their desire for excitement and new experiences. While this can lead to spontaneous adventures, it can also result in making hasty decisions without fully considering the consequences. This impulsive behavior can sometimes lead to regret or difficulties in maintaining stability and consistency in various aspects of life.

Sagittarius are known for their straightforward and blunt communication style. While this can be refreshing and honest, it can also lead to unintentionally hurting others' feelings. Their directness and tendency to speak their mind without filtering their thoughts and emotions can sometimes come off as tactless or insensitive.

Typical Relationships:

Sagittarius individuals are known for their adventurous, enthusiastic, and independent nature in relationships. They value their freedom and seek partners who are open-minded and willing to explore new experiences together. Sagittarius individuals are optimistic, fun-loving, and can bring a sense of excitement and spontaneity to relationships.

Communication is important to Sagittarius, as they value intellectual stimulation and sharing ideas with their loved ones. They are open and honest with their feelings, and straightforward in their approach to love, making them trustworthy and reliable in relationships. They may struggle with commitment at times, as they need their space, and have a natural curiosity and desire for new experiences. However, when they do commit, they are loyal and devoted partners.

Capricorn ♑

Generic Sign Dates:	December 22nd thru January 19th
Element:	Earth
Modality:	Cardinal
Common Symbol(s):	Goat

General Description:

Capricorns are known for their ambitious nature, practicality, and discipline. This sign comes from the mixing of earth (practicality, groundedness, possibly materialism) and cardinal (initiation). The result is a person with a practical approach to life who keeps initiating. They climb higher one step, one initiative at a time, to achieve their goals.

One of the prominent traits of a Capricorn is their strong sense of responsibility. They take their commitments and goals seriously and are dedicated to achieving success in every aspect of their lives. Capricorns are highly organized and possess excellent planning skills, which make them effective leaders and managers. They have a natural ability to set goals, create strategies, and work diligently towards achieving them.

Another important trait of Capricorns is their practicality. They have a realistic outlook on life and prefer to make decisions based on logic and evidence rather than on emotions or intuition. Capricorns have a knack for assessing situations and coming up with practical solutions. This pragmatism helps them navigate challenges and find success in various endeavors.

Capricorns are also known for their patience and persistence. They understand that success takes time and effort, and they are willing to put in the necessary work to achieve their goals. Capricorns can endure setbacks and obstacles with determination, using them as learning experiences to grow stronger and wiser.

Ambition is another key characteristic of Capricorns. They have a strong desire to climb the ladder of success and achieve their ambitions. Capricorns are willing to work hard and make sacrifices in pursuit of their aspirations. They set high standards for themselves and constantly strive for excellence in whatever they do.

Capricorns value tradition and stability. They appreciate established systems and methods that have proven to be effective and are cautious about embracing new ideas or risks without careful consideration. Capricorns prefer a structured and secure environment and aim to establish a solid foundation in their personal and professional lives.

Though Capricorns may come across as serious and reserved, they also have a dry sense of humor and a witty side. They enjoy intelligent conversations and appreciate others who share their wit and sarcasm. Capricorns have a practical and realistic approach to life, but they also have a playful and fun-loving side that emerges in the company of their close friends and loved ones.

Career-wise, Capricorns thrive in roles that require leadership, organization, and strategy. Their determination and hard work make them successful in various fields, including business, finance, law, and management. Capricorns have the ability to handle high-pressure situations with grace and are often seen as reliable and trustworthy professionals.

In conclusion, Capricorns are ambitious, practical, and dependable individuals who possess a strong sense of responsibility and a desire for success. Their dedication and commitment make them excellent leaders and reliable partners. With their pragmatic approach and hardworking nature, Capricorns effectively navigate challenges and achieve their goals, making them an asset in personal and professional spheres of life.

Typical Positive Traits:

Capricorns are known for their unwavering ambition and strong work ethic. They set high goals for themselves and are willing to put in the necessary effort and discipline to achieve them. They have a clear sense of direction and are often focused on long-term success. This drive propels them to work hard, overcome challenges, and reach their aspirations. They exhibit great patience and perseverance in pursuit of these goals. They understand that success often requires time and effort, and they are willing to put in the necessary work. Capricorns can stay focused and committed to their path, even when faced with obstacles or setbacks. Their ability to endure and remain patient contributes to their ultimate success.

Capricorns have a natural inclination towards structure and organization. They thrive in environments where there are clear rules and routines. They possess a strong sense of discipline, which helps them stay focused and motivated towards their goals. Capricorns excel at managing their time, resources, and tasks with efficiency, allowing them to handle demanding situations and meet deadlines successfully.

Capricorns have a practical and realistic approach to life. They possess excellent problem-solving skills and can analyze situations objectively. Their grounded nature enables them to make sound decisions based on logic and reason. Capricorns are not easily swayed by emotions, and they often consider the long-term consequences before taking action. This practicality allows them to navigate challenges with a level-headed and strategic mindset.

They take their responsibilities seriously and exhibit a strong sense of accountability. They are reliable and dependable individuals, often taking on leadership roles or positions of authority. Others trust them to get things done efficiently and effectively. Capricorns are known for their ability to handle tasks and commitments in a responsible manner, making them valuable assets in personal and professional settings.

Common Potential Negative Traits:

Capricorns can sometimes have a tendency towards pessimism and a negative outlook. This is often a result of their practical and cautious nature, where they focus on potential obstacles and challenges rather than possibilities and opportunities. It's important for Capricorns to find a balance between realistic assessments and maintaining a positive mindset. Likewise, they can be naturally cautious and guarded when it comes to trusting others. They tend to take their time to build trust and may have a skeptical attitude towards new people or situations.

Capricorn individuals are known for their strong determination and perseverance, but this can also lead to stubbornness. Once they have set their mind on something or formed an opinion, it can be challenging for them to change their stance, even when presented with new information or alternative perspectives.

Capricorns are highly driven and ambitious individuals who are often dedicated to their careers and achieving success. However, this can sometimes result in workaholic tendencies, where they prioritize work and career goals over personal relationships and self-care. It's important for Capricorns to strive for a healthy work-life balance and prioritize their overall well-being.

Typical Relationships:

Capricorn individuals are known for their practical, ambitious, and responsible nature in relationships. They value stability, loyalty, and long-term commitment. Capricorns are highly dedicated to their partners and are willing to put in the hard work and effort necessary for a successful relationship. They prioritize building a strong foundation and are likely to be reliable, trustworthy, and dependable partners. Capricorns also tend to have high standards and may take a cautious approach to relationships, preferring to take their time in getting to know someone before fully opening up. They also tend to prioritize their personal goals and may require a partner who understands and supports their ambitions. Capricorns may have a stoic exterior, but they deeply care for their loved ones and are often willing to go the extra mile to support and protect them.

Aquarius ♒

Generic Sign Dates:	January 20th thru February 18th
Element:	Air
Modality:	Fixed
Common Symbol(s):	Water Bearer, Man w/ Jug of Water

General Description:

Aquarius is characterized by its intellectual nature, individuality, and humanitarian values. It comes from the mixing of air (ideas, intellect, logic, communication) with fixed (perseverance, steadfast, in-the-now, potentially narrow-focused). The result is a person who is good at compartmentalizing ideas and logic, able to see how they all fit together (or don't).

Individuality is at the core of an Aquarius's personality. They are known for being independent thinkers who value their freedom and autonomy. Aquarians have a natural inclination to challenge convention and break free from societal norms. They have a strong desire to express their true selves and often march to the beat of their own drum. Their originality and creativity allow them to come up with innovative ideas and solutions.

Aquarians are often described as visionaries and forward-thinkers. They have a keen intellect and possess a deep curiosity about the world. Their analytical minds enable them to grasp complex concepts and understand intricate details. Aquarius individuals are highly imaginative and enjoy pondering over philosophical and intellectual matters. They have an innate ability to think outside the box and can offer unique perspectives on various subjects.

One notable trait of Aquarius is their strong sense of social justice. They are deeply concerned about equality, human rights, and making a positive impact on society. Aquarians often engage themselves in various social causes and fight for the rights of the marginalized. They are natural-born activists who strive to create a fairer and more inclusive world. Their genuine compassion for others makes them great advocates for change.

Despite their sociable nature, Aquarians value their alone time as well. They need moments of solitude to recharge and reflect on their thoughts. This introspective quality helps them gain insights into themselves and their surroundings. Aquarians are often perceived as reserved or aloof, but this stems from their need for personal space rather than a lack of interest in connecting with others.

As friends and partners, Aquarians are known for their loyalty and deep sense of friendship. They form deep bonds with those they connect with on an intellectual and emotional level. Aquarians are fun to be around and have a witty sense of humor that can light up a room. They enjoy engaging in intellectually stimulating conversations and are always open to learning from others. However, they might struggle with displays of intense emotions and prefer to maintain an emotional distance.

In their professional lives, Aquarians excel in careers that allow them to utilize their innovative thinking and analytical skills. They are highly adaptable, which makes them thrive in dynamic work environments. Aquarians are excellent problem-solvers and enjoy challenges that push them to find creative solutions. Careers in technology, science, social activism, and creative fields are often well-suited for Aquarians.

Despite their many admirable qualities, Aquarians are not without their weaknesses. Their detached nature can sometimes make them appear aloof and emotionally distant. They might struggle with expressing their own emotions and understanding the emotions of others. They can also be stubborn at times, sticking to their own opinions and resisting change.

In conclusion, Aquarius individuals are unique and independent thinkers who value their individuality and freedom. They possess a strong sense of social justice and have a genuine desire to make a positive impact on society. Their intellectual prowess and creativity set them apart, making them excellent problem-solvers and innovative thinkers. While they may have their challenges, Aquarians bring a refreshing perspective to the world and inspire those around them with their visionary ideas and humanitarian values.

Typical Positive Traits:

Aquarians have a natural talent for innovation and originality. These independent thinkers possess a creative streak that often manifests in their ability to think creatively and outside the box, often challenging conventional wisdom. This makes them great problem-solvers and inventors, as they are unafraid to explore unconventional approaches. This enables them to come up with fresh perspectives and innovative solutions to problems.

Aquarians have a deep thirst for knowledge and are constantly seeking to expand their understanding of the world. They have a natural curiosity and love exploring different subjects, ideas, and philosophies. This intellectual curiosity allows them to engage in stimulating conversations and contribute to meaningful discussions.

Aquarius individuals are characterized by their progressive and open-minded nature. They are receptive to new ideas, different perspectives, and alternative ways of doing things. This allows them to embrace change and adapt to new situations with ease. This often results in a humanitarian outlook, characterized by a genuine concern for the well-being of humanity. Their empathetic nature and passion for equality drives a desire to make the world a better place. In this pursuit, they will often engage in humanitarian efforts and activism.

Common Potential Negative Traits:

Aquarius individuals can sometimes be excessively stubborn and inflexible in their opinions and beliefs, stemming from their fixed modality. They have a strong sense of independence and can be resistant to changing their views, even in the face of new information or evidence. This stubbornness can hamper their ability to adapt and collaborate effectively with others.

Aquarius individuals can exhibit unpredictable behavior, often driven by their desire for freedom and independence. They may suddenly change their plans or commitments without warning, which can be confusing and frustrating for those around them. They thrive on novelty and can easily become bored with routine or monotony, leading to a lack of consistency in their actions and decisions.

Aquarius individuals are known for their intellectual and analytical nature, which can sometimes lead to emotional detachment. They may even come across as aloof or distant. They may prioritize rationality and logic over emotional connections, which can make it challenging for them to form deep, intimate relationships. Their tendency to keep a certain emotional distance can cause them to appear as detached or uninterested in social interactions, making others feel like they are not truly engaged or connected. This can sometimes make it difficult for others to connect with them on a deeper level and may lead to feelings of isolation or misunderstanding.

Typical Relationships:

Aquarius individuals have a unique and unconventional approach to love. They value their freedom and independence and may seem detached or aloof at times. They also have a strong sense of social justice, and may prioritize equality and fairness in their relationships. However, when an Aquarius falls in love, they can be incredibly loyal, open-minded, and committed. They value honesty and authenticity in their connections. Aquarius individuals are often attracted to intellectual stimulation and enjoy engaging in deep conversations with their partners. They seek a strong mental connection and appreciate a partner who respects their individuality. Aquarians may also have a tendency to be unpredictable and desire variety and excitement in their romantic relationships.

Pisces ♓

Generic Sign Dates:	February 19th thru March 20th
Element:	Water
Modality:	Mutable
Common Symbol(s):	Fish(es)

General Description:

Known for their intuitive and compassionate nature, Pisces is a sign that is deeply connected to emotions and empathy. This sign is the mixing of water (emotion) and mutable (adaptability, changing, diverse). The result is a sign that has changing emotions, tending to pick up the emotional state of those around them.

One of the prominent traits of Pisces individuals is their highly intuitive and sensitive nature. They have a natural ability to pick up on subtle moods and emotions around them, making them excellent empathizers and understanding friends. Pisces is known for their compassionate and selfless nature, always willing to lend a listening ear or offer support to those in need. They have a deep understanding of human emotions and can easily relate to the struggles and challenges that others face.

Creativity is a strong suit of Pisces individuals. They possess vivid imaginations and are often drawn to artistic and expressive endeavors. Whether it be painting, writing, or music, Pisces has a natural talent for channeling their emotions and experiences into creative outlets. They have a dreamy and imaginative outlook on life, often finding inspiration in their dreams and fantasies. This creative energy also allows them to think outside the box and come up with innovative solutions to problems.

Pisces individuals are known for their adaptable and flexible nature. They can easily navigate different situations and adapt to various environments. Their ability to go with the flow makes them great companions and easy to get along with. However, this adaptability can sometimes lead to a lack of boundaries and self-identity, as they may tend to absorb the moods and emotions of those around them. It is important for Pisces to establish boundaries and take time for self-care to prevent feeling overwhelmed or drained.

Intuition plays a crucial role in the decision-making process of Pisces individuals. They rely on their gut feelings and inner guidance when faced with choices. This intuitive nature allows them to trust their instincts and make decisions that align with their inner truth. They often have a strong inner wisdom that guides them through life.

Pisces individuals are deeply connected to their spiritual side. They have a natural inclination towards the mystical and unseen aspects of life. They are drawn to spirituality, meditation, and practices that allow them to tap into their higher selves. Pisces may also have a deep interest in exploring the depths of the human psyche and the mysteries of the universe.

Career-wise, Pisces individuals are often drawn to professions that allow them to express their creativity and compassion. They make excellent artists, musicians, writers, counselors, and healers. They are known for their ability to connect with others on a deep emotional level and bring about positive change. Pisces can excel in careers that involve working with people and making a difference in their lives.

In conclusion, Pisces individuals are intuitive, compassionate, and creative. They possess a deep understanding of human emotions and a natural talent for connecting with others. While their adaptability and sensitivity can pose challenges, Pisces has a unique ability to bring beauty, love, and compassion into the world.

Typical Positive Traits:

Pisces individuals are deeply empathetic and compassionate. They have a remarkable ability to understand and share the feelings of others. They are often the ones who offer a listening ear, a helping hand, or a comforting presence to those in need. They often prioritize the needs of others over their own and are willing to go out of their way to support and uplift those around them. Their generosity and willingness to give without expecting something in return make them incredibly valued and loved by those who have the privilege of knowing them. Their empathy allows them to connect with people on a deeper level and provide support without judgment.

Pisces have a strong intuition and a deep connection to their spiritual side. They rely on their inner wisdom and gut feelings to navigate through life. They have a natural ability to pick up on subtle cues and emotions in their surroundings, which often makes them insightful and perceptive. They tend to have a more developed spiritual side which helps them find meaning and purpose in life.

Pisces have a rich inner world and a vivid imagination. They are highly creative and often express themselves through various forms of art, such as writing, painting, music, or acting. Their ability to think outside the box and tap into their imagination allows them to come up with unique ideas and solutions. They often see the world through a different lens and have a talent for bringing beauty and inspiration into the lives of others.

Pisces individuals are adaptable and flexible when it comes to navigating through life's ups and downs. They understand the ever-changing nature of the world and are willing to adjust their plans and perspectives accordingly. They can go with the flow and find creative solutions to challenges, which allows them to find harmony even in the midst of chaos. Their ability to adapt and embrace change makes them resilient and capable of handling various situations with grace and ease.

Common Potential Negative Traits:

Pisces individuals can have a strong inclination toward escapism. Due to their sensitive and emotional nature, they may seek refuge from the hardships of reality through various means such as daydreaming, excessive fantasizing, or indulging in addictive behaviors like substance abuse. This escapism can hinder their ability to face challenges head-on and may lead to a sense of detachment from reality.

One of the other common alternatives when faced with difficult situations or conflicts is a tendency to adopt the role of the victim. Instead of taking responsibility for their actions or finding practical solutions, they might dwell on their perceived misfortunes and wallow in self-pity. This victim mentality can hinder personal growth and prevent them from taking proactive steps toward improvement or resolution.

Pisces individuals have a trusting and idealistic nature. While this can be a beautiful quality, it can also make them vulnerable to being taken advantage of by others. They may place their trust in people who don't necessarily deserve it, which can lead to disappointment, heartbreak, or being easily manipulated.

Pisces often have a hard time making decisions, especially when faced with multiple options or uncertain outcomes. Their empathetic nature leads them to consider the feelings and well-being of others, which can sometimes leave them feeling conflicted and unsure about what course of action to take. This indecisiveness can lead to missed opportunities or a reliance on others to make choices on their behalf.

Typical Relationships:

Pisces individuals are known for their deeply emotional and compassionate nature in relationships. They are highly intuitive and empathetic, easily sensing the emotions and needs of their partners. Pisceans are loving, nurturing, and deeply devoted to their loved ones. They are willing to go above and beyond to support and care for their partners, often placing the needs of their loved ones before their own. They seek deep and meaningful connections and value emotional intimacy. Pisces individuals can sometimes be prone to becoming overly selfless or sacrificing their own needs, so it's important for them to find a balance in maintaining their own well-being while also caring for their partners.

Pisces individuals are extremely romantic, idealistic, and committed when it comes to love. They are deeply sensitive and empathetic, often connecting on an emotional and spiritual level with their partners. They have a deep desire for a soulful and meaningful connection, often seeking a partner with whom they can share their dreams, fantasies, and imaginative world. Pisces individuals are also incredibly supportive and understanding, making them excellent listeners and confidants.

Bibliography

Cahn, J. (2020). *The Harbinger II.* Lake Mary, FL, United States of America: FrontLine.

Continental Mathematics League. (2023). Retrieved November 2023, from Continental Mathematics League: https://www.cmleague.com

Gecewicz, C. (2018, October 1). *'New Age' beliefs common among both religious and nonreligious Americans.* Retrieved November 2023, from Pew Research Center: https://www.pewresearch.org/short-reads/2018/10/01/new-age-beliefs-common-among-both-religious-and-nonreligious-americans/

Hogan, D. (2019, October 6). Faith to Raise the Dead. *Sid Roth's It's Supernatural.* (S. Roth, Interviewer)

Hugh Ross, P. A. (2018, August 10). Hugh Ross vs Peter Atkins - Debating the origins of the laws of nature. (J. Brierley, Interviewer)

Storm, H. (2005). *My Descent Into Death.* New York, NY, USA: DoubleDay.

Turnbo, M. (2022). *The Invitation: Encounters to Help You Enter Christ's Inner Sanctum.* Monee, IL.

Whitfield, P. (2001). *Astrology a history.* London, Great Britain: The British Library.

Greg J. Stenger is available for author interviews. For more information, send inquiries to info@advbooks.com

To order copies of this book or any other books published by Advantage Books online visit AdvBookstore.com.

advbookstore.com

www.ingramcontent.com/pod-product-compliance
Lightning Source LLC
Chambersburg PA
CBHW080247170426
43192CB00014BA/2588